Gunnar Brusewitz

HUNTING

*Hunters, game,
weapons and
hunting methods
from the remote past
to the present day*

STEIN AND DAY/*Publishers*/ New York

First published in the United States of America by
Stein and Day/*Publishers* 1969
Translated by Walstan Wheeler
Translation copyright © Wahlström & Widstrand 1969
Copyright © Gunnar Brusewitz 1967
Library of Congress Catalog Card No. 75-84825
All rights reserved.

Printed in Sweden by Esselte AB, Stockholm

Stein and Day/*Publishers*/ 7 East 48 Street, New York, N.Y. 10017

SBN 8128-1240-9

for INGRID

Although man has been a hunter during the greater part of his existence here on earth, remarkably little has been written about the long history of hunting. It is true that there is an almost overwhelming abundance of books specialising on particular aspects of hunting. General works are so few in number, however, that they can almost be counted on the fingers of one's hands.

The reasons for this are obvious. The history of hunting is such an extensive subject and offers so many different avenues of approach that it is difficult to get to grips with it. It not only includes hunting methods and the various kinds of game but to a very great extent it also covers the history of our own development — art, literature, religion, politics and economics, indeed every imaginable expression of human civilisation.

Bearing this in mind, it might undoubtedly appear to be a hazardous undertaking for a layman to set himself the task of attempting to present an outline, in words and pictures, of hunting in Europe through the ages. Nevertheless, it is now a fait accompli and the person responsible can only offer the excuse that the book does not claim to be exhaustive or scientifically profound. The writer-cum-artist — the one half at times engaged with the other in a stern struggle for space — has tried to give an outline of the main developments in the history of hunting ever since Neanderthal man went out with his club to kill a cave bear for his evening meal. To achieve this aim the author has presented those facts and pictures which he believed to be illustrative and characteristic of the different periods. Costumes and hunting methods were extracted from the vast throng of people and events in mediaeval tapestries or from engravings and paintings. Weapons, trapping equipment and other objects were tracked down in the collections and storerooms of museums. The title of "Hunting" should be interpreted in its widest sense for in this book it also covers trapping methods and matters relating to the zoology of hunting.

The author has always been fascinated by the state of tension which has existed for thousands of years between man and his natural environment. Since the Middle Ages, most of Europe has been under the plough and probably there is scarcely any animal whose distribution has not been affected in some way or other by man, who is sometimes described with innocent cynicism as the lord of creation.

Several species of animals have been completely wiped off the face of the earth, thanks to ruthless persecution. Some species are faced with the immediate threat of extermination (according to the latest estimates, there are in Europe alone 16 species of animals which are in danger of disappearing and for the whole world the figure is 675!) while other species enjoy immensely improved living conditions. The natural animals of prey — the bear, glutton, wolf and lynx — have been forced to retreat as a result of a systematic war of extermination that has been waged for centuries, while at the same time, thanks to cattle ceasing to graze in the woods, an increased amount of food has become available for various animals such as members of the deer family.

The result is nothing less than a danger of overproduction among some species in a number of areas. The hunter and the gamekeeper both have an important part to play in ensuring that the balance of nature remains in a healthy condition.

It was formerly believed that an interest in the history of hunting was almost non-existent among hunters. This belief was probably based, however, on the same narrow-minded attitude which once made Frederick the Great of Prussia declare that hunting is a kind of bodily exercise which makes the limbs strong and supple "but leaves the head empty", or caused the learned Dutchman van Espen to state that "the curious thing about hunting is that it captivates and fascinates people so much that it deters them from indulging in intellectual pursuits", or led Rousseau to describe hunting as "toughening the body but hardening the soul". Remarks such as these must be construed as expressions of an old-fashioned view of hunting enthusiasts since the latter nowadays show an ever-increasing interest both in the history of hunting and in books on the subject — the last-mentioned fact is apparent not least from the considerable rise in the prices of old books.

Even an enthusiastic collector of old hunting literature has little chance today of acquiring a collection on the same scale as his predecessors in the 1920s and 1930s. I therefore owe a great debt of gratitude both to the Müntzing hunting library to which I had access through the kind offices of the Swedish Sportsmen's Association and to the Nordic Museum's library, whose staff rendered invaluable assistance in enabling me to consult rare books.

As regards foreign works, I was greatly helped by the collection of hunting literature in the Oates Memorial Library and Museum at Selborne, Hampshire, where Mr. Cyril Northcliff was always ready to give me the benefit of his expert advice. In addition, the reader will find a bibliography at the end of the book which mentions some of the most important works on hunting in Europe.

To turn to the illustrations in this book, I wish to thank Brynolf Hellner, Ph.D., of the Royal Armoury in Stockholm for allowing me to make drawings of weapons and other objects. I was also shown great kindness at a large number of museums, libraries and collections on the Continent and here I am able to mention but a few of the persons to whom I am most grateful: Karl Sälzle, Ph.D., of Das Deutsche Jagdmuseum in Munich, Dr. R. B. F. van der Sloot of Het Leger en Wapenmuseum in Leyden, M. Henri de Linarés of the Musée International de la Chasse à tir et de la Fauconnerie in Gien, M. Chr. Hallo of the Musée de la Vénerie in Senlis, the Keeper of the Jagdschloss Kranichstein near Darmstadt and officials of the Bavarian National Museum in Munich. I feel that this list of acknowledgements should serve not only as a token of my gratitude but also as a useful guide for anyone interested in the history of hunting who may happen to visit the neighbourhood of the places mentioned.

The never-failing optimism and stimulating interest in the project shown by the publishers have naturally been of paramount importance for the completion of the book. I am exceedingly grateful to Mr. Malcolm Wallerstedt of the Swedish Sportsmen's Association's periodical "*Svensk Jakt*" for ensuring that embarrassing omissions in the contents have been avoided. He very kindly read the text and contributed a great deal of useful advice on the more technical aspects of hunting and on matters connected with cynology.

Last but not least I wish to thank my wife Ingrid for her invaluable help and boundless understanding during the years that "*Hunting*" dominated our lives.

Gunnar Brusewitz

Contents

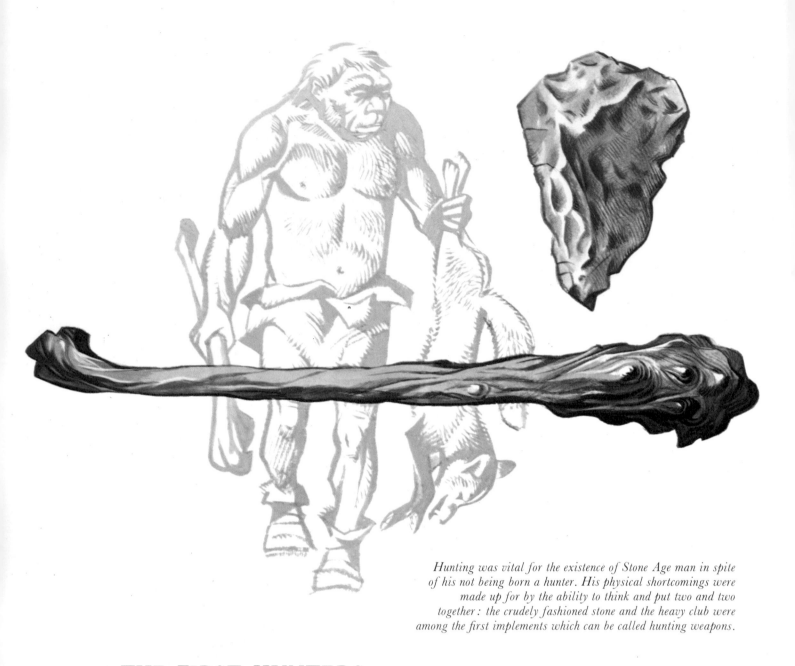

Hunting was vital for the existence of Stone Age man in spite of his not being born a hunter. His physical shortcomings were made up for by the ability to think and put two and two together: the crudely fashioned stone and the heavy club were among the first implements which can be called hunting weapons.

THE FIRST HUNTERS

Man was not born a hunter.

It may be said that, in comparison with beasts of prey, man was completely lacking in the most elementary requirements for catching a fleeing quarry. He was not quick enough to overtake a swift-footed animal; he did not possess tusks or claws with which to seize or kill it and, besides all this, his senses, with the possible exception of his sight, were rather poorly developed. If he had remained at the animal stage, he would, in common with pigs and other omnivorous creatures, have had to be satisfied with living on plants and worms, lizards, eggs and other foods easy to come by.

How is it then that the first Europeans took to hunting? Naturally enough, a definite answer is not possible, but there is much to suggest that in the beginning climatic changes, and the after-effects of these changes, may have obliged man to change his diet and obtain furs with which to cover his body.

At all events, his need of meat gradually developed and, fortunately, with it a sluggish ability to put two and two together, a kind of intelligence concentrated on outwitting animals. With infinite pains man scratched holes in the ground to trap animals and slowly tried also to improve the primitive weapons which he had to use in order to make up for what nature had failed to give him in the way of strength or speed.

So it was that one day a fortunate combination of suitable hereditary gifts created the first hunter. He discovered that he could fashion stones and bones into effective weapons. Then, too, by studying the habits of animals and anticipating their moves, the first hunter was able to make a systematic use of the element of surprise or lure them in various ways into traps. With each succeeding generation the means of obtaining meat developed and it is perhaps not too much to maintain that the very fact that man, partly against his nature, developed into a hunter was of decisive importance in the mental evolution of the human race. Man overcame his physical handicaps by constantly sharpening his wits.

Hunting techniques underwent, of course, many changes during the long period in the history of mankind covered by the Stone Age, owing to the various changes in climate that succeeded one another and led to new physical conditions, new kinds of game, new races of people and new cultures.

The first hunters, named after Neanderthal in western Germany, employed extremely primitive hunting methods for thousands of years, but in spite of this they succeeded in defeating a formidable animal like the cave bear. For a long time the cave bear was the most important prey of the Paleolithic peoples. It was a heavily-built animal, certainly a third as big again as the European brown bear of today, high and big at the withers and with a frontal bone that sloped noticeably backwards. To judge from skeleton finds, the cave bear seems to have been extremely common in some areas: at certain trapping stations as much as 99 per cent of bone deposits derive from the cave bear. There is much to suggest that the hunters of the cave bear killed their quarry either inside or at the mouth of the caves where the bears lived. These animals were generally hunted fairly high up in mountainous country, and this has been interpreted as a sign that hunting took place in the periods between ice ages when the climate was reasonable.

An examination of molar teeth that have been found showed that the hunting season was in the late autumn, perhaps when the bears made their way to the caves to hibernate. The most famous of all bear caves is the one near Graz in Austria where the remains of hundreds of cave bears have been found. By the end of the Mesolithic age the cave bear no longer seems to play an important role, partly perhaps on account of the persecution to which it had been subjected.

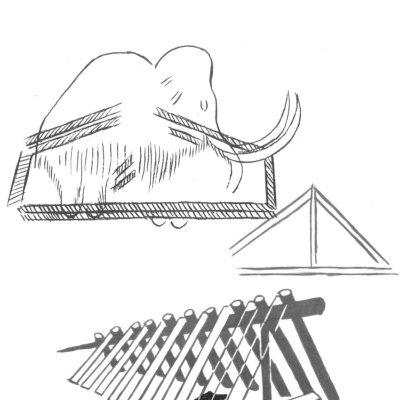

A mural painting at Font-de-Gaume shows how the mammoth was caught in a trap that resembled in some ways the traps still used in Scandinavia in our times. (After Breuil) These traps were often represented by simple drawings of angles placed among the animals on the cave walls. Shown below is a diagram of a deadfall used by the North American Blackfoot Indians. (After Lindner)

The Age of Mammoths

The demands on the energy and constructive imagination of the Stone Age hunters increased in conjunction with the considerable climatic changes which occurred when an ice age succeeded a mild climate. Radical changes in the scenery and altered conditions for hunting ensued. The huge forest elephant and its companion, the primitive rhinoceros or Merck's rhinoceros, disappeared and were replaced by two other magnificent animals, the mammoth and the woolly rhinoceros, both animals of the tundra and adapted to a cold climate. The mammoth left its mark on hunting in central Europe to such an extent that in the history of hunting there is justification in talking about the age of mammoths. It was with the deterioration of the climate during the Mousterian that the hunting of the mammoth started and this animal was a typical kill far into the next archaeological period, the Aurignacian (about 100,000 B.C.). (See Notes.)

During the age of mammoths the central European landscape was radically transformed. The huge primeval forests disappeared and in their place an arctic tundra with sparse vegetation covered large areas of the continent. The summers were hot and the winters extremely cold: in our times it is necessary to go to Greenland to experience a climate like that of this period of the Stone Age.

Under these harsh new conditions, life of course became hard for the Stone Age hunters, but we may assume that not everything was a change for the worse. According to the distinguished German historian of hunting, Kurt Lindner, the climatic changes also meant a cultural revolution of considerable proportions. During the early and milder Stone Age periods the hunter was a fairly lazy type of man, of limited intellectual gifts, who was content to hunt at random within easy reach of his dwelling.

The tundra hunter on the other hand was obliged to be a good deal more active in order to survive. The hunters were now forced, much more than before, to organise their hunting, perhaps using beaters, and this also necessitated some kind of social organisation.

The mammoth came to acquire an enormous importance as game for the European Stone Age hunter and gradually there evolved a rich variety of methods of hunting and trapping this huge animal. A study of the paintings which these highly developed hunting tribes left in caves in different parts of central Europe has enabled us to obtain a

*Pictures of the woolly
rhinoceros, which was a
contemporary of the mammoth,
occur very seldom in cave paintings.
This fact has been taken to indicate that the
woolly rhinoceros was relatively uncommon both
in its occurrence in the countryside and as a quarry
for hunters.*

certain knowledge about their hunting methods.

It is true that these techniques are often merely summarised in a simple symbolic sign denoting the trap or method of capture, but nevertheless it is possible to base a description on them. In the case of one type of deadfall which was clearly fairly widespread, the animal was knocked down by logs on entering the trap. This trap worked on the same principles as those used in Scandinavia for wolverine and lynx. The hunters also caught their quarry in well-hidden pitfalls. Another method they employed was to creep up on sleeping animals stealthily. It is typical of the bone deposits at the large hunting stations that the great majority of the bones are from the female or young of the mammoth, cave bear, rhinoceros and other large and dangerous animals.

These "stations" were of course primarily concentrated in areas where game was particularly abundant and, as far as mammoth hunting is con-

cerned, extremely rich deposits have come to light during the excavation of certain trapping grounds. The most famous one, Předmost in Moravia, was found to contain, for instance, numerous remains of hunts and meals, in addition to the 23,000 objects so far counted which were chiefly connected with the hunting of mammoths. It has been suggested that a large herd of mammoths died or were isolated there during some natural catastrophe.

It is tempting at this juncture to discuss man's role in the extermination and disappearance of some kinds of animals. A ridiculously large number of animal types have obviously been wiped off the face of the earth by indiscriminate hunting on the part of man in historic times. As regards the state of affairs in prehistoric times, however, it is wisest to be more cautious as to the causes. Opinions among experts have varied greatly regarding the rapid decrease of the mammoth, but there are some who firmly believe it was chiefly due to the Stone Age hunters. Others believe that man at this stage of his evolution could never have been the sole cause of an extermination. Climatic changes and their after-effects were, on the other hand, of decisive importance in the chain of events.

17

The Age of Wild Horses

The roaring of trapped cave bears, the trumpeting
of the mammoths and the grunting of the woolly
rhinoceros gradually gave way to another sound
which was to acquire great importance for the tribes
of central Europe: the sound of wild horses galloping
across the wide plains.

The wild horses necessitated adjustment yet again
on the part of the hunting peoples. They were very
suitable game animals for the big, fleet-footed races
that now began to appear. These horses were shy
animals of the steppes and could be captured only
with the aid of cunning. Fire and beaters were used
to force them into enclosed traps or systems of pits.
Above all, they were stampeded over steep cliffs.

The age of wild horses was an important period

in the development of the hunter and a small place
called Solutré, near Lyons in the Rhône valley, has
given its name to a whole archaeological period, the
Solutrean, which began about 50,000 B.C. There is a
hill there which rises gradually from a high plateau
and suddenly ends in a sheer precipice. This was for
many hundreds of years a suicide drop for probably
hundreds of thousands of wild horses which were
driven to their deaths up the gentle slope.

One of the biggest prehistoric hunting stations
discovered so far was established at Solutré. The
remains of more than 10,000 wild horses found there
are estimated to represent a mere tenth or so of the
total number of slaughtered animals. There is much
to suggest that the wild horses constituted more than

the perverse hunting spectacles of the eighteenth century! Nevertheless, the stampeding of elk, reindeer, and red deer over precipices actually occurred in some places in northern Europe as recently as at the beginning of the last century.

In view of the huge bone deposits, originating from the slaughter of wild horses, which have been found in various areas of central Europe, one might be led to suppose that it was the Stone Age hunters who gradually managed to exterminate this animal. This would, however, probably be an exaggeration of the part played by the hunters. The hunting of wild horses was dependent on the migrations and behaviour of the large herds, and success was presumably largely a matter of chance.

There is plenty of artistic evidence from the age of wild horses at the end of Paleolithic times, in the form of cave paintings or carved and engraved objects, to testify to the existence also of other hunting methods than those mentioned. Proof has been found of hunting with snares and slings, and it is surely not improbable that the hunters tried to capture the horses alive so as to have fresh meat available for future needs. The eagerness of some scholars to discover bits of rope round the necks and legs of wild horses in cave paintings may sometimes appear to be somewhat hazardous, however; in some cases it is fairly apparent, at least to an animal artist, that lines which have been interpreted as representing snares are in actual fact merely drawing errors which have been corrected by the cave artist!

The first big increase in hunting the wild horse occurred during the Aurignacian, reaching its climax in the Solutrean and gradually decreased during the Magdalenian, when it was the turn of the reindeer to play a predominant role in the hunting cultures in central Europe.

half of the animals hunted over long periods of the Stone Age. As regards individual types of animals, the reindeer is almost certainly the only one which was later to acquire greater importance for entire periods in the history of civilisation than the wild horses during the Aurignacian and the Solutrean.

It must certainly be said that the method of hunting animals by stampeding them over precipices is by far the most cruel fashion, and reserved, one would have thought, for only the most primitive hunting people. It has been pointed out quite rightly that similar cruelty in hunting is only to be found in

The Stone Age artists often made sketches of the animals on small flat stones, perhaps as cartoons for the wall-paintings. This herd of horses is carved on a stone found at Limeuil, France. The drawing on the right shows approximately what a wild horse must have looked like in reality.

The throwing-stick or spear-thrower was an implement which greatly interested the designers of the Magdalenian period and there seems to have been no lack of imagination when it came to giving an artistic shape to this important article. In this instance a blackcock was the model. Bone sculpture from Mas d'Azil, France.

Weapons

Weapon techniques developed little during the end of the Paleolithic age, and apparently not even during the relatively advanced Aurignacian were hunting methods enriched by any real epoch-making inventions. There is perhaps cause, however, for suspecting that the foundations of the revolutionary changes that occurred in the field of hunting during the Solutrean and Magdalenian had been laid earlier.

It was during the relatively highly developed eras that the golden days of hunting in the Stone Age occurred: tools and weapons were perfected and, also artistically speaking, there began a golden age. The fact that the reindeer was to acquire such

immense importance during the Magdalenian was due, not least of all, to people having learnt to make utensils and tools of different kinds from the bones and antlers of reindeer.

For instance, they constructed spear-throwers, which gave the arm extra throwing power; they made carved daggers and sticks for straightening the shafts of arrows; they made barbed harpoons, launched with the aid of throwing-sticks, and bone signal pipes, the forerunners of the hunting horn of a later age. The great majority of these objects were lavishly decorated and beautifully designed.

Large quantities of arrow-heads have been discovered in layers of refuse from these archaeological

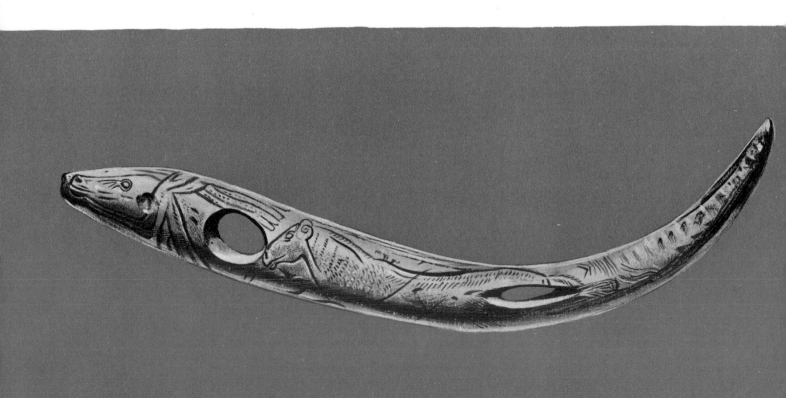

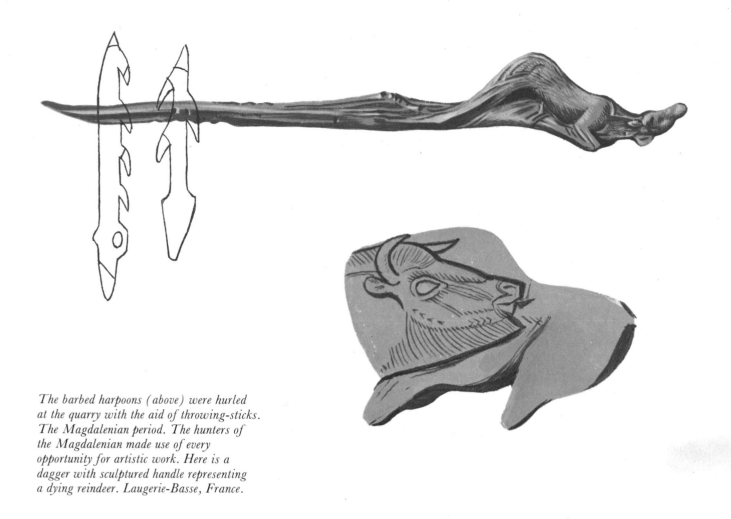

The barbed harpoons (above) were hurled at the quarry with the aid of throwing-sticks. The Magdalenian period. The hunters of the Magdalenian made use of every opportunity for artistic work. Here is a dagger with sculptured handle representing a dying reindeer. Laugerie-Basse, France.

periods, but this does not mean that all the Stone Age hunters were familiar with the bow. As far as can be seen, the latter is of comparatively recent date and did not become common until the Neolithic age in northern and central Europe. The earliest evidence of the use of the bow and arrow is to be found in rock carvings in a number of mountainous areas in eastern Spain, and it is with some hestiation that they have been said to date from the Solutrean, at the earliest.

Thanks to the rich artistic productivity which flourished during the Magdalenian, we have formed a fairly good idea both of the hunting methods used and of the game hunted — even if some archaeolo-

gists have been a bit too quick to discern weapons and traps even in the most obscure of signs.

Other implements which were of special interest for artists were the so-called "staffs of office". At first there was quite a lot of uncertainty regarding the purpose of these implements. Nowadays it is believed that they were used for straightening the shafts of arrows, exactly as Eskimos still do. This stick is made of reindeer antler and was found at Teyjat in France. (After Obermaier)

The reindeer was hunted and caught by the Magdalenian hunters by means of approximately the same methods used earlier in hunting wild horses. The lasso was employed and presumably also other methods of snaring animals, as a drawing of reindeer at Les Combarelles suggests. (After Breuil)

The Age of Reindeer

Of course, the reindeer had featured now and again on the menus of the Neanderthal people, but it was not until the later part of the Stone Age that it acquired real importance, above all during the Magdalenian, when it succeeded the wild horse as the predominant type of game. At the time of the last great glaciation there took place, as already mentioned, a tremendous change in the house-keeping of the Stone Age peoples. The change in climate resulted in changes in the landscape and to some extent in the fauna, too. Enormous herds of reindeer wandered across central Europe and, particularly at the northerly hunting stations, the reindeer accounts for as much as 80 per cent of the analysed bone remains.

There were several reasons for this popularity. Hunting techniques had developed very much during the age of wild horses when several new methods — for example the lasso and the use of snares — had been evolved or perfected, but one of the chief incentives for the hunting of reindeer was the greatly increased production of weapons and tools. For the reindeer is a remarkably useful animal and the various parts of its body can be utilised almost a hundred per cent. It is difficult to imagine how the hunters of the ice age would have been able to survive without an inexhaustible supply of this splendid game.

The men of the Magdalenian hunted and captured the reindeer by the same general methods as those used for the wild horse and it was apparently usual to employ various means of forcing the reindeer out into fast-flowing waters where the hunters could then reach them easily. These tactics were and are still used in several areas in circumpolar regions, for instance in Scandinavia, Siberia and by the primitive caribou eskimoes in North America.

The use of snares and lassoes seems to have been very common for the hunting of reindeer and a very realistic drawing at Les Combarelles (see picture) shows how a bull reindeer was caught with the help of some kind of snare or lasso or perhaps a *bola*, similar to the kind still used by the Indians

weapon seems to have been very widespread. The harpoon reached its target with the aid of a throwing-stick which was hurled at the quarry. When it scored a hit and got a grip with its barbs, the shaft fell off but remained dangling from a long leather strap attached to the harpoon. In this way the animal was slowed down in its attempt to escape.

The reindeer became of greater importance to the Neolithic cultures than any other animal. The elk, which will be dealt with in detail on a later page, played a fairly subordinate part in central Europe and the legendary giant red deer was obviously so uncommon that it was only hunted spasmodically. Bones of elk and the giant red deer found in the refuse layers of hunting stations are almost exclusively the bones of female or young animals. This has been interpreted as meaning that hunting was a question of pouncing on the animals and that the hunters avoided the bulls on account of their antlers and their ability to put up a better defence.

In central Europe the red deer is not often found among the hordes of animals in the cave paintings. In Spain, however, it seems to have replaced the reindeer, which never penetrated so far south, as the typical game animal during the Magdalenian. The red deer was chiefly hunted there with bows and arrows and was probably the first European animal to be killed systematically with projectile weapons.

of the South American pampas, that is to say, a long lasso with one or two round stones fastened at the end. They throw these bolas with terrific force at the running animal and the idea was to make the end of the rope with the stones wind itself round the animal's neck or legs.

Harpoons and arrows were also used during the Magdalenian. To judge from finds, the former

In Spain the red deer replaced the reindeer as the typical animal hunted. It was hunted with, for example, bows and arrows and was presumably the first game animal in Europe to be systematically killed with projectile weapons. Painting in red, Cueva Saltadora. (After Maringer—Bandi)

Not only speed and courage were demanded of the Magdalenian hunter to ensure success when hunting the dangerous aurochs but also careful preparation beforehand.

The Bison and the Aurochs

The bison and the aurochs were of great importance for the Stone Age hunting peoples, but this does not mean that they set their seal on this phase in the history of mankind in the same way as the mammoth, wild horse and reindeer. The bison is one of the game animals most often depicted in cave paintings and it is tempting to believe that this was due to its picturesque and impressive appearance.

During the Paleolithic age it was mostly a matter of chance if these large and dangerous animals were caught and killed. As far as the history of hunting goes, they belong above all to the Mesolithic and Neolithic ages with their more highly developed races of man whose swiftness and intelligence made possible a more regular form of hunting.

In addition to the pits and similar traps referred to in connection with the capture of reindeer and wild horses, the hunters of the aurochs and bison used various other methods, for instance different kinds of deadfalls, perhaps partly reminiscent of those used in mammoth hunting.

Unfortunately the artists of the Stone Age were not very generous with pictures that actually depict hunting scenes, but as far as the bison is concerned there is in fact a carving which provides invaluable evidence for the history of hunting. A piece of reindeer antler from the Magdalenian culture showing a hunter creeping up behind an unsuspecting bull bison was found in a cave in Dordogne. Certain marks on the creeping man have been taken to mean that he disguised himself with an animal skin so as to be able to get sufficiently close to kill the animal with a spear or sling (there is no sign of a weapon in the picture).

If the interpretation of the picture is correct, it is one of the earliest known examples of camouflage in hunting — a technique which was to acquire tremendous importance in the history of hunting right up to our own times.

A very important way of catching animals was also to use simple enclosures and palisades to force the hunted herds over mountain precipices or

A camouflaged hunter creeping up on all fours on an unsuspecting bull bison. Laugerie-Basse. (Musée de St Germain-en-Laye)

24

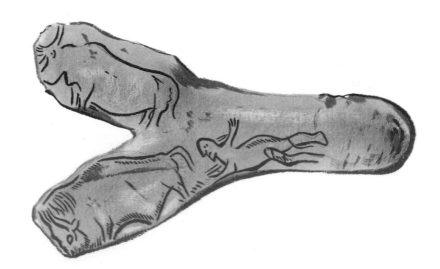

This diagrammatic drawing (above, left) is at Castillo in Spain. It is believed to represent a fence trap, with the opening facing a precipice or stretch of water. (After Lindner) If this is the case, it was probably a sketch for the drawing on the right which shows aurochs being driven along the palisade to the opening and the precipice.

There is reason to suppose that the bisons were also pursued in deep snow until they were exhausted and became an easy prey for the hunters. A brutal method of hunting with dire consequences, which, surprisingly enough, managed to continue right up to our times in many places.

down into water. During their flight the animals reached one of the two extremities of the fences and followed it up to the opening on to the precipice. In other words it was a perfected form of the stampeding practised during the age of wild horses.

In some cave paintings, especially in Spain and southern France, mysterious geometrical signs have been discovered, the precise meaning of which has been in doubt. There is however much to suggest that they actually represent traps of this kind and that their presence in the groups of animal pictures was perhaps connected with some magic ritual and that they were intended to "conjure" the game into the trap.

It was, as a matter of fact, pictures of bisons that led to the discovery of the cave paintings, later world-famous, in the cave at Altamira in Spain. In the late 1870s an amateur archaeologist, Don Marcelino de Sautuola, was busy with excavations in the relatively newly-discovered cave while his five-year-old daughter Maria went on a voyage of discovery in the narrow passages with a candle in her hand. Suddenly she rushed out to her father shouting "Toros! Toros!" She told him that she had seen bulls painted on the walls of the cave and when at last her father, somewhat against his will, went along with her he saw to his amazement that he had wandered into a prehistoric art gallery.

But, of course, after that it was a long time before experts allowed themselves to be convinced of the genuineness and impressive age of the pictures.

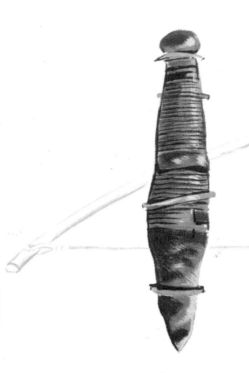

A NEW AGE — NEW HUNTERS

The transition to the late Stone Age, the Neolithic, brought with it a tremendous change, in every respect, in the life of human beings. This period, which is the threshold of our own times, started about ten thousand years before the beginning of our era in central Europe, but the changeover and transformation varied considerably in different parts of the continent.

The new type of man appeared in an age full of crises and fundamental changes. Earlier, the Stone Age peoples had been entirely dependent on hunting for their existence, now the Neolithic tribes tilled the earth and kept domestic animals. They formed village communities and began for the first time in the history of mankind to transform the countryside round their dwelling sites: in other words they started to create farmland. That is why hunting was relegated to a subordinate position economically and it is certainly one of the reasons for the remarkable lack of interest in it by scholars when studying the life of the Neolithic age.

If then there are several gaps in our knowledge

of hunting during the Neolithic age we are at least well informed in one special respect, namely, as regards the lake-dweller cultures in Switzerland, France and southern Germany. An analysis of the refuse in these places has resulted in interesting statistics on the popularity of different kinds of game on the dinner menus.

It was shown, for example, that the advances made in the sphere of weapons, beginning with the sharpened flintstone, resulted in certain game which had been unattainable for the Paleolithic hunters suddenly securing a foothold in housekeeping. This was especially true of small animals such as the beaver, badger, fox and otter, as well as waterfowl of various kinds.

It is significant that the bones of tame animals have been found to predominate in these deposits. In certain villages of lake-dwellers in Switzerland, domestic animals have provided 80 per cent of the bone finds, while the figures are even higher in Neolithic villages in southern Scandinavia. According to Magnus Degerböl, who has examined the Bundsö dwelling site, it was discovered that of a total of 10,000 bones found, only about 150 were from game, mainly red deer, and the rest were from domestic animals.

The red deer played an important role, from a hunting point of view, among Neolithic hunters of central and southern Europe. Next comes the wild boar and then roe deer, beaver, badger and fox,

though the order of precedence taken by these animals varies from place to place. The fox in particular occurs in strikingly large numbers and seems now and then to have been second in importance to the red deer! Traces of knives and teeth on the bone remains of fox shows that this animal held an accepted place on the menu.

Strangely enough, the hare, on the other hand, seems to have been an almost unknown delicacy and finds of hare bones are so rare that one must try to find out the reason. Some experts have expressed the view that the remains of roast hare were given to the dogs, which devoured the bones with such greed that nothing was left over for the archaeologists. But how then does one account for the existence of so many other bones of small animals? Some thought has also been given to the possibility of the hare having been protected, for some reason or other, as a "holy" animal in the lake-dweller cultures, as was the case at about the same time with the Egyptians and other peoples.

Perhaps, however, the simplest explanation is that the hare was rare, purely and simply on account of the obviously large number of beasts of prey.

When it comes to game birds, waterfowl occupy a special place in the lists of game hunted by the lake-dwellers, different kinds of duck, mostly, but also the stork, heron, swan, cormorant, and various kinds of geese including, for example, the snow-

goose, an extremely rare visitor to Europe nowadays. The snowgoose is a bird of the high Arctic, whose annual migration routes perhaps led to Europe in former times: Olaus Magnus mentions it, for instance, in one place in his *Historia de gentibus septentrionalibus.*

(Left) The red deer and wild boar were as a rule the main types of animals hunted by the lake-dwellers in central Europe. Then, in varying order of precedence, came the roe deer, badger, beaver, fox, otter and other small animals.

Thanks to new and more effective weapons, above all the bow, the Neolithic hunter was able to obtain animals other than those which had been available to the Paleolithic peoples. He could kill waterfowl. He could shoot ducks and swans in marshes abounding in bird life, and the fox was one of the favourite dishes on the menu.

There is much to suggest that the dog used for hunting by the Neolithic hunters was the ancestor of the elkhound of our days, and that it has not changed in appearance.

ARCTIC HUNTING

Rock carvings and dwelling sites, of course, enable us to get an idea of how hunting was pursued in northern Europe during the Stone and Bronze Ages, but nevertheless there are numerous question marks, owing above all to the difficulty of dating or interpreting the enormous quantity of pictures and artistic objects.

Many of the primitive forms of hunting seem to have retained their basic features, irrespective of archaeological limits of eras and varying cultural epochs, from prehistoric times until the Middle Ages — in certain cases right up to our times. The basic principles of hunting are simple and primitive and the changes are often insignificant.

The Bronze Age carving at Massleberg in Bohus-län (above) is an invitation to make apparently obvious interpretations, but perhaps one should not be too definite about it after all. This splendid carving has generally been interpreted as a hunting scene where a stag has been brought to bay by a number of dogs while the hunter approaches with his spear. But how is the hunter's mysterious equipment to be interpreted? Is he carrying a shield or is he wearing a kind of disguise? Does the

heavily stressed sex of the stag suggest that this is a scene from some kind of rite?

The Nordic hunter was presumably the first to make methodical use of the dog as an assistant in hunting and there are cogent reasons for supposing that the breed in question corresponds very closely to the elkhound (above, left). Several heads found on dwelling-sites, as well as the dogs in the rock carvings with the strongly marked tails pointing upwards, seem to be proof of this.

From many points of view the elkhound was an ideal comrade for the prehistoric hunting peoples of the north. It is tough, loyal, sporting, patient and sturdy.

It was used by prehistoric hunters to pursue the quarry and hold it at bay until the hunter arrived. A whole pack of dogs was used for this purpose.

Another famous Bohus rock carving with a hunting motif is to be found in Hultane and depicts an archer surrounded by a pack of twelve hunting dogs together with the infuriated quarry. The latter, just hit by an arrow, has been considered by certain scholars to represent a wild boar, but, in my opinion, it is much more like a wolf, with its

characteristic drooping tail thrown into strong relief.

Naturally, it is often a most difficult matter to examine the extremely simplified symbols used in rock carvings from a zoological point of view, but in this particular case I feel that the hunted animal's size in comparison with that of the dogs, which are drawn in a similar manner, points fairly convincingly to its being a wolf.

The rock carving at Massleberg in the province of Bohus in Sweden has been the subject of much debate (above, centre). Several historians of hunting have been eager to regard it as proof that trained dogs held a stag at bay pending the arrival of the hunter while others are more hesitant and suggest that it may just as easily be a scene from some mystic rites.

Another Bohus rock carving from Hultane (below) shows, however, fairly unmistakably a hunter with a pack of twelve hunting dogs.

Elk and Reindeer

The more or less nomadic hunting tribes who made their way northwards, following the retreat of the ice sheet, found an enormous amount of game at their disposal. In order to obtain meat and skins, they soon invented methods which compensated for their lack of weapons. In the far north reindeer hunting acquired vital importance and the reindeer was a prerequisite for human life in arctic regions.

In common with the Stone Age people on the continent, the peoples of the north were extremely successful with pitfalls and the stampeding of herds of animals over cliffs. Both in Norway and in neighbouring areas of western Sweden entire systems of neatly walled pits lined with stones were constructed in the mountain valleys in places where experience had shown that reindeer would pass. These pits were

two yards deep, two yards long, and about a yard wide, and were covered over with willow branches and brushwood. They were apparently very effective and came to play a big part in the food gathering of mountain dwellers long after the invention of fire-arms; in fact, as far as one type was concerned, until the last century.

It is, perhaps, a little difficult for us to understand that our ancestors could have influenced the numbers of wild animals. Without doubt, however, the mass slaughter of reindeer and elk as a result of the pit systems, for example, the stampeding of entire herds over mountain precipices and similar techniques have played a far from insignificant part in the decrease and, in some cases, extermination of certain types of animals.

The reindeer pits, carefully lined with stones or walled, were normally dug on rocky ground on mountain slopes where it was known that the herds were in the habit of wandering. Elk pits were not walled and were usually placed in valleys or on islands in the middle of moorland bogs.

(Left) The figure from the Rödöy carving in Nordland in Norway is considered by many experts to represent an authentic skier. The protuberances on the head are interpreted as a camouflage of reindeer antlers to allow the hunter on skis to approach the herds of reindeer unnoticed. (After Gjessing and Hallström)

The elk played a very important part in the imagination of our ancestors. It is the commonest animal in magic hunting rites. This exquisite stone elk head from the province of Uppland in Sweden was presumably part of a ceremonial club. (The National Historical Museum in Stockholm.) There are also similar heads in Finland. The elk on the left with "lifeline" is taken from a rock carving in Tröndelag in Norway. (From Kunst der Eiszeit.*)*

The trapping of wild reindeer with the aid of carefully prepared pits was in fact so rewarding that a trapping station in the mountains was valued as highly as a farm in the village.

Skis, the use of which has been traced back to Neolithic times, also had a particularly adverse effect on the supply of game in northern Scandinavia, where hunting on crust snow was extremely profitable, especially in the case of the heavy elks which crashed through the crust as they fled.

> Surely nowhere in the wide world,
> beneath the blue sky can there be
> anything in the lonely forest,
> any kind of four-footed beast,
> that a hunter wearing these skis
> can fail to overtake with ease.

These lines are to be found in the ancient Finnish national epic, the *Kalevala*, and the method of hunting animals by exhausting them in crust snow survived into our times. As far as Sweden is concerned, this extremely cruel form of hunting was not forbidden by law until 1836.

Even long after the invention of fire-arms, hunters chiefly employed spears, used also as ski-sticks, or the bow, which was handier to carry about than the clumsy shot-gun. Often they were content to carry nothing but a knife or axe with which they killed the exhausted and defenceless quarry.

Presumably the "silent" weapons were considerably more efficient than shot-guns, for the latter were slow to load. A Norwegian source tells us that a peasant managed to kill 150 red deer with a bow and arrow during the course of a winter in the middle of the sixteenth century.

Traps and Deadfalls

The transition from the Neolithic to the Bronze Age
was not remarkable in the history of hunting and,
generally speaking, many scholars are indeed
doubtful whether a distinction should be drawn at
all between the Bronze Age and the preceding era.
The manufacture of stone weapons was perfected
and flourished *simultaneously* with the beginning of
the Copper and Bronze Age, and the metal, which
was relatively difficult to obtain, never achieved
any major importance for hunting. At the hunting
stations in the "copper belt" on the continent the
proportion of bronze objects was five for every
thousand stone implements!

In the northern countries trapping animals was
of considerably greater importance than hunting,
and as recently as our own times a distinction was
still drawn in the north between "hunting" and
"trapping" animals, even if the people of northern
Sweden had one word for the meanings, the ancient
verb "*skoga*".

Pitfalls and other primitive forms of trapping

were dealt with on an earlier page. During the
Bronze Age new and more complicated traps,
technically speaking, appeared, some examples of
which have been preserved in peat-bogs.

These traps were made of wood, especially oak or
beech, and fitted with one or two springs of pliant
wood. They were placed on animal tracks and by
water-holes and their use seems to have been very
widespread. Apart from finds in Scandinavia, they
have also been found in Ireland, Scotland, Germany, Italy, Poland and the Ukraine. There was
at first some uncertainty as to how they were
sprung and which was their right way up; they
were more than a metre long, and descriptions with
minor variations are to be found in old hunting
literature.

Thanks to a Polish scholar's research on these
age-old traps, which were actually used by trappers
in Poland as recently as in the 1920s, we have a
fairly good idea of how they worked. In southern
areas of the Scandinavian countries they were used

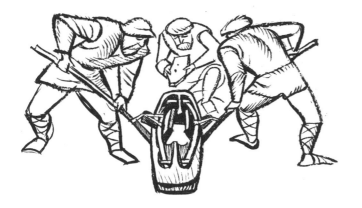

Three men setting a spring trap. The whole trap is then turned over and placed in position on the track used by game. (Below) Rock carving from Drammen in Norway, which has been interpreted as representing a spring trap. (After G. Berg)

for catching red deer and possibly also elk and reindeer. On the continent they were in addition used for wild boar.

For the largest kinds of traps with double springs, three men were required for the work of preparation. They used stout poles to set the jaws and then they put the actual tripping-board in position. The trap was then turned over and placed in a depression in the ground and was presumably covered with earth and branches.

When the animal put its foot in the rectangular hollow, it pressed down the tripping-board and the jaws snapped shut. It is not known for sure whether the trap was secured to the ground; this was perhaps unnecessary since in any case the heavy and clumsy wooden contraption did not allow the trapped animal to move any distance. The Polish traps, at any rate, do not appear to have been secured since bears are said to have managed sometimes to drag the heavy traps away with them and escape.

It is perhaps fairly probable that other types of traps were also used, although it is strange that none have come to light. In a number of rock carvings in Norway mysterious symbols have been found in pictures of animals. One explanation given for these symbols is that they represent a kind of trap, but so far this is mere speculation. The elliptical patterned pictures occurring in certain Bronze Age rock carvings have been interpreted by some people as spring traps.

All in all, it is difficult, for reasons easily understood, to determine when the various trapping and hunting methods were invented or developed; it is merely assumed that they are of very ancient date. At the time of the earliest documents (provincial laws, chronicles, and place-names), they occupied a self-evident place in these documents.

The hunters and trappers in the northernmost parts of Europe used all their ingenuity to obtain skins and meat; this effort on their part was of vital importance as long as the rearing of cattle was still only at an experimental stage.

They snared reindeer and even bears, constructed self-releasing spears for elk, dug and walled entire systems of pits along the tracks followed by wild animals, set deadfalls for small fur-bearing animals and so forth. As has already been said, probably no one will be able to tell the exact date when more advanced methods began to appear, but when the inhabitants of the north had reached the threshold of the new age — the Iron Age — the trapping methods had long since been developed and tried. Even if the new metal age meant a far-reaching revolution for the whole of mankind, the majority of the old hunting and trapping methods nevertheless continued to exist through the centuries.

Apparently already during the Neolithic and Bronze Ages the deadfall and the wild reindeer snare were among the more important of all the many methods of hunting practised. The deadfall was used above all to catch small fur-bearing animals, and in Finland the snare is believed to have also been used for catching bear.

HUNTING IN CLASSICAL TIMES

While hunting in the northern half of Europe continued to be pursued strictly for economic reasons, it had already developed into a popular sport and pastime for the people of antiquity, and it is certainly no exaggeration to say that the European sport of hunting has its roots in Rome and Greece.

Thanks to the detailed descriptions to be found in classical art and literature we have a fairly good idea of how hunting as a sport was practised in classical times.

The spear was the most important weapon used by the amateur hunter and it would seem that the bow and arrow belonged to utilitarian hunting and an earlier phase of civilisation. Light javelins and heavier thrusting-spears for use at close quarters were employed. The heroes and demi-gods of classical literature are often shown engaged in successful struggles with wild boars and lions, which were considered to be by far the most dangerous of wild animals.

Were there lions in Europe in historical times or were they merely a form of allegorical embellishment in literature? There are scholars who have doubted the physical existence of lions but it is now regarded as an established fact that there really were lions, at least in the mountain regions between the river Achelous in Aetolia and the frontier river Nestus between Macedonia and Thrace between 500 and 300 B.C. This view is based above all on a passage in Herodotus, who is considered reliable, relating how during Xerxes's war against the Macedonians his supply camels were attacked by lions at Thermes (Thessaloniki).

Otto Keller, who has devoted particular attention to the animals of antiquity, maintains that the fondness shown by the lions for camel meat reveals their

Arabian origin. Keller believes that, at the time of the Persian attacks on the Greeks, lions followed the enormous baggage-train all the way into the Balkans, where they then remained and increased. How they managed to cross the Hellespont is a question that has so far not been answered.

When the lion gradually disappeared, the energetic hunters had a fully acceptable substitute in the wild boar, which in some cases was given proportions that place it on the dividing line between myth and reality. For the killing of boars like that, heroes of the stature of Theseus and Hercules were required. The most renowned was the Calydonian boar which was given the *coup de grâce* by Meleager and whose precious remains became relics in various monasteries and churches. The tusks were reputed to have been of such an impressive size that it is nowadays seriously asked whether they were not in

When the latter had found a wild boar they started to bark and waited for the huntsmen, who put them on a leash and spread out a coarse net in a half-circle behind the boar. The dogs were then released, whereupon they at once went to the attack, and the boar fled into the net, got entangled and was killed by the most skilful huntsman.

Providing, of course, that everything went according to plan. But it might also happen, according to Xenophon, that the enraged boar ploughed straight through the howling pack of dogs and rushed towards one of the huntsmen who then had to engage it with the thrusting-spear. In such cases the huntsman held the front of the spear in his left hand and the shaft with his right. His feet were set wide apart so as to parry the heavy jolt when the animal touched the point of the spear. If the thrust failed

One of the most beautiful scenes of a lion hunt is inlaid in silver and gold on a dagger which was discovered in one of the famous royal graves at Mycenae. It dates from about 1600 B.C. (The National Museum, Athens.)

actual fact mammoth tusks that the pious monks kept in their treasure hoards!

Nevertheless the more or less veracious description of these wild boar hunts give us a good idea of how these dangerous animals were hunted in classical times. Xenophon (430–355 B.C.) was the first author of a handbook on hunting whose work has survived and he gives us extremely detailed accounts of how wild boars were hunted.

Usually several huntsmen hunted together and to assist them they had Laconian dogs of the most powerful kind. Sometimes they also had a large dog, almost reminiscent of a wolf.

To begin with, the dogs were kept on a leash with the exception of two which were used as trackers.

the huntsman threw himself down with his head close to the ground and another member of the party rushed to his aid, giving the boar the *coup de grâce*.

The best time for hunting was the autumn and winter when the boars were well fattened. This also applied to hare hunting, which was done in a similar manner, but in this case a stick was the only weapon employed. Consequently both the wild boar and the hare became allegorical symbols for the seasons.

The huntsmen followed the hounds on foot, thereby underlining the true sporting nature of the hunt. Broadly speaking, this ancient form of hunting was the origin of the method of hunting wild boar and red deer which still survives today.

With Net and Horse

Xenophon also gave a very knowledgeable and likely account of hare hunting and his description shows that the hunters of classical times, when hunting for pleasure, were more interested in the actual hunting than in the spoils of the chase.

In Xenophon's view the huntsman should wear comfortable, light clothes and footwear and should also carry a stick in his hand. He should be accompanied by a man with a net. The dogs are put on the leash when the company approaches the hunting grounds, the man with the net unrolls it and stands on the look-out by it. It is then time to release the swiftest tracker dog; but first Artemis, the goddess of hunting, must for safety's sake be promised her share of the expected kill.

After being flushed from its hiding place, the hare is pursued by the dogs in full cry, an expression coined already in classical times, and the huntsman follows the pack as quickly as he can, shouting encouragement to the dogs. Any attempt to hinder or head off the hare is doomed to failure. Instead, the huntsman exploits the hare's habit of running in a zig-zag course and gradually returning to the spot where it was flushed. When the huntsman hears that the hunt is returning, he shouts to the man with the net to be on the alert and shortly after he is told by the latter that the hare has run into the net. The captured hare may be given to the dogs to kill.

By way of a summary, Xenophon writes that everyone forgets what it is that generally thrills him when he sees the hare being tracked, flushed, pursued and captured in the net. If fighting large beasts of prey at close quarters was an occupation for heroes and adventurous spirits, hare hunting, on the other hand, was mostly considered as a pastime and sport, but this did not prevent the hare from also being a tremendously popular table delicacy in ancient Greece and Rome. The hare was regarded as the best of all four-footed animals (from the gastronomic point of view). In the words of the Classical Latin saying, *"inter quadropedes gloris prima lapus"* (of all quadrupeds the hare is the most excellent). Besides, roast hare was said to have a beautifying effect on anyone eating it. More about this will be found in the chapter on the hare.

The hunting methods used by Greeks and

Detail of frieze on a bronze urn from Hemmoor depicting a hunter with thrusting-spear waiting for a lion to attack while, behind him, a bear is fighting aurochs. (After Willers)

The sling, one of the various weapons used by the peoples of antiquity, is of ancient date. It did not, however, play a very great part in hunting as a pastime since it was clearly regarded as the weapon of a peasant or shepherd. Detail of Etruscan mural at Tomba della Caccia e Pesca. (After Arturo Stenico)

Romans in Greece and Italy, about the nature of which we have acquired such splendid information thanks to pictorial art and the classical authors, were to have a great influence on hunting on the continent in the Middle Ages, at all events so far as hunting as a pastime was concerned. When the Romans colonised central Europe they introduced their hunting methods which gradually fused together with those of local or non-European origin.

A number of finds of richly-decorated bronze urns have been of great interest for research into the history of hunting. They were discovered in various parts of central Europe and date from the middle of the seventh century B.C. Very lively hunting scenes depicting stag chases are incised on these urns. The particularly interesting point about them is that the huntsmen pursue the quarry on horseback. This was a method which was apparently unknown in Greece and Italy, where, as mentioned above, the huntsman was always depicted as following the chase on foot. The weapon used was without exception either a spear or lance. According to this method, the dogs tracked and chased the stag. The huntsmen then killed or captured the animal when the pack had eventually managed to stop it and bring it to bay.

The main features of this procedure became the foundations of hunting at force which was to be the predominant form of hunting for sport until as late as the beginning of the nineteenth century.

Hunting on horseback probably had its origins in northern Europe, as well as among the horse-taming tribes of the Asian steppes. In the Balkans it

was practised by the Illyrians, who in their turn had presumably been inspired from the east, and from Illyria coursing spread rapidly to neighbouring countries and civilisations. At the end of the Iron Age this form of hunting was to be found in most central European countries.

A book on hunting which is of great value to our knowledge of hunting in central Europe was written by Flavius Arrian, who was born in Bithynia — in modern Turkey—in A.D. 95. His *Cynegeticus* describes Celtic hunting and has been preserved in its entirety. It gives us an extremely good picture of the various methods of hunting practised in the countries of antiquity.

Glass bowl with coursing motif from Cologne. Third century A.D. (After Lindner)

The Show's the Thing

Arrian was a devoted admirer of Xenophon, and when he eventually obtained civic rights in Athens he adopted the name of Xenophon the younger. His *Cynegeticus* is in actual fact merely a revised version of the older Xenophon's famous hunting handbook of the same title, but it also includes interesting additional matter on how hunting was practised by the Celts and Scythians. In giving this supplementary information, he shows great respect for his distinguished predecessor and assures his readers that neither an oversight nor carelessness was the reason for Xenophon not mentioning the swift Celtic hounds; he had simply not heard of them.

In the nineteenth chapter Arrian writes that hunting is pursued by all Celts who are well off and lead a life of ease. Early in the morning they send out people to discover the hare's form. As soon as they have been informed by the trackers where the hare is hiding, they hasten to the spot, release the hounds and pursue the terrified animal on horseback.

But, as Arrian is aware, not everyone is able to afford horses and lengthy preparations for coursing. The poor must be satisfied with following the drive on foot or possibly with one horseman. The author also mentions that a badly organised hunt may easily lead to undesirable episodes and he gives a vivid picture of the confusion that arises if the huntsmen are unable to control their excitement when the hare is flushed and unleash their hounds in any fashion, with the result that the hare can only run a few yards before it is seized by the excited pack. There must be a master of the hunt who decides in advance which of the hounds are to be released, for otherwise the best part of the show is lost.

We get some interesting information from these short chapters of Arrian's *Cynegeticus*. In the first place, his work is the first written document on hunting conditions in Europe outside Greece and Italy and it is also the first evidence of hunting techniques being influenced by social standing. The rich rode on horseback and used trackers. The poor followed the chase on foot. It was to become apparent before very long that hunting was immensely dependent on the social distinctions between the high and low born. By Celts Arrian meant the tribes that lived near the Danube.

The view that hunting is sublime entertainment is also underlined in the section on hounds, where it is mentioned that the finest entertainment is lost if the hare is caught too early owing to the carelessness of the people in charge of the hounds.

It was therefore above all for the sake of the *show* and not for the spoils of the chase nor from love of seeing blood flow that hunting took place. This attitude towards hunting for sport and recreation recurs in several places in the oldest cynegetic literature. One survival of this attitude is, as a matter of fact, to be found in fox hunting in England.

Arrian writes in one chapter that it is a sin to let the pack loose on an uninjured hare that has got entangled in the net. He quotes his namesake, Xenophon, who recommends the huntsman to let the hare escape for the glory of the goddess of hunting and also, if possible, to try to recall the hounds and leash them until the next hare has been found in her hiding place and a new show can be arranged.

We are also given a detailed description of stag coursing as it was practised by the Goths, Scythians and Illyrians in the countries around the Danube and modern Serbia and Bulgaria. This form of hunting took place on the whole in the manner illustrated in the pictures on the urns, mentioned above, from the Hallstatt culture. The stag was driven out into open country with the help of beaters and hounds, and thereafter the hunt continued on horseback. Arrian points out that it is true that the Scythian and Illyrian horses were thin and scraggy in comparison with the Thessalian and Peloponnesian thoroughbreds, but, on the other hand, they were tough and possessed great staying power.

When the stag is exhausted, the huntsman can either kill it with a javelin or, if he wishes to keep the animal alive, capture it with a lasso. The reason for the second alternative was that tame decoy stags were probably also used for hunting. The task of the captured stag was to entice his wild brothers within range of the hidden huntsman in the rutting season. This was a very popular form of hunting in the Middle Ages, and even if Arrian does not mention it in his book it is surely not being too bold to assume that this type of hunting existed already in his day.

Perhaps Arrian thought that the use of a decoy stag for hunting was beneath the dignity of the true sportsman. For, as a matter of fact, he says elsewhere that a man with good hounds and horses does not have any time for traps, snares, or any kind of cunning and tricks for that matter, but prefers to use speed to vanquish game. Hunting is a spectacle which has no connection with vulgar deceit: the trapping of animals with snares, on the other hand, may be likened to brigandage. Comparing the two methods, he says that the latter is like an attack by crafty pirates while the former resembles an honest heroic deed, such as the naval battle of Salamis!

It is no exaggeration to say that the hunting tactics which Xenophon and his successor, Arrian, helped to formulate were destined to set the standards for amateur hunting in Europe for a long time ahead: in fact, as regards certain basic features, right up to the present day.

Beater with length of patchwork cloth. Detail of the famous hunting mosaic at Lillebonne in France. Second century A.D. *(After Duchartre)*

On account of its size and beauty, the Greenland falcon (above) was the most prized of the ten birds of prey used for hawking.

spread of falconry in Europe, and the first definite proof that it had become a popular pastime among people of rank in Gaul dates from the fourth century, when items in letters and proclamations clearly indicate that not only was falconry practised, but also that it was held in very high esteem. A Burgundian law from the beginning of the sixth century stipulated that anyone stealing a hawk or falcon would be liable to a considerable fine; alternatively, the falcon would be allowed to peck out six ounces of flesh from the thief's hind-quarters!

The first of many bans on the clergy indulging in falconry also dates from about the same period. The papal decrees do not appear to have been observed very well, since there is plenty of evidence that the passion for falconry sometimes attained such proportions that the worthy prelates even took their

FALCONRY

It is impossible to ascribe a definite date or even century to the birth of falconry in Europe on the basis of what we know at present, but there is much to suggest that it was practised by Germanic tribes somewhere between A.D. 100 and 500. It is true that the people of antiquity, according to Aristotle, occasionally used hawks for hunting marsh birds, but they employed methods other than those of the falconry practised at that time, and presumably for the previous two or three thousand years, on the steppes of Turkestan. It was from this area that this special type of hunting was later to spread to countries in the East and West.

The Germanic tribes were responsible for the

Frederick II's immensely detailed work on hunting birds was completed about 1250. Detail of the illuminated manuscript. (Bibliothèque Nationale in Paris.)

falcons into church and put them on the high altar during Mass!

Falconry apparently spread to Scandinavia by routes other than those followed in the case of the southern parts of the Continent, but as regards the age and nature of the Northmen's use of birds for hunting a lot of facts have emerged. John Bernström, a Swede, who has made a thorough study of falconry in northern Europe, has good grounds for maintaining that so far no acceptable evidence has come to light that the people of the north used trained falcons for hunting in ancient times. There are several reasons for this, not the least being topographical, since large unbroken plains are

by some beautiful pieces of ironwork from chests and a church door in Rogslösa in the southern Swedish province of Östergötland, all executed by the same craftsman. The broad outlines of the method were as follows: the quarry was first pursued by dogs and afterwards attacked by the hawks, which went for the animal's eyes, thereby preventing it from escaping. This meant that the hunter had time to catch up with it and kill it with his spear.

This method of hunting has survived until the present day in the steppes of central Asia, where it is used by nomadic tribes. We are told that it was not very difficult to train hawks for this cruel form

In northern Europe, noble game was hunted with the aid of trained hawks whose task it was to stop the quarry by pecking out the eyes.
(Detail of church door, Rogslösa church, province of Ostergötland, Sweden. Twelfth century.)

necessary for the pursuit of falconry if the breathtaking beauty of the sport is to have full play. Nowadays, a different interpretation is given to the symbols on runestones and the sections of the oldest chronicles which for a long time were taken to indicate the existence of falconry in northern Europe.

The birds of prey used by the people of the north for hunting were apparently specially trained *hawks*, whose hunting technique is most suited to the undulating and forest-clad countryside of Scandinavia. Falcons attack their prey in the open, stooping on it with great force, while hawks approach their quarry with feline stealth making full use of natural cover.

There is a certain amount of pictorial evidence which shows very dramatically how hawks were used for hunting game in northern Europe during the Iron Age. The best examples of this are provided

of hunting. The hawk was allowed to starve for a few days and thereafter it was always fed on meat which was either attached to the head of a dead animal or placed in the latter's eye-sockets. Gradually the starving bird learnt always to make for the eyes of its quarry.

Mention is made of hawks or falcons in several places in the old chronicles: King Adils of Uppsala, for example, who is believed to have lived in the sixth century, is credited with having had thirty hawks, but it is uncertain whether they were used for hunting or merely served as heraldic emblems.

We also know that Hakon Jarl paid Harold Bluetooth a yearly tribute of a hundred gold marks and sixty falcons or hawks for his portion of Norway. Bluetooth referred to Norway as his "hawk island".

By way of summing up, it may be said that it was during one of the first centuries after the birth of Christ that the interest in falconry awoke on the

Frederick II, king of Sicily and Jerusalem, was one of the most brilliant personalities of the Middle Ages. (After a miniature in the Vatican Library.)

He was a distinctly empirical naturalist and it is just because *De Arte Venande Cum Avibus* is a practical handbook that it seems so surprisingly modern even after seven hundred years.

Neither did Frederick II have any exaggerated respect for the great authorities, and this is noticeable in many parts of the book, for example, in the section dealing with the annual migration of birds, where many of his observations were not confirmed by scientific research until modern times. He discounted, for instance, Aristotle's view that certain birds hibernated, and he corrected the Greek gently on several other points. He knew that northern birds migrate earlier than those of the south and that migration is dependent on weather conditions and climate, as well as on the availability of food. He also knew that the leading birds in flocks of geese and cranes change during migration. He was aware, too, that waterbirds cover themselves with fat from a gland in order to keep the water out. In addition to all this, he presented a very lucid study of different aspects of the flight of birds.

The primary aim of all this patient accumulation of learning was to make Frederick conversant with the nature of birds so as to enable him to use his knowledge of them to establish mastery over his falcons and their intended prey.

In spite of all the wars, politics and other matters which annoyed or stimulated Frederick II, it must nevertheless be said that he had every facility for pursuing his hobby. It was on the wide, treeless plains of Apulia, Calabria and Carpania in the south of Italy that he had his domains, dotted with gloomy castles which he delighted in building. He had twenty strongholds in Apulia alone and he was unable, of course, to refrain from erecting small mansions in their vicinity, intended solely for recreation and hunting.

It is ideal country for falconry. Here we find that

continent, to which it had spread from the East, while the origins of hunting in northern Europe with hawks were to be found elsewhere.

During the seventh century falconry developed considerably in the parts of central Europe controlled by Rome, particularly in England and France (Gaul). As a result of the crusades to the Holy Land princes and knights became acquainted with the highly developed art of falconry existing there, and the first golden age of falconry coincided with the passionate interest evinced in the sport by Frederick II in the thirteenth century. He collected his experiences in *De Arte Venande Cum Avibus*, in many ways an extremely remarkable book on falconry, containing instructions and recommendations which have very much influenced falconry in Europe up to the present time.

Frederick II was, without any doubt, one of the brightest stars in the constellation of European monarchs during the early Middle Ages. Apart from being constantly engaged in wars, crusades and various political and religious controversies, he pursued with great success his interest in mathematics, natural history, architecture, philosophy and falconry.

breathtaking expanse of sky and plain necessary if the spectacle is to assume its most dramatic and beautiful form.

Despite Frederick II's efforts, however, falconry never took root in Italy in the same way as in other parts of Europe. It was, of course, pursued by the nobility and princes, but it proved to be extremely difficult to find skilful falconers in the country. Possibly the reason for this was that the Latin peoples simply lack that patience and tender affection for the birds without which falcons cannot be trained with any real success.

To a greater extent than other kinds of hunting, the pursuit of falconry was dependent on social conditions. It was an occupation for the privileged classes and the falcon rapidly became one of the status symbols with which people of wealth and rank surrounded themselves. The falcon often appeared on seals and in portraits in order to indicate the owner's high station in life.

The English statutes of the Middle Ages stipulated very meticulously the kinds of hawks and falcons which the different levels of society were allowed to possess (below) and the office of royal falconer was reserved solely for the most noble families of the land.

The importance of falconry during the Middle Ages is illustrated by a frequently related story from a chronicle. Following a prophecy to the effect that he was destined to rule the world, Jenghiz Khan despatched a messenger to Frederick II, commanding the latter immediately to declare his submission. At the same time he offered Frederick a high appointment in his kingdom. The Emperor's reply to the Mongol ruler was that the only office which he deemed himself capable of holding was that of chief falconer, and that high appointment was, after all, in the hands of Jenghiz Khan's eldest son. The chronicler reached the conclusion

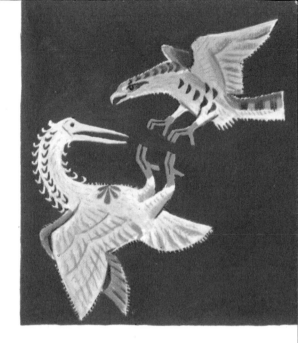

that it was this fact which upset the plans to place the West under the yoke of the East.

Heron hawking with falcon (above). Detail of tapestry from the early sixteenth century. (Cluny Museum, Paris.)

(Below) Social division of hawks and falcons (one of many) : King — white Greenland falcon, prince — male gyr falcon, duke — peregrine, lady of rank — merlin, priest — sparrow hawk, knight — goshawk.

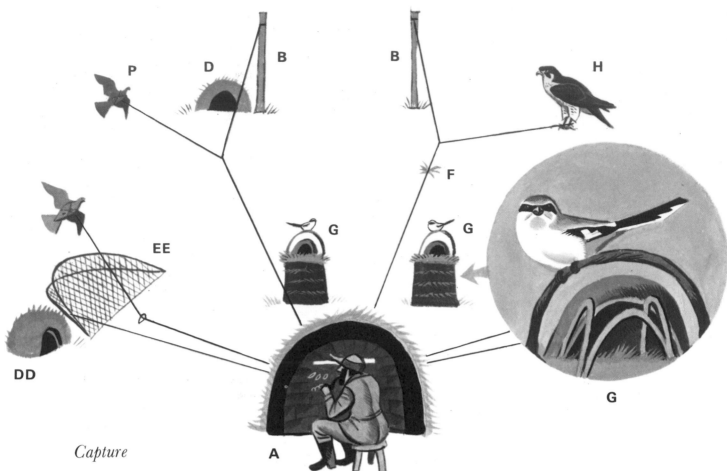

Capture

Frederick II trained both fully-grown falcons and nestlings. In addition, he tried to get domestic hens to hatch falcon eggs so that he would be able to follow the development of the birds from the very beginning. All falconers are agreed, however, on one point: the best hunters are always those birds that are caught fully grown, for they have received their training in the art from their parents. Anyone who has had an opportunity of seeing how an adult falcon teaches a young bird the art of hawking will readily understand that there is no better teacher. Besides, a falcon which has been taken from the nest will never attain the same impetus in its stoop as a falcon captured wild.

In order to soothe the captured falcon and facilitate taming it must be kept in darkness for some time. In the Middle Ages a falcon's eyelids were sewn together with a fine needle but later a leather rufter hood was used. (Musée de la Chasse, Gien.)

Wild falcons were sometimes caught at the nesting site and sometimes during migration between their winter quarters and breeding area; these falcons were termed passage falcons. Icelanders are said to have sometimes managed to capture three or four hen birds on the same nest during one and the same season, because the male was able to find a new mate surprisingly quickly after the old one had disappeared. The female birds were always most in demand on account of their much greater size.

Passage falcons were caught in particular in Holland, known since ancient times as the falconers' country par excellence of Europe. There are many methods of capture but the somewhat complicated technique which will be described here was used by Karl Mollen, the last and most famous of the many prominent falcon-catchers. Mollen was active in Valkensvaard in Northern Brabant by the Belgian frontier. He died in 1937.

Description of picture above: (After J. E. Harting 1883)

(BB) Two poles twenty-five feet high. A thin line, which can be adjusted from inside the hut (A), runs from the top of the poles. A decoy-bird (pigeon) is tethered to one of the poles, (P) and a live falcon (H) to the other.

(F)—A bunch of feathers attached to the line.

(D)—A small hut where the decoy-bird can shelter from the rain or when the falcon appears.

(DD)—One hundred yards to the right and to the left of the hut (A) two small cotes big enough for a pigeon each.

(EE) A bow-net which is adjusted by the falcon catcher from the hut (A). The pigeons in (DD) are at first kept shut up but can easily be brought out from the hut.

(GG)—Great grey shrikes whose task it is to sound the alarm when the falcon appears. It is preferable to use two shrikes so that they egg one another on.

When all the necessary preparations have been made, the falcon catcher picks up the lines to (P) and (H), one in each hand, and waits for the falcon to put in an appearance. Long before the human eye can spot it, the great grey shrikes have seen the falcon and flap their wings anxiously on their perches and utter their alarm notes. The catcher then pulls the right-hand line at once and makes the falcon (H) take wing. It flies round the pole in narrow circles and at the same time the bunch of feathers (F) moves like a bird trying to escape.

The idea now is that the wild falcon will notice his colleague's "chase" and come closer out of curiosity. When he has got within approximately 200 yards, the falcon catcher pulls the tethered falcon down to the ground and releases in its stead the decoy pigeon (P), which is intended to make the passage falcon interested in earnest. If this happens and the falcon aims for (P), increasing his speed for the attack, (P) is pulled in quickly and allowed to shelter in its hut. The falcon now slows up in surprise, but catches sight of one of the pigeons by (DD) which suddenly appears near the bow-net. The falcon wheels round, stoops on the pigeon and ends with its prey on the ground near the net. Now all the falcon catcher has to do is to pull the falcon and the captured pigeon extremely cautiously within reach of the net and then jerk the line attached to the net and capture the bird.

All this may seem unnecessarily complicated, but experience has shown that this method produces the best results. When one recalls that birds of prey are at present included in the list of birds that are most seriously threatened with extermination owing to biocides, egg collectors and other forms of persecution, it is a relief to know that falcons are no longer caught at Valkensvaard. The extensive and undisturbed plains which were a prerequisite for trapping have been broken up into numerous fields and farms, and consequently falcon trapping is no longer feasible there.

Prey and Technique

Falconry was something to watch: it was a *show*, more so than any other type of hunting. The seizure of the prey was not the main point; it was not even desirable. When the falcon had defeated its quarry, the show was over and if the victim was in good condition it was released.

Flying falcon at herons was by far the most popular form of hawking. Of the various methods used, the interception of herons on the way between their fishing grounds and their nesting colonies was the most common. It was not unusual for hunting lodges to be built near the routes taken by the herons so as to allow the various acts of the drama to be followed in comfort from the roof or terrace. A well-trained falconry team must indeed have afforded a thrilling display of co-operation between master and falcon: an advanced ballet in which the falcon was the prima ballerina and the falconer the choreographer.

When a heron was bound for its nest and young, its crop heavy with freshly-caught fish, a blast on the falcon-master's trumpet was the signal for the first act. The hoods were removed from the falcons and the birds were launched into the air, where they soon spotted the heron and prepared to stoop. As a rule gerfalcons and peregrines were used for catching herons and other large birds.

Hawking herons is not entirely without its dangers for falcons, for the heron has a special ability to ward off attacks from above by making a snakelike movement with its neck and stabbing with its dagger-shaped bill. However, two or three falcons were often used simultaneously on these hunts and they assisted one another in exhausting their victim until it was eventually forced down to the ground.

There was a particularly great danger of the heron injuring the falcon on the ground and, in order to protect the valuable bird, specially trained dogs were used to prevent the heron from hurting the falcon. The training of hounds for falconry was one of the most difficult tasks of the falconer. He had to teach both hound and falcon to trust each other; he had to make sure that each of them knew his precise role. As far as the hound was concerned, his task was merely to assist the falcon but under no circumstances touch the quarry himself.

It may be said that the royal hunting lodge at Loo in the Dutch province of Gelderland was a kind of centre for heron hunting with falcons in central Europe, for it was there that the Royal Loo Hawking Club (founded on English initiative) arranged heron hunts on the classical pattern between 1839 and 1853. The season occurred in June and July, when the young were being fed in the heronry, and almost fifty falcons were used, a quarter of which sometimes flew astray and disappeared. The costs were high. Each year about 8,000 pounds of beef

and close to 1,500 pigeons were required to feed the falcons. On an average 200 herons were killed each season at Loo, but one year the figure rose to 297.

The use of falcons to hunt kites was regarded as being *"le vol royal"* — hunting fit for kings; in some areas it was considered to be definitely superior to heron hunting. From a purely aesthetic point of view the flight of the kite is one of the most exquisite to be seen. She literally floats through the air, steering the whole time with the aid of slight flicks of her elegant swallow-tail. On warm, calm days she can rise to an immense height.

In order to enable the falcon to attack, the kite had to be forced down to a more convenient height over the ground. This was done with the assistance of an eagle owl on whose feet a fox's tail had been tied, partly in order to restrict the owl's movements but partly also to make it visible at a long distance. When curiosity causes the kite to descend towards the strangely equipped eagle owl, the falcons are released, the kite immediately climbs and the falcons chase her until they gradually succeed in reaching a suitable height above her from which to stoop. Now follows attack after attack against the long-winged bird of prey, as regular as the blacksmith's strokes on the anvil with his hammer, in the words of a famous falconer, d'Arcussia by name. Eventually the kite and the falcons fall to the ground, the falconer gallops up on his horse and lifts up the kite which regains her freedom.

The glove was made of strong ox or deer skin to protect the falconer's hand from the
falcon's claws. This glove from the middle of the seventeenth century is covered with
blue velvet. (*Musée de la Chasse, Gien.*)

In Europe the falcon was always carried on the left hand. Presumably the reason for the
noble lady wearing the glove on the wrong hand is that the tapestry weaver saw the
picture in a mirror when copying it on to the cloth.

Margaret of Anjou being given a mallard by her falconer who has just brought in the
falcon with the aid of the lure. (*"The hunting tapestry"*, *c. 1440*, Victoria and
Albert Museum.)

"I have bought me a hawk and a hood and bells and all and lack nothing but a book to keep it by," Ben Jonson writes in *Every Man in his Humour* (1598). It was probably easy to make up for this deficiency as at that time the market was flooded with compendiums, some more magnificent than others, on hunting with hawks and falcons. Interest in falconry reached its zenith in the Middle Ages, and the splendour that attached to it was enormous. At first it was open to all sections of the community, but it very soon became in fact a privilege of the wealthiest classes. Already in the ninth century the falcon had established its unrivalled position as a status symbol and there was scarcely a royal personage who did not draw attention to his high rank by having his picture painted with a falcon on his wrist. Monarchs allowed their most distinguished falconers to precede them in processions, a tradition which survived until modern times.

The cost of falconry at royal courts gradually rose to incredible sums. The falconers at the court of Francis I (1515–1547), for example, cost 40,000 livres a year. This sum was probably the equivalent in modern currency of well over 70,000 pounds.

In England, in particular, the interest in falconry shown by highly born ladies appears to have been remarkable during the later Middle Ages. One of the more famous works on falconry, incidentally the first book on hunting to have been written in the English language, was the *Boke of Saint Alban* by Abbess Juliana Barnes, printed in 1486. This work provides an interesting sidelight on the clergy's often demonstrated passion for hunting in various forms, although the Papacy constantly issued warnings and forbade the sport. It is true that J. E. Harting has provided good grounds for doubting the abbess's authorship as regards the whole work but she undeniably supported its publication.

It even happened during the sixteenth century that the coveted post of chief falconer was held by a woman — Mary of Canterbury. There appeared at the time of the marriage between Margaret of Anjou and Henry VI a series of tapestries, full of detail and interesting to students of the history of hunting, which were woven in Tournai about 1440. After leading a Sleeping Beauty existence for several hundred years these tapestries were discovered at the turn of the present century. They were restored and are now at the Victoria and Albert Museum in London. The scenes are clearly from illustrations in *The Hunting Book of King Practice and Queen Theory* written a century or so earlier by Gaston Phoebus under the title *Les Livres du Roi Modus et de la Reine*

(*Left*) *Sparrow hawk on bow-perch;* (*right*) *French perch from nineteenth century.* (*Musée de la Chasse, Gien.*)

Ratio qui parle de chasse at de pestilence, which according to the cynegetics expert, Gunnar Tilander, dates from 1374–1377.

The vast increase in interest in falconry led, not unexpectedly, to rivalry between the huntsmen and the falconers. The former began to enjoy a smaller share of the limelight at royal courts. In Gaston Phoebus's hunting handbook, referred to above, it is stated that the huntsmen were in the habit of calling the falconers "fleapickers", on account of their having to spend a fair amount of time after each hunt removing lice from the falcons. The falconers got their own back by pouring scorn on the huntsmen, saying that they always reeked of the kennels.

A learned man who was asked to say which form of hunting was the best gave the following verdict:

"It is true that the eye, the mirror of the soul, is the most noble of the senses and therefore falconry should be regarded as the best, but nevertheless hunting to hounds must be awarded the prize since they alone give pleasure both to the huntsman's ear and to his eye at the same time."

Gyrfalcon, of northern Scandinavian race, on falconer's deerskin glove. The feathered hood is the Dutch type. The lure (above) exists in many versions. Hidden from view is the fork for the piece of meat with which the falcon is lured down to the ground.

(Below, right) Dutch and Indian hoods, rufter hood and Indian bell. (After Lascelles.)

It is difficult to realise just how much falconry influenced the lives of the upper classes for several hundreds of years. It permeated pictorial art, literature, legislation, and cultural life as a whole. It is impossible, for example, for a translator to do full justice to a piece of Shakespeare when putting it into any foreign language whatsoever without a knowledge of the terminology of falconry, for his dramas are so full of allusions to and metaphors connected with this sport.

For instance, in one well-known line Hamlet says that "I am but mad north-north-west; when the wind is southerly, I know a hawk from a handsaw". "Handsaw" is a corruption of the mediaeval English "heronshow" or "herounsew", that is to say

modern English "heron". Shakespeare simply used an old falconer's expression meaning that when a falcon and a heron climb into the sky with a north-westerly wind the falconer is dazzled by the afternoon sun (that is when the hunting is done) and is unable to distinguish between the two birds as easily as when the wind is in the south, for instance. Shakespeare's dramas are full of similar references to various points about falconry which, for reasons easily understood, are a mystery to a translator without a basic knowledge of the art of falconry.

The falconers had an extensive jargon, rich in secret expressions whose origins are lost in the mists of history. In former times there were innumerable technical terms and it may be assumed there was not a single move made by the falcon, not the most insignificant phenomenon of its behaviour, which did not have a special term in the vocabulary. Although in modern times it has been possible to remove the majority of exaggerations and superfluous expressions, the terminology of falconry continues to be extremely wide in the various civilised languages.

The standard equipment of the falconers included the deerskin *glove, hoods* of various kinds, for example simple rufter hoods for newly caught falcons, and magnificent hoods of various designs. The *lure* varied greatly in design. Usually it consisted of two wings fixed to a strong leather-covered pronged stick with a strap approximately three yards long. During training the falcon learns to associate food with the lure, for it is fed on meat attached to the prongs. When the falconer wants to bring in the falcon he waves the lure about or throws it up in the air. The falcon then turns and catches it in mid-air. The lure must be sufficiently heavy that the falcon cannot lift it and fly away with it. The lure is the falconer's most important item of equipment and in Germany, as a matter of fact, it gives its name to this method of hunting (Ger. Federspiel).

Jesses, strips of leather for the legs, which must be worn the whole time by the falcon.

Bells to be attached to the legs. The best are said to be made in Lahore in India.

The *cadge* was mainly used for large gatherings when several falcons had to be transported to the field. The man who carries this frame is called a *cadge-bearer*, a precursor of the *golf caddy*. The frame is fitted with four legs so that it can be stood on the ground.

The *block* and the *bow-perch*. The former is for falcons to rest on and the latter for hawks. There are numerous varieties of these two perches.

The *hawking bag* or *falconer's bag* is fairly large and spacious and is very striking in appearance. It is designed to hold two live pigeons, bits of meat or other edible matter which are given to the falcon when he has stooped on a bird or has been enticed to the lure.

An old English proverb says that "it is easier to train a gun than a hawk", and great demands were indeed placed on a good falconer. In Sigmund Feyerabend's famous work *Neuw Jag- und Weydwerck Buch*, of 1582, the requirements are summarised as follows: "He must be straightforward, friendly, gentle, lovable and in addition possess several other desirable characteristics. He must have a bold but mild nature and he must be extremely interested in hawking. When the falcon is disobedient he must not flare up and shout at him, abuse him, shake, prod or hit him. The falconer must instead be forbearing and patient, but he must correct the falcon's mistakes in a kind and gentle way, and give him a thorough and skilful training. He must be hard-working, spare no pains or shirk any task, day or night, and always think of his falcons. Whether the weather is fair or foul, whether it is warm or cold, he must always be eager to work."

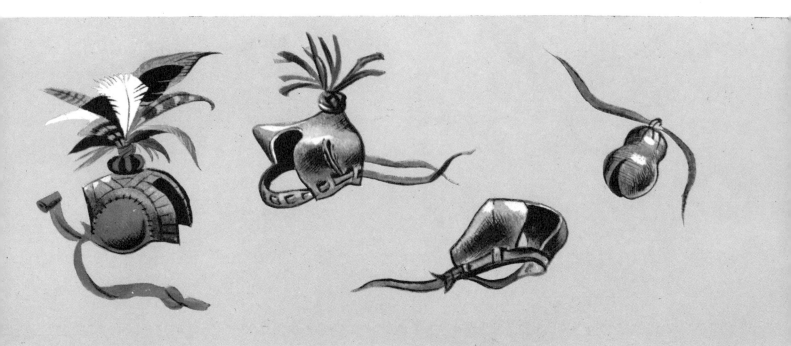

At first only the handler may approach the newly-caught falcon. He must move slowly, talk to the falcon a lot so that the latter recognises his voice and every time he gives it food he must use special words of command or whistles. He must constantly study the falcon's behaviour so that he gets to know its character, for falcons may vary enormously individually and there is no standard recipe for training them.

In the beginning, the falcon is of course very frightened and ill at ease and the falconer should therefore take him to lonely spots when he needs fresh air. In order to soothe a nervous falcon it was, and still is in some parts of the world, the custom to squirt a mouthful of water over him. This makes his muscles contract and he is obliged to close his wings and quieten down, at least temporarily.

This method was indeed recommended by Frederick II as early as the thirteenth century.

When the falcon has begun to get accustomed to falconers went so far as to take their protégés with to start carefully accustoming him to other people and in that way, little by little, to the hustle and bustle of everyday life. During the Middle Ages the falconers went so far as to take their protégés with them to the alehouse, where they quickly felt as much at home on the back of a chair as on their perch in the cage.

There exist the most detailed instructions on the treatment of falcons in the event of various accidents or complaints but the majority of the prescriptions had no other effect than to line the purse of the medicine man. When it is recalled what enormous sums of money princes spent on their darlings it is really quite easy to understand that all kinds of superstition and quackery flourished unrestrained. In English books on falconry a constantly recurring ingredient of the medicine was something called "mummy", but nowadays people are extremely uncertain as to what this substance actually was. When a distinguished falconer not so very long ago asked a colleague whether he knew what mummy really was he was given the illuminating reply: "Mummy is mummy."

Experienced falconers possessed, however, an extraordinary ability to cure or prevent certain complaints affecting falcons. The birds were kept out of draughts, they were carefully dried and kept warm when it rained, they were given the right

(*Above, from left to right*) *Falconer's servant with
cadge, huntsman with eagle owl for kite hawking.*
(*Inset*) *The Elector Clement Augustus of Cologne
(1723–1761) and his Greenland falcon.*
(*After Wood-Fyfe.*)

quantities of feathers or hair with their meat so as to
ensure that their digestive organs functioned in the
same way as when the bird in its wild state had to
obtain food itself. There was also an ingenious
method of replacing broken wing-quills so that the
falcon recovered its normal powers of flight.

During the moulting season discarded feathers
and quills were retrieved, carefully numbered and
stored out of harm's way. When a bird broke a particular quill, a spare quill was fetched from the
store, and cut into the right length. One end of a
fine needle was inserted in the stem of the reserve
quill and the other end in the stub of the old wing
feather. The two halves were then forced together
into one whole feather, after which the falcon was
able to fly again without any trouble at all. (Page
54.)
This operation was called imping. Shakespeare
makes clever use of this well-known falconer's trick
in a metaphor in *Richard II*:

"If then we shall shake off our slavish yoke,
imp out our drooping country's broken wing"

It takes about six months of intensive work to get
a falcon fully trained for hunting. It is trained each
day to stoop on tame birds and to return without

(*Below*) *Scottish falconer on horseback.*
(*After an etching by C. Turner, 1816.*)

The Lanner falcon was one of the commonest birds of the Chase during the Middle Ages. It was usually called "the bluefoot" owing to the colour of the legs and feet of the young birds. This falcon nested in central Europe until the mid-eighteenth century. The method of attaching the jesses to the falcon's feet dates from the early Middle Ages.
A broken feather could be repaired by means of imping, for which a wing feather, retrieved during the moulting season, was used.

fail when the falconer calls and waves the lure. It is a lengthy business and a training that requires the utmost patience from both the falcon and his master. Whatever one's attitude to this sport, particularly when the unfortunately rapid decrease of birds of prey in many parts of Europe is borne in mind, it is nevertheless an unforgettable sight to see the falcon leave his master's glove and fly off with rapid beats of his wings on a practice flight across the fields, and a little while later return obediently and stoop on the lure. There is a kind of secret understanding between man and falcon, an understanding born of our natural instincts which has never ceased to provide a fascinating spectacle and method of hunting.

It was mentioned on an earlier page that the female falcon, because of its size, was more popular with the falconers. It was always the female bird to which the word falcon applied. The male was

called a tiercel (Lat. *tertius*), and this term has survived in the language of falconers ever since the days of Frederick II. The origin of the word is obscure. As a rule, it is taken to mean that the male is smaller than the female bird by a third, a considerable exaggeration. According to another explanation, which is sheer superstition, one of the three nestlings normally found in a falcon's nest is always a male!

What birds of prey are used for falconry? For a start it may be said that the actual word "falconry" is misleading since nearly all birds of prey, with the exception of owls, have been used for this kind of hunting. Apart from the various types of falcons, sparrow hawks and goshawks have been the most important as far as Europe is concerned.

The mainly white *Greenland falcon* was the most highly esteemed. It could be used for flying at all kinds of birds.

54

Next in order of merit came the *Iceland falcon* and the Scandinavian *gyrfalcon*, more or less equal in status, but there was a preference for the most lightly marked examples.

They were replaced in the south-eastern parts of Europe by the *saker falcon*. It was, however, considered unreliable and difficult to tame and was therefore, despite excellent hunting qualities in other respects, less popular than the preceding kinds.

One of the most common hawking birds during the Middle Ages was the somewhat smaller *Lanner falcon*, which was usually called the bluefoot owing to the colour of the legs and feet of the young birds. In a detailed commentary on a mediaeval translation of Albertus Magnus, Kurt Lindner dealt with the role played by the Lanner falcon, the bluefoot, in falconry in central Europe, and pointed out that the range of this type of falcon, which nowadays is only to be found in Italy and the western Balkans, covered large areas of the European continent during the Middle Ages. It was not until the middle of the eighteenth century that it disappeared completely from Germany, presumably as a result of an energetic campaign to destroy birds of prey. It was very much used at royal courts but was never looked upon as one of the "noble falcons", being regarded as slow and difficult to train but possibly of some use for partridge hunts (d'Arcussia).

It may be mentioned that the French name for this falcon, Lanier, according to Gunnar Tilander's research, means "weaver" in mediaeval French. This trade was considered unworthy of men and the word gained a derogatory sense when applied to a falcon.

The *peregrine*, which was used a lot for hawking, was the same size. It was, however, completely different in character and more audacious.

The *hobby*, *merlin* and *kestrel* are the smallest types of falcons. The merlin was used above all by noble ladies, and the kestrel was recommended chiefly for novices in the art of falconry since it was very easy to train. Curiously enough, Louis XIII used it for catching bats!

The *goshawk* is an efficient hunter which, it is true, was unable to provide as magnificent a show in the skies as the falcons, but on the other hand it was greatly appreciated in the kitchen as a household hunter. Hoods were never used for hawks.

During the Middle Ages, hawks were particularly popular in France as birds of the chase. According to Shakespeare, the French let the hawk stoop on "all that moved". Only the large, audacious female birds were used — under the rules of class distinction they were reserved for the junior clergy —

and they were apparently capable of dealing with nearly everything in the way of small game birds, although, of course, they did not provide a spectacular show. Their speciality was, in fact, hunting for the table: they were reliable and fairly efficient at this. If done in the right way, it provided the peasant falconer with a pretty reasonable additional income. Charles d'Arcussia, who was a distinguished falconer in the mid-seventeenth century, wrote that, at the height of the quail migration in western France in the early autumn, an experienced hunter, using his sparrow hawk, caught as many as seventy quail in a single day; the birds were so fat that they were hardly able to lift their wings!

In England, too, right up to the present day, the sparrow hawk has frequently been used to frighten away thrushes from cherry trees in the summer, which underlines their ability to act as "flying cats". "I have a fine hawk for the bush", runs a line in *The Merry Wives of Windsor*. These words undoubtedly refer to the sparrow hawk which, in contrast with the "long-winged hawks", preferred to hunt in wooded country.

Hawks differ from falcons in that they make use of both their hearing and their sight when searching for their quarry. For this reason, a hood is never used for a hawk, as it is more difficult for it to get its bearings when the hood is removed.

A full-grown golden eagle weighs about thirteen pounds and consequently it is tiring to carry it on one's hand for any length of time.

In open country a fox has no hope of escaping from an attacking eagle. The latter's flying speed has been clocked at 120 miles an hour.

Eagles

It is true that eagles head the "roll of honour" in several mediaeval books on falconry — according to the *Boke of St Albans*, the eagle was reserved for emperors — but nevertheless they played an extremely insignificant and sporadic part in the art of falconry in Europe.

Frederick II mentions the eagle in his book on falconry, but emphasises that for various reasons it is unsuitable for hawking. For one thing, it is too heavy and big to carry on one's hand and, besides,

it upsets the smaller birds of the chase and makes it difficult to hunt in company with them. In Asia where eagles are very much used for hawking, they always hunt with the eagle on its own in view of its difficulties in "co-operating" with other birds of the chase.

The golden eagle, imperial eagle and Bonelli's eagle are the chief kinds used for hunting. The Bonelli's eagle is by far the most suitable for this purpose on account of its small size and ability to

56

learn, while the imperial eagle — despite its splendid name — is considerably less popular. Experts describe the latter as being slow and cowardly and credit it with characteristics which put it only on a slightly higher plane than the kite.

Hawking with eagles does not afford the breathtakingly beautiful sight provided by swooping falcons: the chief purpose of this form of hunting is to obtain food for the table. The Kirghizes, who live west of the Caspian Sea, have been particularly fond of training eagles, and they use them mainly for hunting wolves, foxes, hares and badgers as well as several kinds of large birds, especially the extremely shy bustards. The Mongolian chieftain, Timur (Tamerlane), who lived at the end of the fourteenth century is said to have hunted swans with eagles in the neighbourhood of Bukhara.

A newly-caught golden eagle sold for up to three horses, and a trained eagle for two camels. In south-eastern Europe the people of the Carpathian mountains were among those who used eagles for hunting far into the twentieth century.

Eagles were trained in much the same way as hawks: in other words, the bird was at first allowed to starve, after which it was fed on meat placed in the eye-sockets or on the heads of dead animals. Before the eagle was let loose on the quarry the huntsman had to be sure that it had really caught sight of it: otherwise, the eagle might easily pounce on the huntsman's horse and try to peck out the latter's eyes. Apparently this kind of mishap was not particularly uncommon. A fox skin was used instead of a lure to persuade the eagle to return.

When a trained eagle attacked a deer or wild boar, it usually planted one foot in the small of the animal's back and the other in its shoulder or neck and tried to open up a wound in the fleeing animal's side. In this way the quarry was forced to the ground on account of its injuries. When hunting foxes or wolves, the eagle gripped the animal's back with one foot and when the quarry turned its head it felt

In Asia the eagle is carried on a perch attached to the handler's belt or on a pole fastened between the stirrups of two horsemen.

the eagle's other foot grip its muzzle so that it had to stop.

Eagles are considered to be more difficult to train than falcons, perhaps partly owing to their being greater individualists. They are extremely sensitive to the way in which they are treated and apparently are remarkably resentful. When they get old, it is not rare for them to become irritable, so that it is wise for the owner to be careful how he handles his bird. The latter-day successors of Frederick II, for whom the art of falconry is a hobby for a select few, have actually achieved good results with the training of eagles for hunting both in Europe and America. One of the most successful and famous was the Englishman, Hugh D. Knight, whose eagles became world-famous thanks to the cinema and the press.

The pre-eminent position of falconry as a pastime in mediaeval Europe can only be compared with that of football today. But, on the other hand, falconry was so dependent on the feudal system, on the hitherto little cultivated continent, that any future development was out of the question. Large-scale hunting with falcons needs open and undulating park-like country alternating with copses and streams and rivers.

With more and more land coming under the plough, falconry found its freedom of movement very much restricted; this was perhaps one of the most important of the many reasons why the beautiful sport with birds and lures began to lose its glamour and popularity in one country after another. In all probability the French Revolution was the final blow to the mediaeval form of falconry: in modern Europe the falconer's art seems to be an archaism.

The attempts that were made in the nineteenth century and later to infuse fresh life into falconry were of little account, relatively speaking. It is true that Napoleon very soon realised the value of falconry as an imperial status symbol, but his attitude to the noble sport was unfortunately a somewhat depraved one. On one occasion he wantonly shot a falcon which had just risen into the air to hunt. When he saw the dead bird, he merely exclaimed in amazement: *"Quel bel oiseau!"*

The interest in falconry remained alive longest in England, although very feebly at times, and it was without doubt very much thanks to Englishmen that the famous Dutch falconry traditions managed to survive until the middle of the nineteenth century.

Holland had been for centuries a kind of centre for falconry enthusiasts, and the small town of Valkenswaard supplied the whole of Europe with well-trained falcons and distinguished falconers. During the golden age of the town there lived there some thirty families who in some cases had specialised for generations in the catching and training of falcons. The last of these legendary falconers, Karl Mollen, died in 1936.

The Royal Loo Hawking Club was founded in 1839 by English, Dutch and French falconry enthusiasts. Under the patronage of William III of Holland the club hunted heron with falcons in the grand style of the old days at the royal hunting lodge, Het Loo, near Valkenswaard. The club was also responsible for an enduring monument to its activities by entrusting two naturalists, H. Schlegel of Germany and A. H. Vorster de Wulverhorst of Holland, with the task of producing a work on falconry, which was printed between 1844 and 1853; thanks to the wonderful life-size colour lithographs, it is considered to be one of the most valuable (and most expensive) works in the whole of the rich literature on falconry.

The club had to be disbanded in 1853 and the falconer's art declined for some years, until in 1864 the English Old Hawking Club was founded for the purpose of hunting with falcons on Salisbury Plain and, later on, also in other suitable places. It was very active as recently as 1926 when it, too, was obliged to close down on account of the high costs. The membership fee was in the region of £350.

The Deutscher Falkenorden was started in 1923 in Germany on the initiative of former prisoners of war who had come into contact with falconry in Russia and Turkestan. It soon came under the powerful patronage of Herman Göring and this also resulted in the construction of the Reich-falkenhof in pure Germanic style. Thanks to its leader, Renz Waller, falconry was raised to a very high level in Germany, but then the war came and everything was ruined. Nevertheless, Waller brought off the feat of getting peregrine falcons to nest and hatch out young two or three times during the war. His famous goshawk "Medusa" actually survived the war and did not die until 1949 when it was twenty-one years old.

The interest in the falconer's art also survived the war in Europe. Clubs and private individuals keep falconry alive in several places in spite of the fact that it is becoming increasingly difficult to obtain falcons on account of bird protection laws and the growing rarity of the birds.

The Deutscher Falkenorden has been resuscitated and a new Falkenhof has been built close to the old Hessian hunting lodge, Kranichstein, near Darmstadt. So the blasé tourists of today can go there and witness the marvellous sight of falcons with delicately tinkling bells being recalled from high in the sky by falconers with lures. In France the "Association Nationale de Fauconniers et Autoriers Français" (ANFA) was founded to promote and preserve the falconer's art. The association has about 250 members and they are entitled to wear the silver club buttons bearing a gyrfalcon and the proud motto "Rien sans pennes".

In England, too, falconry societies have appeared since the war and Phillip Glasier's stimulating book, *As the Falcon her Bells*, should help considerably in increasing interest in the sport.

It may therefore be said that this ancient art continues to survive, as if by a miracle, through the centuries in spite of all the things that are happening to the countryside and people. The sense of contact with the Middle Ages is never so deep as when one sees the beautiful display of co-operation between the falcon and his master.

The falconer's art was often handed down from generation to generation, sometimes for century after century. Peter Ballantyne (above) has been called the last of the Scottish falconers. His father taught him to carry a falcon on his hand "as soon as he could stand on his two legs" and he was active in this profession until his death at the age of 86. (After Lascelles.)

(Below) In modern times, too, falconers have striven to surround themselves with a certain, but perhaps comparatively modest, glory. This is a bronze and pewter uniform button made for Doctor Luc Arbel's falconry team at the beginning of the twentieth century. (Musée International de la Chasse à tir et de la Fauconnerie, Gien.)

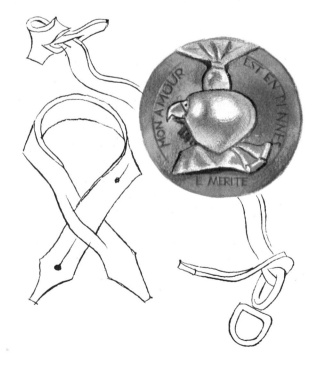

Using a line smeared with bird-lime to catch quails squatting on the appearance of a trained hawk. (Freely adapted from Pietro Olina's Uccelaria, *1622.)*

Hunting Birds

Various birds of prey were also used with the emphasis more on the utilitarian aspect than was the case with falconry. On such occasions their task was twofold: either to frighten the quarry into squatting tightly on the ground so that the hunter could easily reach it, or to entice the bird into making a daring attack, thereby enabling the hunter from his hiding place to catch it in one of several ways.

The use of birds of prey for this kind of hunting dates back a very long way. According to the Pseudo Aristotle, rather cunning tactics were employed to hunt marsh birds in Thrace in Greece. At certain times of the year, presumably during the migratory season, crowds of people went out into the marshes and beat about in the reeds with sticks, shouting and making a lot of noise. This frightened large numbers of birds into taking wing, but they were immediately forced down to the ground again by the numerous birds of prey which were usually to be found in the neighbourhood. "The moment had now come for everyone to pounce on the squatting birds and hit them with sticks: the catch was then taken home, once some of it had been left for the birds of prey."

This use of the well-known instinct of birds to squat tightly at the sight of a predatory bird gradually produced an organised method of hunting with the use of tame, trained birds of prey.

An Italian handbook on hawking from the beginning of the seventeenth century describes how two men caught quails with a hawk. One of the men carried the hawk on his hand while his companion very cautiously pushed a long stick, with a line at the end, smeared with bird-lime, towards the quails squatting in the grass. This strange method of using a bird of prey may appear to be reasonable in theory but hardly feasible in practice, yet in times when there was an abundance of birds of the fields it was in fact a very widespread and effective method.

The author of the present work was once trying very carefully to approach a little ringed plover on open heathland near a lake with a view to photographing it. The bird ran in fits and starts in front of me but would not let me get closer than between twenty and thirty yards. Suddenly it stopped dead in its tracks, made itself as small as possible and cocked an eye at the sky. I followed his gaze and caught sight of a large female goshawk streaking over the shore. As a rule, therefore, birds look on human beings as the less dangerous threat.

Trained falcons and hawks were also used in conjunction with a drawnet — *a tirasse* — for catching birds. This was a very ancient and primitive technique, primarily based on co-operation between the men, the bird of prey and a specially trained dog.

The dog discovered where the covey of partridges was hiding in the grass and pointed to the spot; the bird of prey was released or placed on top of a high pole, taken along for the occasion. The pole was then planted in the ground where it could easily be seen by the birds. The hunters then dragged the three or four-yard-wide tirasse along the ground between them while the dog, moving cautiously, manoeuvred the squatting or running flock of birds into the net. It was essential that the dog drove the birds along in front of it and did not frighten them. Sometimes a piece of wood was fastened to its palate to prevent it barking.

The use of an eagle owl or other type of owl to catch crows and birds of prey is an ancient method. The oldest cynegetical literature contains a large number of variations on the same theme, which, on the whole, differ little from the type of hunting with eagle owls still practised in many places — apart from the fact that fire arms were not used in ancient times! Bearing in mind how greatly the whole eagle owl species is threatened, it is a relief to note that a well-made decoy eagle owl infuriates its attackers in almost the same way as a live bird.

Owls, and in particular the eagle owl with its ear-tufts and flaming eyes, cause many kinds of birds to explode into a blind rage. The use of the eagle owl as a decoy dates back to the world of antiquity. Before the development of weapons made wing shooting possible, they were largely caught with the aid of twigs smeared with bird-lime. (After a woodcut in Petrus von Crescens' Opus ruralium, 1493.)

The majority of birds of prey behave extremely aggressively towards the eagle owl. This fact was readily made use of by the bird-catchers who caught them with the help of a tame eagle owl and a high net.

Originally, eagle owls were used as decoys almost solely for the *trapping* of birds; a considerable time was to pass before the improvement of fire-arms made wing shooting possible in combination with the use of the eagle owl.

During the Middle Ages, this was very much a form of hunting for the common man — in *The Hunting Book of King Modus* it came under the heading of "bird-hunting for the poor man". Apparently, it was most usual to place lime rods among the trees and bushes near the eagle owl and the hunter's hide. The use of lime to catch birds will be described in greater detail in the chapter on small birds; the lime was made mainly from mistletoe berries and smeared on branches or sticks on which the birds alighted when attacking the eagle owl.

The use of an eagle owl or other kind of owl for trapping birds is based on the fact that most birds hurl themselves furiously upon these nocturnal birds whose mobility is greatly limited in daylight. According to Henri de Ferrières in *The Hunting Book of King Modus*, the best time for trapping birds was shortly before sunset.

When the hunter has put the eagle owl in position, he enters the hide and imitates a bird's shrill warning cry by blowing into his cupped hands, using a leaf or piece of grass as a membrane — a skilful bird-catcher should be able to vary his call according to the kind of bird he is trying to catch. This method of trapping birds with the aid of bird-lime was used already in the days of antiquity and spread across the continent thanks to the Germanic tribes. It was also practised in Scandinavia during the Middle Ages.

Ferrières assures us that the use of lime to catch birds was sometimes so profitable that the rods and branches had to be cleared of birds, and more lime smeared on three or four times in the course of one spell in the hide. As many as 120 jays were once caught in a single day.

Another and very widespread method of trapping birds involved the use of tongs or *cleft sticks*. In this case the hunters — in contrast with those using bird-lime — took an active part in catching the birds. Use was made of the attacking bird's habit of alighting on branches in the immediate neighbourhood of the owl for the purpose of scolding the latter at close quarters. As a rule, this was a form of hunting for several men at a time.

The cleft stick was about one and a half yards long and split lengthwise, so that it could be closed quickly like a pair of pincers with the aid of a piece of string which zigzagged between the two sections of the stick. The decoy was placed close beside or on the actual hide, which had to be big enough for three or four hunters to stand comfortably upright inside. The cleft sticks protruded from different parts of the hide. When a bird settled on one of them it was up to the man holding the stick to pull the string quickly so that the two sections gripped the bird's feet or claws.

Thrushes especially were caught in this way. The most suitable time was during the early autumn, when large flocks of migrating thrushes were in the habit of descending on vineyards to gorge on the grapes. According to Ferrières, the best results were obtained towards the end of the wine harvest when only the odd vineyard or two was still untouched and where, consequently, all the thrushes in the neighbourhood congregated.

A curious variation of this trapping method is to be found in an illustration of Aesop's tales in a German edition of 1501. It shows a one-man hide which can easily be moved and used on the move! Here the owl is placed on the actual cleft stick. The practical value of this portable trapping hide seems, nevertheless, to be rather dubious. Hunting with an owl or other decoy bird is in the very nature of things dependent on a fixed spot in the open, to which birds can be enticed. The picture is doubly interesting, however, since it is also a sort of transitional form between the hide and camouflage.

The eagle owl was particularly valuable for the

Catching birds with cleft sticks and a decoy owl. Detail of woodcut in Livre du Roy Modus, *1486. (After Lindner.)*

trapping of hawks, falcons and other birds of prey. For this the owl was placed close to a high net with a fine-threaded and rather large mesh, in which the birds easily got entangled when they stooped on the owl. The hunter had to remain hidden close to the net so that he could rush out quickly to the trapped bird before it had time to escape. In later years the owl was also used in conjunction with the war which was waged indiscriminately against birds of prey of all kinds, in the name of game protection, far into the present century. Without any doubt, the efficiency of the eagle owl as a decoy played a far from insignificant part in reducing the number of birds of prey, in many parts of Europe, to a mere pitiful fraction of what it once was.

Bird-catcher with cleft stick, decoy owl and portable hide.

A cart bumping along through a wood does not worry game nearly as much as a hunter on foot. The branches on the vehicle doubtless have no other effect than to make the red deer curious and stop to have a look. (After Gaston Phoebus, Bibliothèque Nationale, Paris.)

DISGUISES

The use of protective camouflage for hunting has been practised since the Stone Age — it is perhaps almost as old as hunting itself.

The need for concealment in order to come close to the quarry underlines man's peculiar position in nature. What he lacks of the beast of prey's inborn instincts and hunting talents he has to make up for with cunning and craft. In many places protective disguises are still used, but their heyday was when the very short range of weapons obliged the hunter to approach the quarry as closely as possible.

In spite of the development of the art of disguise and the numerous variations on the theme being among the most fascinating aspects of the history of hunting, there is still room for research in this field. Only the most important methods will be described on this page as the subject will be treated more fully in the pages that concern the hunting of the different species of animals.

Primarily, the body or clothes were smeared in mud and earth so as to resemble the ground as much as possible — this simple trick is still used by primitive tribes — or the hunter perhaps hid behind twigs which he attached to his clothes and held in front of his face. It was at a very early stage that the hunter wore grey or green clothes — white when

Cows were not as co-operative as horses for hunting purposes, but with the help of a couple of servants and a cowhide the master himself could make an absolutely splendid dummy stalking cow. (After Stradanus.)

64

there was snow on the ground — in order to differ as little as possible from the surrounding countryside. "The green hunting jacket" is steeped in ancient tradition!

Disguises developed and improved. Soon there was a whole series of methods for different conditions. Three main groups are recognisable: *the use of local surroundings* (this also includes different types of non-mobile hides); *trained animals* behind which the hunter can approach the quarry unseen or with which he can entice other animals of the same kind to approach him; and thirdly *animal-like* disguises.

The disguises that fit into the local scenery include both non-mobile and portable hides. To the latter group belong the hunting-carts covered in

importance of trained hunting animals is apparent from the value attached to them already in the early mediaeval laws.

Several kinds of animals were used for stalking — in addition to red deer, even such animals as the aurochs and bison, presumably difficult to train — but the most usual was the horse, on account of its ability to learn. A well-trained stalking horse which did not react when a matchlock musket was fired close to its head was a great asset and a worthy present from one king to another. When Frederick II of Denmark happened to hear in 1571 that John III of Sweden was interested in hunting, he sent him a stalking horse as a present, "admittedly not very beautiful but well trained in its duties".

Sture Lagercrantz in his survey of the use of

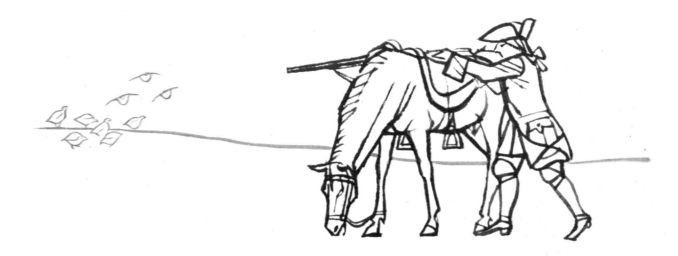

leaves (see above, left) which were described by Gaston Phoebus in about 1400. In the case of certain shy animals of the plains, it was found that an ordinary farm cart could be an excellent form of camouflage for the hunter — in the same way as the modern motor car is an absolutely splendid hiding-place. Other mobile hides include rafts covered with reeds, which slowly drifted within firing range of water birds, and sleighs which were used for hunting in the winter in snow-covered regions.

The use of captive or trained animals to enable the hunter to approach his quarry began at a very early stage in the history of hunting. This method had long been familiar to the hunters of antiquity, and red deer, in particular, were used to trick their wild cousins into joining them. The borderline between decoy animals and animals used as a live "disguise" is somewhat elastic: they were often used for both purposes at one and the same time. The special

Apart from a strap running from its head to one of its forelegs, the stalking horse had no headgear at all. While grazing, its task was to approach the unsuspecting birds on the ground.
This strange disguise for the hunting of snipe occurs in one of the Roi Modus *manuscripts (Berlin).*
The less the hunter resembles a hunter the better.

Hunter disguised in a cowhide driving partridges into a hoop net. (After Pietro Olina, Uccelaria, *Rome 1622.)*

disguise in Swedish hunting pointed out that stalking horses were mainly used for partridge hunting — but in wooded parts of the country they were also sometimes used for hunting blackcock at their display grounds, as Linnaeus, indeed, tells us in his *Scanian Journey,* 1749. Nevertheless, if we are to believe Olaus Magnus's descriptions from the first half of the sixteenth century, stalking

horses were also used for swan and capercailzie hunting.

As mentioned above in the section on bison hunting during the Magdalenian culture (page 24), a reindeer horn carving, believed to depict a hunter disguised in animal skins stalking his quarry, was found in Dordogne. In other words, the animal disguise is of ancient origin. It occurred, and still occurs, here and there among hunting peoples all over the world. It often happens that the hunter, in addition to wearing this disguise, also imitates the quarry's call-note. This will be described in greater detail in the chapter on seal hunting in the Baltic Sea.

In Europe a cowhide was the disguise most commonly used for hunting. Its use varied according to the nature of the hunt. Since it was awkward to drag around in rough country — especially if the hunter had to see to his weapon at the same time — it came to be used most as a combined disguise *and* dummy stalking cow; that is to say, one or two helpers acted as a stalking cow and concealed the hunter (see picture on page 64). The hunting that appeared on the continent during the Middle Ages was definitely for the country gentleman and provided a welcome variant form of sport.

The cowhide also played a great part in the catching of ground birds, particularly partridges, with nets. There are numerous pictures from the Middle Ages and far into the nineteenth century showing how the hunter, disguised as a cow, drove the coveys into nets. As a matter of fact, as recently as the end of the last century, a Swedish nobleman regularly caught partridges in the autumn in this old-fashioned manner, in order to feed and protect them during severe winters! This was thus a measure intended to further the conservation of wild life.

The idea arose very soon of replacing the unwieldy cowhide with a simple screen on which a picture of a cow was painted. Before long, there appeared a rich and varied collection of the most peculiar, and often far from illusory, cattle which were to be seen advancing slowly across the landscape. Behind them were concealed hunters with or without weapons. Apparently these living screens were mainly used in conjunction with nets for catching birds. The chief reason for this was that the hunter used both hands to control the screen and, consequently, was unable to handle a weapon at the same time.

Finally, at the beginning of the nineteenth century a much improved version of the dummy stalking cow was devised. The hunter was now able, on his own, both to control it and shoot from it. So he no longer had to use his servant as a cow. The version that appeared in Sweden was named "Greiff's dummy cow", after its inventor. This dummy cow was made of sacking covering a framework of hoops and laths and was painted flesh colour. The horns and eye sockets were made big enough to take a gun barrel. The forelegs were fixed to a wooden board on wheels, so that the whole apparatus could be pushed along with ease. The picture below shows how the whole thing worked. Naturally, the illusory effect was considerably reduced if the dummy cow appeared with its side turned towards the quarry.

The use of this latter-day descendant of the animal masks of the Stone Age never became widespread, however, in Sweden: it was mainly in use among the landed gentry for whom the sport of hunting was a full-time occupation. Two or three years ago, I made an appeal in the columns of the press for information about, or any remnants of, "Greiff's dummy cow", but the result was very poor. The last recorded occasion on which a dummy stalking cow was used for a proper hunt in Sweden was in the mid-1920s, in Skäne during the goose-shooting season. My informant told me that the use of this dummy stalking cow for hunting soon stopped, however, presumably because of the unwelcome amusement that the disguised goose-hunter caused as soon as he was spotted by the local population.

Without doubt, there was no one who gave any thought to the fact that this brought to an end one of our most ancient methods of hunting, with its origins dating back more than 50,000 years before the beginning of our era.

Hunting horns from different epochs:
(Left to right) Ox horn (twelfth century), oliphant
(fifteenth century), and tracker dog handler with call
(1780s, after Ridinger). (In the foreground) eleventh-
century oliphant at the Rijksmuseum, Amsterdam.
(On next page) Huntsmen from 1760 and the 1840s.
(After Chabot.) (In the foreground) a hunting horn
from the 1780s in Kranichstein, Darmstadt.

THE HUNTING HORN

As soon as hunting became an organised affair, the need arose for calls to enable the hunters to maintain contact with one another. Calls of reindeer antler or bone have been found in deposits of the Mesolithic Age. They gave a thin, penetrating whistle.

In order to obtain a mightier sound, and to make it audible further afield, use was soon made of the long curved horns of the wild ox. When hunting for pleasure gradually acquired a high degree of importance from the social point of view, the hunting horn became an attribute of the country gentleman. It was of course mainly lords and princes who were able to arrange large hunts with a lot of participants, and it was necessary to use hunting horns to keep the field together. Lindner tells us that their use is never mentioned in law matters concerning the common people.

One of the greatest virtues of a nobleman in the Middle Ages was the ability to play a pretty note on a horn, and eyewitnesses agree that the French were the masters of this instrument. Horn music played an active part in enhancing the beauty and drama of hunting, and in all mediaeval accounts of hunting one senses the strident notes of oliphants and aurochs horns in the background.

The *Roi Modus* stresses that the best thing about boar hunting was the beautiful hunting music it produced. When the hounds found a scent, the hunt took on a gay air and a terrific chorus of barking, shouting and the sounds of horns were heard. When, later, the reserve pack of hounds also joined in, the noise might be so great that it drowned the sound of thunder. The court chaplain, Gace de la Buinge, thought that this music was more beautiful than the Hallelujah chorus in La Sainte Chapelle.

Was it perhaps this enjoyment of noise that made the cynical Erasmus of Rotterdam write the

68

following in *In Praise of Lunacy*?

"Fools are also they who do not find any pleasure in anything other than hunting and who boast about the pleasure they experience when they hear the abominable noise of the hunting horn and the howling and whining of the dogs."

The *oliphant* (the Old French word for ivory) was a kind of luxury version of the ox horn and almost attained the rank of regalia. Several famous oliphants have been preserved and are included in clerical and secular treasure chests. The dying Count Roland used an oliphant to summon his uncle, Charlemagne, thirty leagues away (about eighty-four miles). After a series of adventures this oliphant reached Frohsdorf castle in Austria. The mighty uncle's oliphant is in the safekeeping of Aachen Cathedral.

When the Merovingian king Guntchramn — in chronicles, it is true, often called "the Good", but with a legendary lack of tolerance — was robbed of his hunting horn, he at once threw a number of innocent suspects into the dungeons and confiscated all their belongings. This story gives us an idea of how greatly he valued this instrument.

The longer the horn was, the further the sound carried, and when ox horns and oliphants were replaced by the metal horn, *corno di caccia*, at the end of the Middle Ages, they received the distinct curved shape which became the model for the French horn and the slender *hunting horns*.

With the big hunts in the seventeenth and eighteenth centuries, hunting horn music enjoyed its last golden age. The clear resounding blasts on trumpets are inextricably connected with the red-coated huntsmen and silver-green parkland of the tapestries.

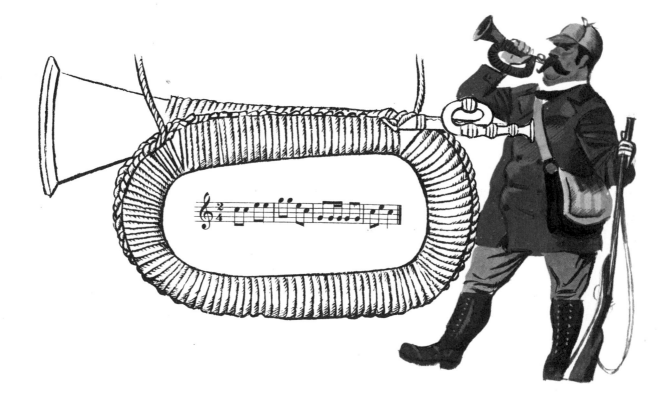

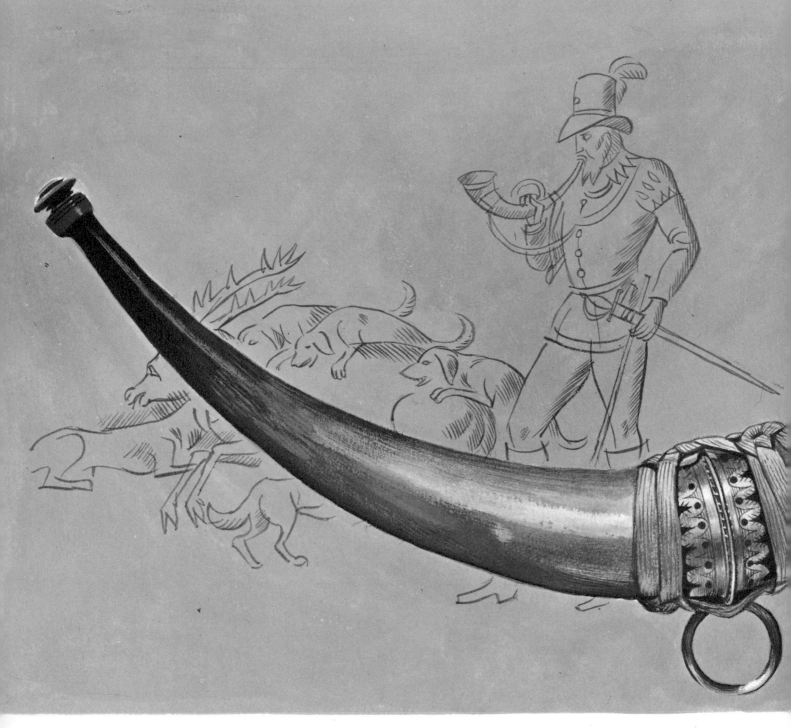

*In all probability this splendid hunting horn in the Royal Armoury in Stockholm
once belonged to the last aurochs in Europe. It reached Sweden with other war booty
during the Polish campaign of Charles X Gustavus and is dated 1620.*

During the nineteenth century, when a more democratic wind blew on the hunting scene, the horns quickly shrank in size and gradually became what they are today — calls serving the same purpose as the reindeer antler and bone pipes of the Stone Age hunters!

The Royal Armoury in Stockholm has in its keeping a hunting horn with an interesting history. It was already mentioned in the original inventory and was described there as "huntsman's horn chased with silver, gilded, bearing an inscription and a small red band on the outside".

According to Professor J. A. Lundell, the translation of the inscription runs as follows: "*Aurochs horn from the last aurochs in the Sochaczew district, from Vojvoden in Rawa, Stanislaw Rodziejowski, at that time starets in Sochaczew, in the year 1620.*"

Its outer curve is 47·5 cm and the circumference of the mouth, 17 cm. It was originally a gift to a member of the Polish house of Wasa, but found its

way to Sweden as loot during the Polish war of Charles X Gustavus, and, according to research carried out by E. O. Arenander, there is much to suggest that it really is a horn from the last living aurochs in Europe.

By the early Middle Ages, aurochs were already so rare in western Europe that they were reserved for royal hunts. In the chronicle of the Franks we read that King Guntchramn, mentioned above, who lived at the end of the sixth century, one day discovered that aurochs poaching was going on in his woods in the Vosges. He quickly decided that a certain chamberlain was responsible for the heinous deed and had him stoned to death, "but afterwards the king suffered bitter remorse at having, for such trivial reasons, rid himself of a good servant whom he found difficult to replace". The incident bears witness to the high esteem in which the aurochs was held as royal game.

In the sixteenth century, there still remained a small number of aurochs in the huge frontier forests between Poland and Lithuania, where they were jealously guarded by the princes of Masovia, and the salted meat, horns and hides of aurochs soon became highly appreciated presents from Poland to various royal households all over Europe. In 1564 there were, to be precise, eight old bulls, three young bulls, twenty-two cows and five calves still alive. Obviously, however, they did not breed very well, since by 1602 the number had dropped to four animals and in 1620 there was only an old cow left. There is much to suggest that it is this very one that is mentioned in the inscription on the remarkable horn in the Royal Armoury!

Hunting horn from the late seventeenth century. (The Royal Armoury, Stockholm.)

WEAPONS

The Bow

According to the distinguished French authority on weapons, P. L. Duchartre, the bow was for at least 116 centuries one of the most important weapons of the European hunter. The first definite evidence of the use of the bow is a Neolithic rock painting from south-eastern Spain (see page 22). On the other hand, however, the numerous arrowheads which have been found in strata of old civilisations might equally well have been launched with the aid of spear throwers or throwing sticks.

On the continent bows were mainly made of yew or larch; in Scandinavia, mainly of fir and birch. It was soon discovered that the range of the bow could be increased by lengthening it, and *longbows*, one and a half metres in length, have been found even in the Swiss Stone Age dwelling sites. During the Middle Ages, the longbow was the main weapon in the English armies, and archery was for several hundred years a national sport which was enthusiastically cherished by the kings of England. Edward III forbade, on pain of imprisonment, all "useless" sports — not least football — which might in the slightest way entice the younger generation away from archery. A sixteenth-century English theologian pointed out that it was not possible to become a good shot if one was not brought up in the use of the bow and arrow from childhood.

The hunter discovered, at a very early stage, that the tension of the bow increased substantially if it was strengthened by gluing together two staves of wood of varying degrees of suppleness. In his account of his Lapland journey in 1732,

Carolus Linnaeus gave a detailed description of how the Lapps made bows of resinous fir and birch staves which were joined together with glue obtained by boiling the skin of perch. This shows that the bow was still of great importance to the population of the far north of Scandinavia long after fire-arms came into general use in the south. The bow disappeared for good in the latter regions at the beginning of the seventeenth century, while it was used in Lapland until the end of the eighteenth century, when it was replaced by the steel cross-bow. Arrows were still used for squirrel hunting well into the nineteenth century.

The composite bow was a perfection of the reinforced bow. The under part was covered with thin pieces of horn, while the back was covered with sinew or rawhide. During the drying process the ends of the bow stave were twisted forwards and this gave the bow its characteristic profile when drawn (see picture).

There has been a lot of discussion regarding the age of this design: perhaps it already existed during the later phases of the Stone Age. It was widely used in the ancient world, and was praised for its great elastic strength and impressive range. (The world record is considered to be held by a seventeenth-century sultan, 940 metres!)

As a rule the arrow was about half as long as the stave and was provided with four rows of feathers at one end. The quiver, which was of wood or leather, had room for about twenty arrows, but in mediaeval pictures hunters are often shown with one or two

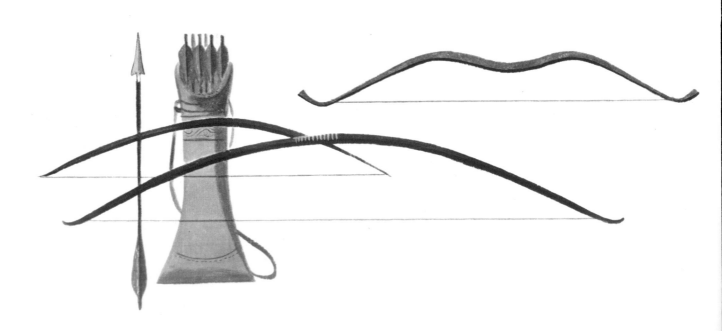

During the Middle Ages, they used longbows, short bows — for hunting on horseback — and the stiff composite bows (left, top). The longbows had an effective range of approximately 100 yards. In England, the home of Robin Hood, this weapon survived a particularly long time. It was used in warfare until 1627.
The arrows were usually half the length of the bow. Ulysses drew a huge composite bow to strike terror into the hearts of Penelope's suitors in the twenty-first poem of the Odyssey.

arrows stuck loosely in their belts (picture above).

According to the *Roi Modus*, hunting with bow and arrow was considered one of the most noble forms of hunting as a sport, and in the section on "hunting of four-legged game by the gentry", mention is made of a number of methods which have remained in use since the replacement of the bow by fire-arms — stalking, driving, shooting from raised platforms, to name but a few.

There is no doubt that the bow was an exceptionally effective weapon in the hands of a skilful shot. Two American ethnographers, who taught themselves to construct bows and use them, had no difficulty in killing such large animals as the grizzly bear and lion with this weapon! Linnaeus tells us in his account of his Lapland journey how amazed he was to see the Lapps using their simple wooden bows to shoot sparrows "at the very top of a fir tree".

The *Roi Modus* tells us that it was King Setmodus who, according to legend, invented the bow. The king had a son, by the name of Tarquin, whom he taught to use the bow at the age of eight. In time, Tarquin became a champion marksman. Setmodus gave his son nine rules on how to string a bow,

fashion the arrows, take aim and draw the bow-string.

"It is best not to shoot until just after the stag has passed," he says, "since an arrow that strikes behind the shoulder kills more quickly than one that hits the front part of the animal. If a stag has merely been wounded by an arrow, it must be followed on horseback and then it is important to ascertain, from the traces of blood, how badly wounded it is."

It is apparent from the above that already in the Middle Ages almost the same rules applied for finding the wounded quarry as in the age of modern fire-arms.

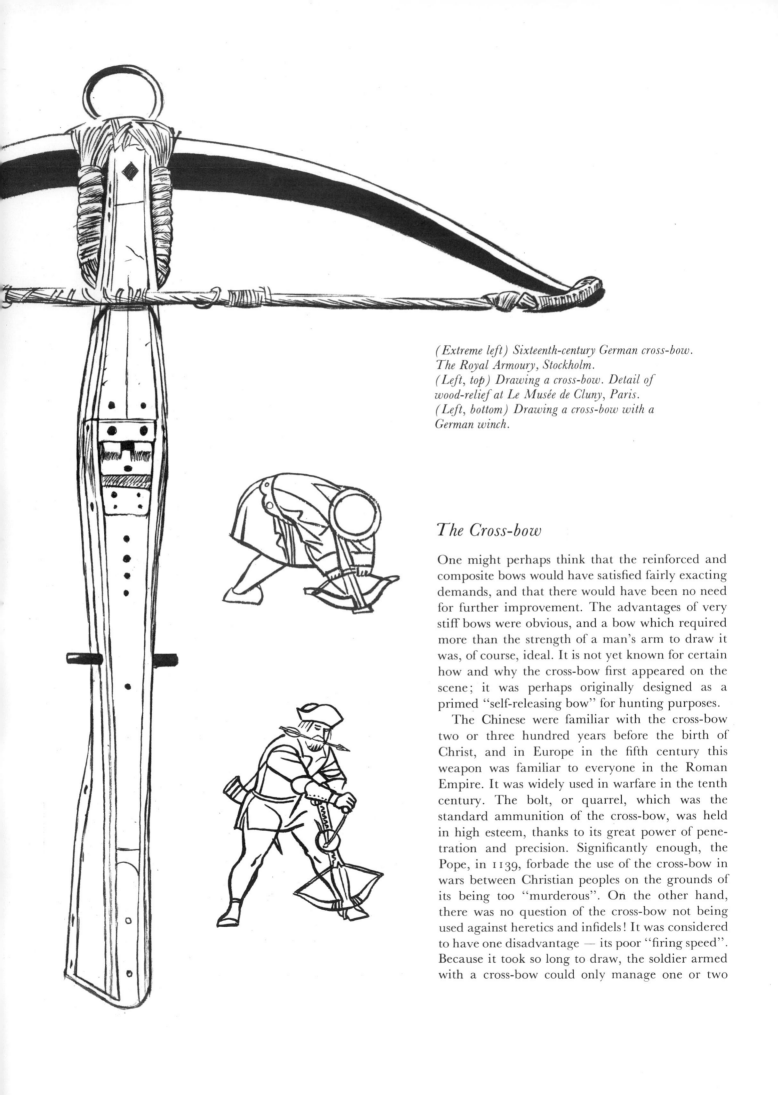

(*Extreme left*) *Sixteenth-century German cross-bow.
The Royal Armoury, Stockholm.*
(*Left, top*) *Drawing a cross-bow. Detail of
wood-relief at Le Musée de Cluny, Paris.*
(*Left, bottom*) *Drawing a cross-bow with a
German winch.*

The Cross-bow

One might perhaps think that the reinforced and
composite bows would have satisfied fairly exacting
demands, and that there would have been no need
for further improvement. The advantages of very
stiff bows were obvious, and a bow which required
more than the strength of a man's arm to draw it
was, of course, ideal. It is not yet known for certain
how and why the cross-bow first appeared on the
scene; it was perhaps originally designed as a
primed "self-releasing bow" for hunting purposes.

The Chinese were familiar with the cross-bow
two or three hundred years before the birth of
Christ, and in Europe in the fifth century this
weapon was familiar to everyone in the Roman
Empire. It was widely used in warfare in the tenth
century. The bolt, or quarrel, which was the
standard ammunition of the cross-bow, was held
in high esteem, thanks to its great power of pene-
tration and precision. Significantly enough, the
Pope, in 1139, forbade the use of the cross-bow in
wars between Christian peoples on the grounds of
its being too "murderous". On the other hand,
there was no question of the cross-bow not being
used against heretics and infidels! It was considered
to have one disadvantage — its poor "firing speed".
Because it took so long to draw, the soldier armed
with a cross-bow could only manage one or two

As the cross-bow became increasingly powerful and more difficult to draw, there was an ever-increasing simultaneous demand for efficient drawing devices. The fourteenth century saw the construction of various types, including the "German winch", which was intended for the heaviest steel bows. In Scandinavia this device was employed to draw cross-bows used as missile traps until the mid-nineteenth century. (Bayerisches Nationalmuseum, Munich.)

shots a minute, against the archer's six or seven.

The first cross-bows were rather simple weapons with wooden bows; according to Olaus Magnus, however, this type was still in use in Scandinavia in the sixteenth century. Nevertheless, there was a rapid increase in the demands made on this weapon and, by the thirteenth century, relatively easily handled cross-bows of horn had made their appearance. These bows were covered with calfskin, sinew, whalebone etc., and, in addition, were fitted with a comparatively advanced form of firing mechanism. They were called hornbows.

Various devices — the stirrup, the English winch, the Samson belt and, for the heaviest steel cross-bows, the German winch, were used for loading these extremely stiff bows.

In the course of the sixteenth century, various parts of the sporting cross-bow began to be copied from fire-arms; the weapon was fitted with a diopter sight, a quick-release trigger, a covered groove for the bolt, a built-in stirrup and a cheek rest on the stock. Previously, the weapon was fired from the shoulder or the armpit.

The cross-bow was very much a weapon of war — to begin with, anyway — and it did not play any important part in the history of hunting during the Middle Ages. The majority of hunters appear to

have preferred the quick-firing and handy conventional bows.

The *stonebow*, on the other hand, was widely used during the sixteenth and seventeenth centuries. It was of Asiatic origin and was represented in Europe by two distinct types: an Italian version, easily recognisable by its greatly decurved forestock, and a central European variant with a straight stock of steel. They were easy to carry and could be drawn by hand. The Spanish, in particular, are said to have been extremely fond of using this weapon when shooting partridges with dogs. Dr. R. B. F. van der Sloot, of the arms museum in Leyden, who has himself tried out the central European type of stonebow, assured me that its performance was extremely good.

It was above all in France and Italy that a unique method of hunting with stonebows evolved. It was done at night by lamplight. The ideal number of participants was three; the lantern-man, who carried his oil lamp, with a reflector, in his left hand, and a swatter, reminiscent of a badminton racket, in his right hand; a boy with a cowbell; finally, the crossbowman with his stonebow. The boy's task was to use the cowbell to make birds, hiding on the ground, stir. The lantern-man shone his light on trees and bushes where the small

75

*Small elegant cross-bows were made for lady hunters.
The weapon depicted above belonged to Queen
Christina. The inlay on the stock shows that it was also
used for target practice. (The Royal Armoury,
Stockholm.)*

birds sat on their roosting perches, paralysed by the light. Frightened by the noise of the stonebow, they flew towards the lantern; it was then an easy matter to knock them down with the racket.

The cross-bow is one of the more persistent of mediaeval weapons. This fact may perhaps be construed as proof of its many excellent qualities. It was still frequently used about 1700 — with poisoned bolts — on chamois hunts in the Alps; a type of hunting with a long history. As a matter of interest, it may be mentioned that the Emperor Maximilian of Austria (1459–1519), the leading hunter of his day, killed 600 chamois with the cross-bow. The cross-bow, with a bow of steel which was used at the time, had a range of up to 310 metres and could kill up to 150 metres.

The cross-bow lingered on for a long time as a hunting weapon in the northernmost parts of Scandinavia. It achieved particular importance in the hunting of wild reindeer and squirrels. There was a different bolt for practically every kind of game, with the weight, type of head and other details specially modified for the species in question. For squirrels, martens and other fur-bearing animals, blunt-headed bolts were used, so as not to damage the fur. According to Sven Ekman, who has made a study of the hunting methods employed in the northern Swedish province of Norrland, the use of the cross-bow seems to have survived longest for hunting squirrels — a favourite quarry. There is evidence that the weapon was still used there at the

beginning of the nineteenth century.

The squirrel hunter usually took a "bolt servant" with him, whose function was to retrieve the bolt after it had been fired. Specially trained dogs were also used for the same purpose; Olaus Magnus mentions this fact. The cross-bow was drawn with the aid of a Samson belt.

In appearance, the cross-bows of the far north sometimes differed in one respect from the continental types in that the stock was greatly extended so that it could also serve as a ski stick. According to a seventeenth-century writer, when the stock was used for that purpose, it was fitted with a plaited disc like those on modern ski sticks. It was fired from the hip.

A very powerful and primitive type of cross-bow has been used up to the present day by the Norwegian coastal population for hunting whales that have entered the narrow fjords by mistake. The bolts employed for this purpose are often used earlier against whales and are then retrieved from the bodies, without being cleaned and, therefore, cause blood poisoning.

As a matter of fact, poisoned cross-bow bolts were also used in other parts of Europe at a relatively late date. The seventeenth-century Spanish writer, Martinez del Espinar, tells us that Spanish hunters often used to coat their bolts with a powerful vegetable poison for hunting red deer and wild boar. In the Alps the same method was employed for hunting chamois and ibex.

On the very first matchlock guns (top) the slow match was attached to a simple double-arm lever, which inserted the burning match in the touchhole in the top of the barrel. Later, the powder pan was moved down to the side and was fitted with a cover which prevented the powder from running out and moisture from entering. The beautifully decorated gun above is dated 1674. (The Royal Armoury, Stockholm.)

The diagram of the lock shows how the gun was fired. The shooter moved the powder pan cover (A) to one side and, with the trigger (B), depressed the serpentine (C) with the slow match (D) forward to the priming powder (E). In favourable weather the gun seldom misfired.

FIRE-ARMS

The invention of fire-arms was undeniably one of the most important milestones in the long history of hunting, but it would be an exaggeration to maintain that they had an immediate and significant effect on hunting. The cross-bow had been so perfected that the first primitive guns had difficulty in providing real competition: in addition, they took too long to load and they were far from accurate.

The first portable fire-arm was constructed in the middle of the fourteenth century, and consisted of a metal tube for powder and shot inserted in a wooden stock. At the base of the tube there was a small hole for the priming powder which, when ignited by a length of burning hemp rope — a slow match — fired the shot. It is self-evident that it was not possible to take careful aim with the weapon since the shooter was fully occupied with the business of getting the priming powder to ignite.

It was not long before the disadvantages of this

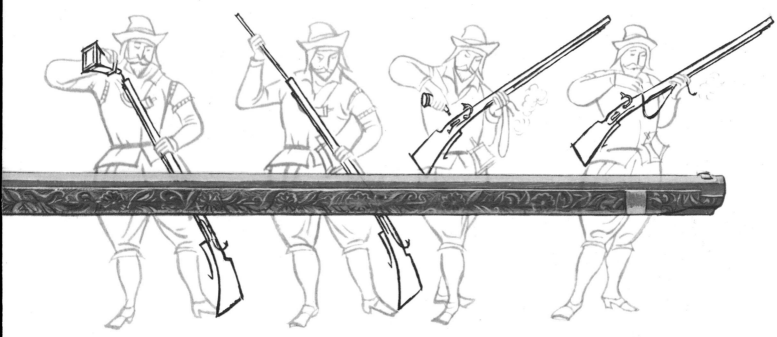

method were realised and the weapon was fitted with a holder for the slow match — the serpentine — and, later, also a lever trigger with which the serpentine could be operated without the shooter having to take his eyes off the quarry or the enemy. In time the trigger was built into the gun-stock, and was combined with the spring release and the powder pan. The result was the first matchlock. The design of the trigger remained for a long time the same as that of the cross-bow trigger. (See Notes.)

Time was to show that the matchlock construction was difficult to surpass. It is true that other types of locks with the most ingenious devices were invented; but after a number of improvements, including the powder pan cover which prevented the powder from getting wet and otherwise spoilt, there was no doubt that this simple gun was, in spite of everything, the most reliable. Despite the fact that the elegant and complicated wheel lock guns and flintlock muskets began to be manufactured at the beginning of the sixteenth century,

Loading the matchlock guns was a lengthy business, as may be seen from 116 elegant engravings by Jacob de Gheyn. Here we see how the powder was poured into the barrel, the charge rammed down with the ramrod, the powder pan filled with a carefully measured amount of fine powder, and finally the moment came for applying the burning slow match in the serpentine which was then cocked, ready for firing.

the matchlock maintained its position as the leading fire-arm for another two centuries.

During the periods of transition between the different types of locks, wealthy hunters often used to rely on combinations in order to be on the safe side. Consequently, during the sixteenth and seventeenth centuries it was very common for hunting guns to be fitted with both wheel and match locks. It was not possible to use the clumsy rest in the hunting-field; on the other hand, many natural supports were available. One method was

The periods of transition between the different types of locks are uncertain and difficult to determine. They often merged with one another and gave rise to combination locks of, for example, this type. If the intricate and delicate wheel lock failed to work, the old reliable slow match was held in readiness. Combined wheel and match lock of German construction from circa 1600. (The Royal Armoury, Stockholm.)

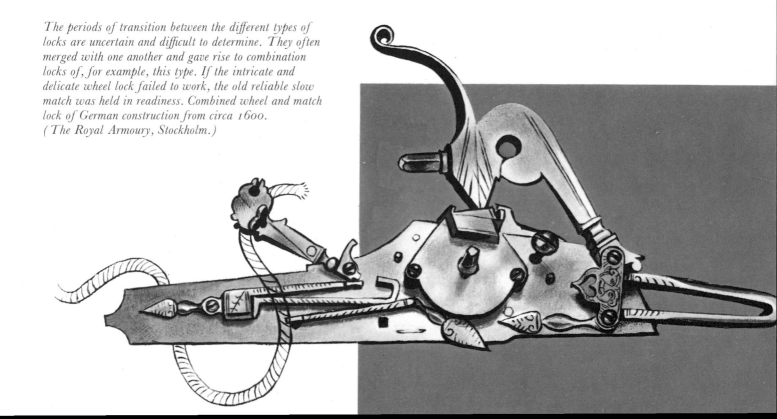

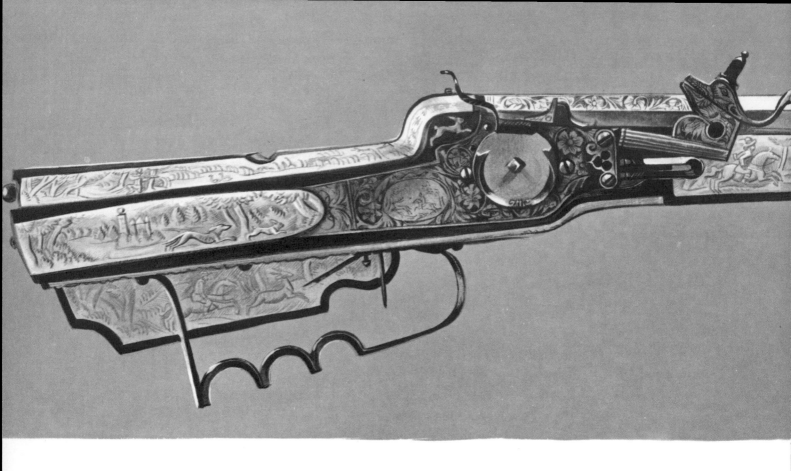

to rest the weapon on one's shoulder, so as not to feel the recoil. The French expert on hunting weapons, P. L. Duchartre, pointed out that it was usual for the gun butt to rest on a person's left shoulder and, as evidence of this, he mentioned the early and very detailed pictures of peasant hunters which Stradanus produced some time in the middle of the sixteenth century. This line of reasoning is not, however, absolutely watertight, since there is evidence that the copperplate engravers were often careless enough to reverse the drawings when transferring them to the copperplate. It is conceivable that Stradanus took this fact into account and made a deliberate mistake in his drawings, but it may be added that there are both left-handed and right-handed marksmen, not only in drawings but also in engravings. It would therefore seem that we may reject the theory that people *generally* shot from the left shoulder.

Wheel Lock Muskets

The wheel lock was invented in about 1500. One of the very first examples is a combination of a wheel lock musket and a cross-bow, mentioned with the cross-bow on page 77 and housed at the Bavarian National Museum in Munich.

The manufacture of wheel lock guns seems to have started originally in Nürnberg, but it can hardly be said that the invention was an immediate success. (See Notes.)

As a matter of fact, this type of gun remained in use longer than any other kind of fire-arm and the last specimens were to be heard down in South Germany at the beginning of the nineteenth century.

A typical South German wheel lock musket from the middle of the seventeenth century is depicted above. This weapon and a twin one are usually

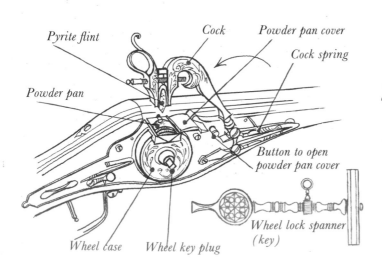

Pyrite flint
Cock
Powder pan cover
Cock spring
Powder pan
Button to open powder pan cover
Wheel case
Wheel key plug
Wheel lock spanner (key)

Expressed simply, the wheel lock worked in the following way: the wheel was wound with the aid of a chain, similar to that on a modern bicycle, which in its turn was wrapped around the square-shaped spindle on the wheel axle with the aid of a wheel lock spanner or key. The chain was connected to the powder pan alongside the upper edge of the wheel. When the wheel started to turn, the powder pan cover was automatically pushed aside and the cock — the "doghead" — with a pyrite flint between its jaws, was forced down against the wheel, producing sparks which ignited the priming powder and fired the shot. The advantage of this lock was that the huntsman was able to use the weapon without revealing his presence by the glow of a slow match.

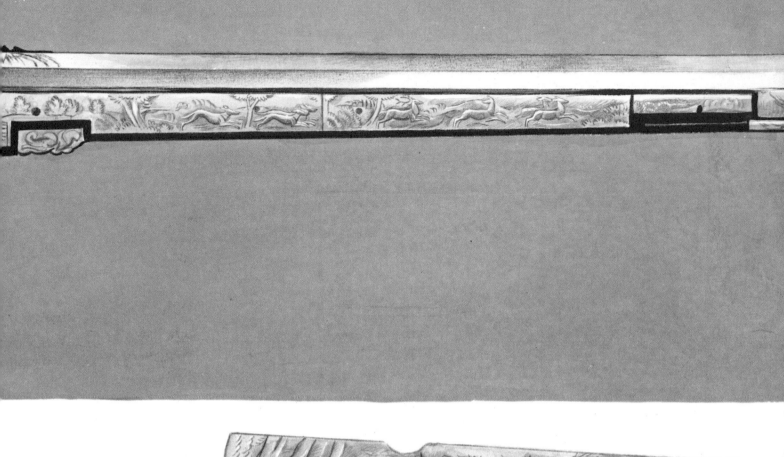

referred to as Charles XI's ivory muskets and form part of the Royal Swedish Armoury's collection. The barrels are about 77 cm long and are of 12·7 mm calibre. There was, in all probability, nothing wrong with their firing properties, but there is much to suggest that they were hardly ever used. They were, for instance, far too sensitive, and may indeed be regarded as decorative objects primarily. Nevertheless, they are interesting from a historical point of view, not only as examples of the great splendour with which hunting endowed the accessories of the chase at that time, but also on account of the detailed illustrations of hunting scenes which have been handed down to posterity in the magnificent ivory carvings covering the entire gun-stock.

As Dr. Brynolf Hellner, the superintendent of the Royal Swedish Armoury, has pointed out, the hunting episodes, nineteen in all, which are depicted on the two guns, have no connection whatever with hunting in Scandinavia, and perhaps not even in South Germany. They are based on scenes borrowed from engravings and illustrations which have served as models on innumerable occasions for the embellishment of weapons and other hunting accessories.

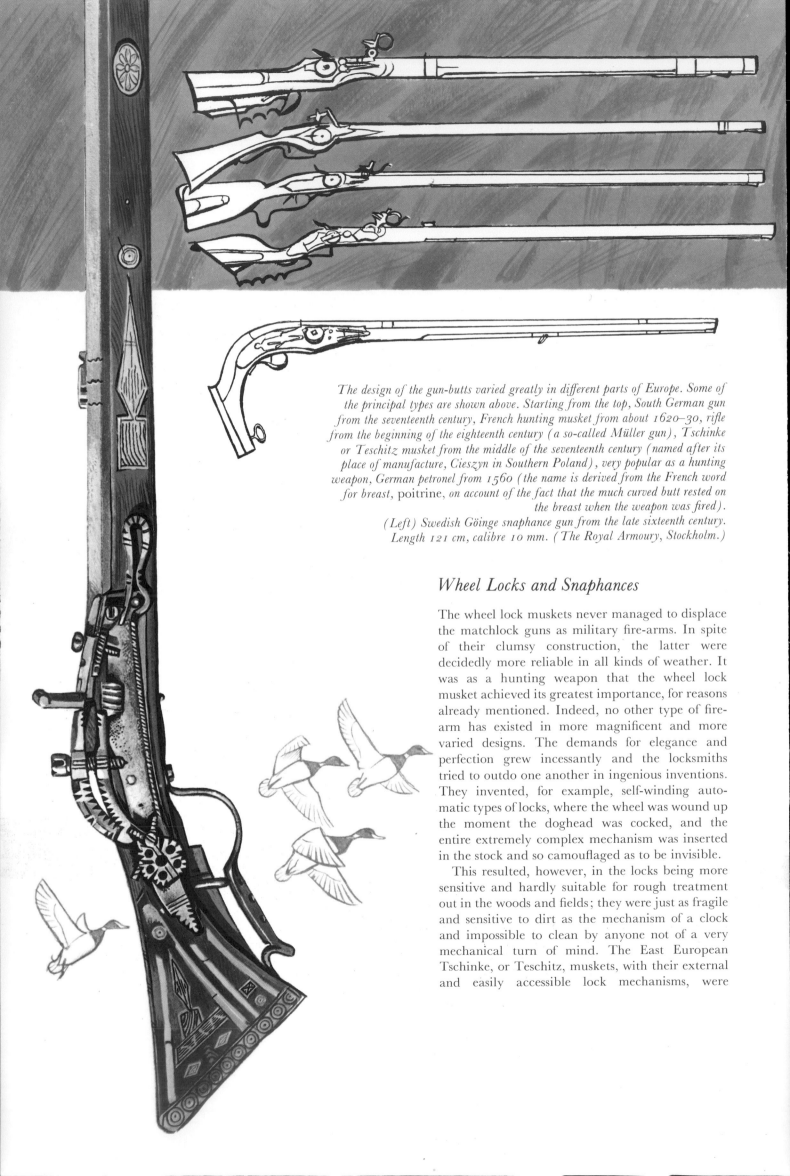

The design of the gun-butts varied greatly in different parts of Europe. Some of the principal types are shown above. Starting from the top, South German gun from the seventeenth century, French hunting musket from about 1620–30, rifle from the beginning of the eighteenth century (a so-called Müller gun), Tschinke or Teschitz musket from the middle of the seventeenth century (named after its place of manufacture, Cieszyn in Southern Poland), very popular as a hunting weapon, German petronel from 1560 (the name is derived from the French word for breast, poitrine, *on account of the fact that the much curved butt rested on the breast when the weapon was fired).*
(Left) Swedish Göinge snaphance gun from the late sixteenth century. Length 121 cm, calibre 10 mm. (The Royal Armoury, Stockholm.)

Wheel Locks and Snaphances

The wheel lock muskets never managed to displace the matchlock guns as military fire-arms. In spite of their clumsy construction, the latter were decidedly more reliable in all kinds of weather. It was as a hunting weapon that the wheel lock musket achieved its greatest importance, for reasons already mentioned. Indeed, no other type of fire-arm has existed in more magnificent and more varied designs. The demands for elegance and perfection grew incessantly and the locksmiths tried to outdo one another in ingenious inventions. They invented, for example, self-winding automatic types of locks, where the wheel was wound up the moment the doghead was cocked, and the entire extremely complex mechanism was inserted in the stock and so camouflaged as to be invisible.

This resulted, however, in the locks being more sensitive and hardly suitable for rough treatment out in the woods and fields; they were just as fragile and sensitive to dirt as the mechanism of a clock and impossible to clean by anyone not of a very mechanical turn of mind. The East European Tschinke, or Teschitz, muskets, with their external and easily accessible lock mechanisms, were consequently the most popular hunting weapons since they were easy to clean even out in the open air.

The need for reliable and easily handled weapons gave rise to various kinds of locks and, during the sixteenth and seventeenth centuries, there were several very different types in use at the same time, not only in various parts of the continent but also, as we mentioned above, on the same weapon. The snaphance probably made its appearance at approximately the same time as the wheel lock, with which it had certain features in common. The snaphance, too, ignited the priming powder by means of sparks produced by a glancing blow but, in this case, the pyrite was replaced by a flint, and the revolving wheel by a stationary frizzen which protruded from the powder pan. The mechanism was therefore considerably less complicated, but this fact did not have any effect on its firing efficiency.

Most arms experts agree nowadays that the snaphance was invented in the Low Countries during the first half of the sixteenth century. The Dutch word *snaphaan*, "snapping cock", was quickly adopted by Germans, Englishmen and Scandinavians, while at the same time it was also applied to the lawless soldiers who roved about Europe in the seventeenth and eighteenth centuries. The snaphance became popular among the latter as an easily handled weapon when grabbing poultry from farms. The frizzen, which was struck by the cock, was sometimes called the hen. The Swedish snap lock was one of the earliest snaphances and it is easily recognisable by the protruding cock.

Without any doubt, the snaphance muskets had many advantages over the wheel locks, not least because less had to be done by hand; according to one widely-held view, the snaphance was the first gunlock in which manipulations by hand, when the shot was fired, were entirely replaced by mechanical devices.

An important advantage of the snap lock was the safety device in the form of a half-cock which was invented by gunsmiths in the Mediterranean countries during the sixteenth century, thanks to which it was possible to fasten the cock in a half-cocked position by means of a locking device in the lock metal. This arrangement meant that it was safe for the shooter to wander around with his gun loaded and, when necessary, to open fire without any time-consuming preparations. Naturally this was a feature which was appreciated by the hunter in particular.

On the whole, it may be said that the snaphance was a forerunner of the type of lock which has remained in existence up to the present day. In contrast with the matchlock and the wheel lock, the cock had its head turned away from the shooter. The snaphance was a percussion lock; the cock did not fall down towards the powder pan in the manner of the cock on the matchlock, nor was it depressed against a rotating wheel. An important period in the history of fire-arms began with the appearance of the snap lock.

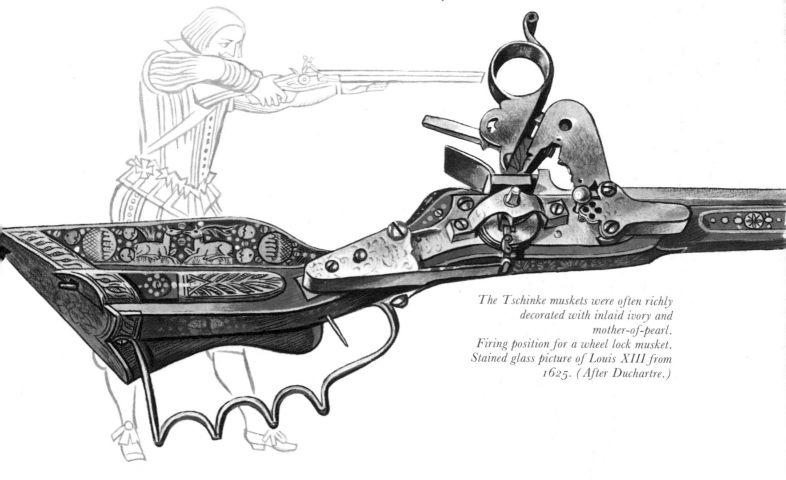

The Tschinke muskets were often richly decorated with inlaid ivory and mother-of-pearl.
Firing position for a wheel lock musket. Stained glass picture of Louis XIII from 1625. (After Duchartre.)

The Flintlock

The flintlock was derived from the snaphance. In his famous work *The Flintlock, its Origin and Development* (1939), Torsten Lenk maintained that the flintlock is a snaphance in which the frizzen and the powder pan cover are combined in one unit and where the cock, thanks to a locking device, can be either fully or half-cocked.

The combined frizzen and cover was an ingenious invention which at once obviated the most irritating problem facing soldiers and hunters, namely the difficulty of keeping the powder in the pan dry under unfavourable weather conditions. Previously, it was necessary to push the powder pan cover to one side immediately prior to the cock being depressed to ignite the priming powder, an operation which could easily jeopardise the whole result if rain was falling or wind blowing. On the flintlock the powder pan cover was pulled out and pushed

upwards at right angles. When the cock with the flint was depressed towards the frizzen, the latter was knocked backwards and in this manner also opened the cover of the powder pan. In other words, the igniting of the priming powder and the opening of the cover took place almost simultaneously, a fact that greatly increased efficiency. A good flintlock musket misfired on an average only once every ninth shot and it was seldom necessary to change the flint more than once in thirty shots.

It is true that the cross-bow, wheel lock, matchlock, snaphance and flintlock were all used simultaneously during the first half of the seventeenth century, but towards the end of the century the flintlock became the dominant fire-arm both for hunting and for military operations. As a matter of fact, one of its most stubborn rivals was the oldest type of fire-arm, the matchlock, the musket "which

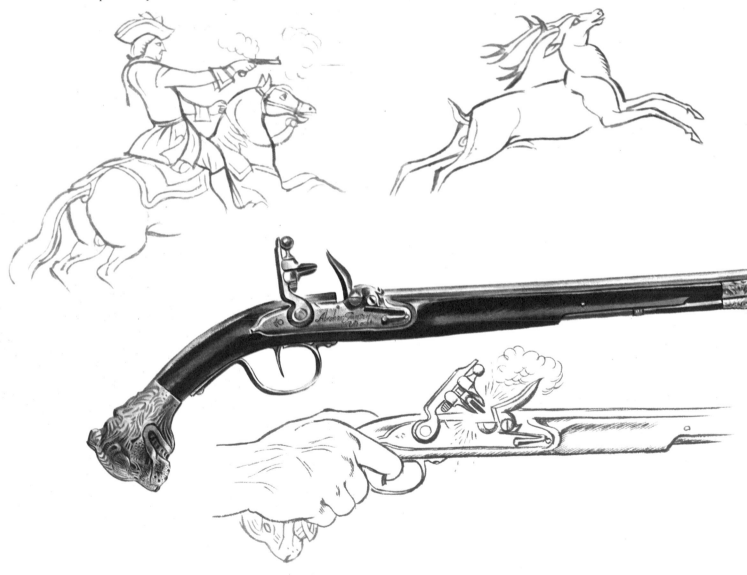

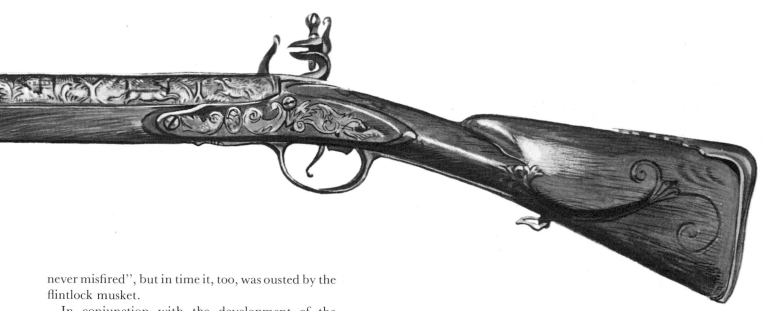

never misfired", but in time it, too, was ousted by the flintlock musket.

In conjunction with the development of the handy and readily fired flintlock musket there was also an increased interest in wing shooting, an occupation which had been practically out of the question with earlier clumsy fire-arms. Furthermore, bird shooting was long regarded as being something almost unworthy of a gentleman hunter since it could not be done in "a sporting manner". Typical of this point of view is a small pamphlet published in 1621 by an Englishman named Gervase Markham under the telling title *Hunger's prevention, or, the whole arte of fowling by water and land*. In other words fowling was an occupation for paupers and the lowest classes of society. The manner in which it was normally done was for the hunter to creep, usually with great difficulty, as close as possible to a large and tightly-packed flock of birds, whereupon he fired an enormous charge of metal right into their midst.

A mere half-century later, bird shooting with

pointers and setters became a highly esteemed sport, enthusiastically pursued by the aristocracy. One of the reasons for this rapid change in values was the improvement of fire-arms and the new fashion of using small shot. After a good deal of opposition this technique had begun to spread northwards from the Mediterranean countries; for a long time it had been considered unsuitable for a hunter and had been mostly used by poachers.

Wing shooting demanded, however, great skill on the part of the hunter and consequently acquired the status of a fully acceptable type of sport.

(Left) Magnificent hunting pistols are fairly common in arms collections, but they were probably used more frequently for shooting at targets than for hunting. The few pictures in existence of hunters armed with pistols show that these weapons were used especially for stag and wild boar hunting. This pistol is from the arms museum in Leyden and was made in Utrecht in the seventeenth century.

(Right) In England, in particular, bird shooting became immensely popular after having been considered, long into the seventeenth century, scarcely a sporting occupation, suitable only for the lowest classes of society. As a result of the improved weapons, facilitating rapid wing shots, bird shooting and the use of pointers and setters immediately acquired a reputation as good sport.

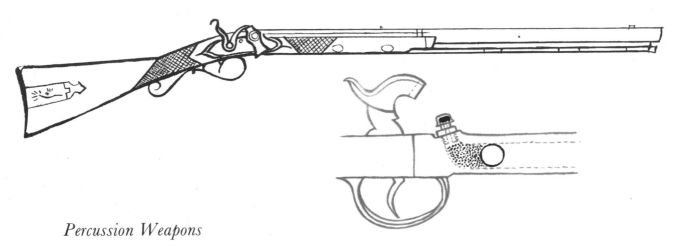

Percussion Weapons

1786 saw an invention which was to have far-reaching consequences for hunting and the art of shooting. The French chemist, Claude Berthollet, discovered, during his experiments, that potassium chlorate exploded when struck a sharp blow. This could not be used in gunlocks, except for igniting the priming powder. Besides, the explosions were so violent that the method could not be put to practical use. Berthollet's invention, however, opened the way for a rapid development of the percussion lock and the percussion cap, and this led to a much more efficient gunlock in the early nineteenth century.

Mercuric fulminate was discovered by E. C. Howard, an Englishman, in 1799, and shortly afterwards the first *pill lock* was constructed — in this lock the priming powder was ignited with the aid of a small pellet containing a percussion compound, which was attached either to the musket cock or to the touch-hole. It is true that this new lock fired much more efficiently than the old flintlock, but nonetheless it was not possible to avoid the time-consuming loading procedure.

According to a rather vague historical record, it was a German Franciscan monk, Berthold Schwartz, who invented both gunpowder and the fire-arm in the early fourteenth century. There is full docu-mentary evidence, however, that another pious Christian, the Reverend Alexander Forsyth, a Scottish minister, was the inventor of the pill lock, which was the earliest type of percussion lock. When the hammer struck a tube leading to the powder pan, the pellet containing the percussion compound exploded and the flash ignited the charge in the gun barrel.

Forsyth patented his invention but, sad to say, his lock was not an immediate success with conservative British huntsmen. For example, there was anxiety about the obvious risk in the fact that the percussion compound chamber had to contain a very powerful charge — it was advertised as being sufficient for twenty-five shots.

There was also a considerable amount of discussion in hunting periodicals on the advantages and disadvantages of the new lock. A letter to *The Gentleman's Magazine* in 1817 is typical of the attitude.

The writer of the letter cannot see that the much-vaunted weapon has any advantages and he counters all objections with devastating arguments. Those who maintain that it shoots more powerfully are told that a good flintlock gun shoots quite powerfully enough. His answer to those who argue that it shoots faster is that an experienced sportsman

(Right) Pauly breechloader (1812–1830). (Musée de la Chasse, Gien.)
(Below right) Dutch patroonkocher *with compartments for four charges, (centre) wooden charge-holder which was fastened to the sportsman's thigh. From the seventeenth century. (Leger en Wapenmuseum, Leyden.) (Left) Sixteenth-century paper cartridge with ball at one end. (After Peterson.)*

with a well-constructed flintlock finds the difference in speed is so slight as to be of very little interest. Finally those who point out that the great thing about Forsyth's lock is that its performance is equally good in windy weather or pouring rain are silenced with the crushing reply: "Gentlemen do not go sporting in such weather!"

The result was that the flintlocks retained their popularity among the older generation of hunters for decades after the appearance of the new weapon in the shops.

Younger and less prejudiced sportsmen, both in America and in Europe, were all the more enthusiastic and, according to Robert Held, already in 1815 or thereabouts a good twenty-five per cent of all first-class weapons in England were fitted with the pill lock.

Gradually, the pill lock improved considerably, thanks to the invention of the percussion cap, but the percussion weapon was nevertheless still rather clumsy to use. Olle Cederlöf tells us that there were no fewer than eighteen stages in the loading of a Swedish percussion gun from 1840 and that the

firing speed was approximately one shot a minute. In addition to everything else, the range was about the same as that of the old steel cross-bow — if not worse. Experiments showed that the range increased considerably if the calibre was reduced, but then of course problems arose regarding the still current muzzle-loading system.

The self-sealing unit cartridge was soon developed as a solution to all these problems and in its turn it paved the way for breechloaders. This meant that some time in the mid-nineteenth century the modern sporting gun had become a reality.

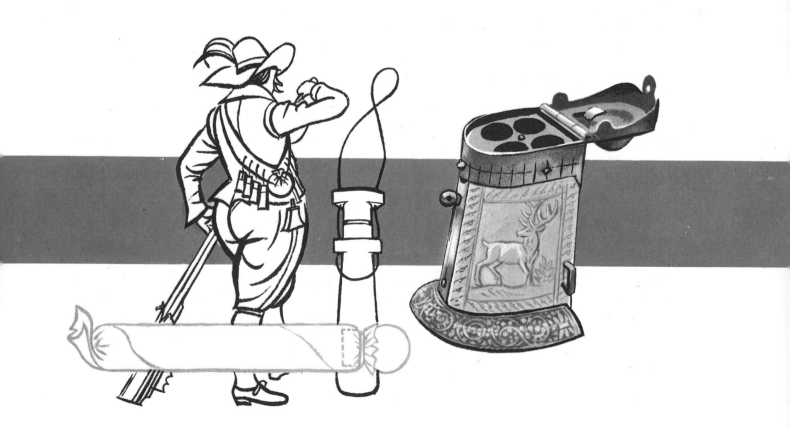

Fowling Pieces

Fowling was for centuries equated with the poor
man's sporting activities. As already mentioned,
the main reason for this was the shortage of suitable
weapons. It was a sport that required the hunter to
creep behind bushes and reedbeds and to use
various tricks that were unworthy of a gentleman
and exposed him to ridicule.

This does not mean that bird shooting was not
practised by the upper classes during the infancy of
fire-arms. It was, however, primarily a form of
target practice and, for reasons easily understood,
the targets were, in the main, sitting or swimming
birds — preferably those in the middle of dense
flocks.

It was a widespread belief that the longer the gun
barrel, the further the ball would travel. It was also
believed that the calibre should be large enough to
take a charge permitting a mighty and destructive
long-range shot. There are many specimens of
seventeenth- and eighteenth-century fowling pieces
almost nine feet in length and with a calibre
reminiscent of that of small cannon! Nevertheless,
the sportsman was advised to creep as near his
intended quarry as possible without frightening it.
Only then was it possible that he might be successful
with his cannon charge.

These heavy guns were used above all for goose
shooting — terrestrial birds were shot on the
ground with short-barrelled guns — but otherwise,
in the higher strata of society fowling in the sixteenth
and seventeenth centuries was done with falcons.
Those occasions when a hunter was lucky enough to

hit a bird encountered by chance when he was out
with a gun were not counted as hunting in the true
sense of the word.

All in all, bird shooting in the infancy of fire-
arms was a game of chance and it is understandable
that sportsmen indulged in this occupation only
when other entertainment was lacking. Apart from
the general clumsiness of fire-arms, the sluggish
gunlocks were another source of irritation. Presumably, the time lag between the ignition of the
priming powder and the arrival of the ball at its
destination must have seemed endless to a keen shot.
Frequently, the bird managed to fly away in the
meantime.

In the section on disguises, mention was made of
the stalking cow and its relatives which old hunting
handbooks considered to be an indispensable prerequisite for bird shooting in open fields. The
stalking horse was frequently used in England,
where the interest in bird shooting has always been
somewhat greater than elsewhere. As already
mentioned, it was a horse, specially trained for the
purpose, behind which the hunter crept as close to
the flock of birds as possible.

Shakespeare is full of quotations in which the
stalking horse or disguises for bird shooting are
mentioned. In *As You Like It*, the stalking horse is
only a disguise: "He uses his folly like a stalking-
horse, and under the presentation of that he shoots
his wit."

It was in the early seventeenth century that the
overlarge goose guns began to appear. The largest

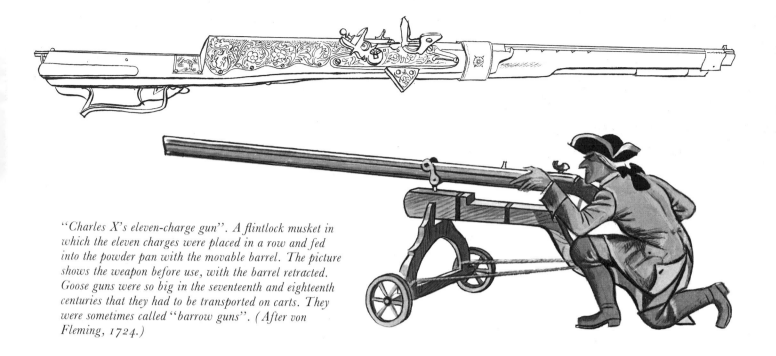

"Charles X's eleven-charge gun". A flintlock musket in which the eleven charges were placed in a row and fed into the powder pan with the movable barrel. The picture shows the weapon before use, with the barrel retracted. Goose guns were so big in the seventeenth and eighteenth centuries that they had to be transported on carts. They were sometimes called "barrow guns". (After von Fleming, 1724.)

of them were fitted on gun carriages and trundled towards the geese; once the cannon had been concealed with the aid of some suitable camouflage, of course (see page 223). They were loaded with quite a few pounds of heavy shot and, in all probability, thundered like howitzers when the hunter fired.

Gradually, as fire-arms improved, there arose, however, an interest in the most difficult type of bird shooting — wing shooting.

Here, too, it was mainly the English who went in for the sport and already in the early eighteenth century there was such a passionate interest in it that wing shooting actually received literary acclaim from a certain A. B. Markland, in 1727, under the title of *Pteryplegia: or, the Arte of Shooting-flying*.

At first, wing shooting was made more difficult because sportsmen used single-barrelled guns and because the loading procedure was still so time-consuming. Fowling pieces were so long and of such heavy calibre that the fitting of double barrels would have made them too unwieldy. (There were rare cases of multicharge guns having been manufactured a good deal earlier. See picture above.) Naturally, wealthy sportsmen employed attendants who reloaded the guns and always had a loaded

weapon in reserve — see picture on page 232 of Ludwig VIII of Hessen-Darmstadt shooting woodcock during the autumn migration — but the lone hunter had to be content with one shot at a time.

Gradually, however, experiments were made with various types of double or multi-barrelled fowling pieces. In the case of multi-barrelled guns, a single lock was used and the clustered barrels revolved, but there were also other combinations. There was, for example, a French flintlock type from the late eighteenth century with four barrels and a similar number of locks! It was essential to remember which barrel had been fired last!

When the pill lock and percussion cap were invented and percussion powder facilitated considerably faster shots, the length of the gun barrels was also shortened a good deal. They became easier to handle and so it was now possible to construct double-barrelled fowling pieces without making the weapon too heavy.

The Powder Horn and the Bullet Mould

The powder horn is about the same age as the fire-arm, but its very earliest design had little in common with the traditional type. The oldest kinds of powder were very sensitive and highly explosive and so were difficult to carry around. For this reason, the raw materials — sulphur, charcoal and saltpetre — were often taken along in barrels and the powder was mixed on the spot, as required.

The first powder horns were probably large leather sacks or boxes intended only for powerful cannon charges.

It was only when the first small arms were manufactured at the beginning of the fifteenth century that the need arose for what we nowadays mean by the term powder horn. It apparently did not take very long before powder horns developed a characteristic shape. The materials used in their manufacture varied, but there was a preference for bone and horn, particularly for cow horns, which had been hot-moulded into a less bulky shape. The earliest powder horns were fitted with simple wooden plugs at the ends. Early in the sixteenth century, however, various types of mechanical opening and closing devices were tried out for the mouth of the flask. Later on, these devices were perfected with an automatic powder measure in the form of a flap valve at the mouth of the tube.

Boxwood powder flask from about 1700. A pack of hounds are harrying a wild boar hog round the entire flask. Wild boar hogs occur on a large number of powder flasks of this type, presumably because the design is eminently suitable for this purpose. (The Bavarian National Museum, Munich.)

One of the oldest and commonest forms of the powder horn was the flattened cow horn. Here we see an early eighteenth-century version. Engraved on the side is a lively hunting scene with mediaeval costumes. The mounting is of iron and the nozzle is fitted with a spring-operated cap. (Jagdschloss Kranichstein.)

1. *Powder flask dated Augsburg 1580. It is of gilded bronze and is richly ornamented.*
2. *German powder flask from the early seventeenth century made of stag horn and inlaid with silver. St Hubert is depicted on the flask.*
3. *Combined powder flask and wheel lock key from the 1550s.*
4. *Powder horn from circa 1600.*

From the end of the sixteenth century, and for more than 200 years, the basic construction of the powder horn remained unchanged. Nevertheless, there was no lack of imagination in varying the exterior, both as regards the material and the decoration. The manufacturers of powder horns were spurred on to outdo one another and this resulted in masterpieces of craftsmanship. The latter now have their place among the most treasured possessions of museums.

These powder horns, examples of artistic perfection, were just as much a kind of status symbol as were the magnificent fire-arms. They were intended for royal courts and wealthy customers and were indeed used in particular for ceremonial occasions and as popular gifts in the highest circles of society. The powder horns used by the nobility for less formal hunting expeditions were of a decidedly simpler kind, often the traditional cow horn type illustrated above. It was considered so practical that it became standard for both hunters and soldiers in England and America at the beginning of the eighteenth century.

It is, of course, impossible to bring any systematic order into the bewilderingly rich profusion of powder horns. An attempt has been made, however, to classify them under the most common main types so as to give collectors wishing to specialise a better idea of what there is in this field. Even a rough classification is likely to result in a very long list and here we shall merely mention some of the most important types.

Entirely without ornamentation. The main value of these lies in the rich variety of designs.

The shell type. The design and ornamentation is provided by a strictly stylised mussel.

Huntsman and hounds. This is one of the most usual pictorial motifs, especially, perhaps, on the long kinds of powder horns.

Game. Intricate compositions of wild boar, stags, ibex, foxes being pursued or held at bay by large packs of hounds, are among the commonest motifs, particularly on the splendid specimens from the eighteenth century.

Ornamented overall. A dense network of trailing plants or stylised patterns cover the whole horn, often in the form of ivory inlay against dark wood. Occurred especially on powder horns for wheel lock muskets of the *Teschitz type* in the seventeenth century.

Unusual materials. Here every imaginable curiosity is allowed full scope. Horns of bearskin, undressed tortoiseshell, hard rubber etc.

Mythological scenes. Variations on the theme of Diana, together with hunters and hounds, were favourite subjects for the engravers of powder horns. Saint Hubert depicted with a stag seems to have been particularly common in Germany while the powder horn with allegorical motifs was manufactured in many places in northern Italy — the Alps and the Dolomites — in the eighteenth century.

Combinations. Powder horns with every kind of gadget, such as a built-in clock, wheel lock key, etc.

Leather Covered. The metal horns which came into use particularly during the nineteenth century were

detailed information about the equipment of these humble hunters. They were mainly intended as sketches for tapestries and other fabrics for which Stradanus painted patterns for the Medici family, but they were also copied in a variety of versions by copperplate engravers for large-scale distribution. Our knowledge today of the apparel, equipment and so forth of the hunters of the sixteenth century is to a large extent due to the energetic Dutchman.

The two large powder horns were fastened by means of a strap over the one shoulder and were handy for the shooter to use. When the gun was loaded and the hunter crept cautiously towards his quarry, the horns were pushed back over his shoulder so as not to hinder his movements.

One would have thought that hunters would have been delighted at the arrival of the new breechloader which was introduced at the beginning of the nineteenth century. This meant that the whole clumsy and irritating procedure of loading was replaced by a simple method. Nevertheless, conservative hunting circles adopted a sceptical attitude towards the new invention; in the course of decades of constant hunting, many a man had perhaps become an expert in the art of loading a

often covered with leather. This was a great advantage for the hunter. For one thing, the horn did not rattle in his pocket and in addition it was more pleasant to handle on cold winter days.

It is not very surprising that we know a considerable amount about the hunting weapons and accessories of the uppermost classes of society, since these articles have been preserved in armouries, museums and private collections. On the other hand, however, we know comparatively little about the common man's hunting equipment in olden times. Contemporary paintings were mainly concerned with the gentry's hunting activities. Fortunately, however, there was a Dutch artist by the name of Giovanni Stradanus who settled in Florence and, during the latter half of the sixteenth century, produced a large number of drawings of the hunting practised by the peasantry, which provide us with

The costly and splendidly sculptured powder horns were replaced in the early nineteenth century by much simpler metal flasks, frequently factory-made and with a manual finish given to the de luxe version. The master craftsmen disappeared and the poor success of those who tried to continue the craft is shown by the front of this de luxe powder flask from 1851. (Jagdschloss Kranichstein.)

flint-lock musket and found it difficult to adapt himself to a quick-firing weapon. Despite the quick perfection of the snaphance musket through the breech-loading system, and despite the appearance of ready-loaded cartridges in the 1830s, there was still a demand for the old powder horns. There was many an old gentleman huntsman who spoke in scornful terms of the new fire-arms and believed that they were of no benefit to the "true sportsman".

So it was then that in many conservative hunting circles, particularly in England, it was still considered, during the latter half of the nineteenth century, not truly sporting to hunt with the new handy guns.

It is not until the end of the nineteenth century that powder horns, ramrods, bullet-bags, primers and all the rest of the equipment required for the loading of the hunting gun may be considered as finally relegated to the museums.

The business of loading the gun was almost as important as the moulding of the bullet. A few pages from some prayer book, some mortar from a church wall or anything else that happened to have a connection with the Almighty, were very popular as plugs for inserting in the gun before the charge. In some parts of Sweden wasp nests, if available, were also used as plugs because "they packed so well". There was probably a good deal of superstition underlying it all; perhaps the idea was that the wasp's stinging properties would be transferred to the bullet or that there was some connection with the old belief that wasps were "the devil's birds"!

If the shot missed its mark, despite the observance of all these good rules, there was only one natural explanation for the failure; the gun was "bewitched". Someone who bore a grudge against the hunter had simply cast a spell on it. (See Notes.)

In addition to the powder horn, there were a good few other articles and tools in the equipment of the hunter of past centuries, since preparing a gun for firing involved quite a lot of technical know-how. Besides, for several centuries the hunter had no alternative to making the ammunition

himself and for that purpose he used bullet moulds of different sizes depending on the gun calibres he used.

During the seventeenth and eighteenth centuries, these bullet moulds were simplified and gradually acquired the shape of a pair of pincers (see picture below). When calibre sizes were standardised, this meant that no moulding implement needed more than one bullet mould. It was not until the introduction of factory-made cartridges some time in the mid-nineteenth century that the bullet moulds became obsolete, even though quite a few poor hunters in remote country districts continued to mould their own bullets far into the present century.

Mention must also be made here of the black magic and superstition which flourished for centuries in connection with bullet moulding and the loading of a gun.

In order to ensure that the bullet found its mark, the lead was melted together with certain metal objects which were believed to have supernatural powers. These objects included iron from meteorites, lead from the mullions of a church window — the latter was most effective if stolen during High Mass, when the priest was standing at the altar! — metal scrapings from nails on a gallows or the needle that had been used to sew the shroud of a recently deceased girl, not to mention other macabre ingredients.

The custom of "lacing" the molten lead with various oddities from the world of nature — a live bat, or (in more humane cases) only its heart and liver, the heart of a swallow, hoopoe feathers, earthworms, blood from the hunter's right hand, cantharidin, grains of wheat, and a whole host of other choice titbits — was fairly widespread.

Eighteenth-century bullet mould from the arms collection in the Kranichstein Castle armoury.

CLOTHING AND ACCESSORIES

Hunting costumes, as indeed all clothing fashions, have changed a good deal over the centuries. It is possible, however, to discern two distinct main groups in hunting fashions. On the one hand, there are the clothes of subdued colour, the purpose of which is to enable the stalker to merge into the local scenery; on the other hand, there are the colourful costumes of the chase, worn in order to heighten the spectacle, which gradually became more and more like uniforms.

Recent research has shown that animals do not register colours in the same way as human beings. It would therefore be equally suitable to wear bright colours for elk hunting, for example, and thereby possibly reduce the danger of shooting accidents. The suggestion has been made, but would probably be difficult to put into practice, since the majority of hunters would no doubt consider it bad taste to wander about the woods in a red or yellow jacket, for instance. As regards hunting fashions, most hunters are stalkers to the core!

Since ancient times the main colours for hunting garb have been green and grey. They have also been used for disguise and camouflage up to the present day.

The Emperor Maximilian felt very strongly on the subject of the hunter's attire. The following extract is from *Haimlich Gejaidt Puech*:

"You must wear grey and green clothes, partly grey, partly green. They are the best colours for deer and chamois. You must always take a change of footwear with you; in addition, four shoe trees, so that if you tramp about in snow in the mountains and your shoes get wet, you put the trees in them and get out the dry pair of shoes. — You must also have woollen stockings which you can pull over your shoes and breeches when you are high up in the

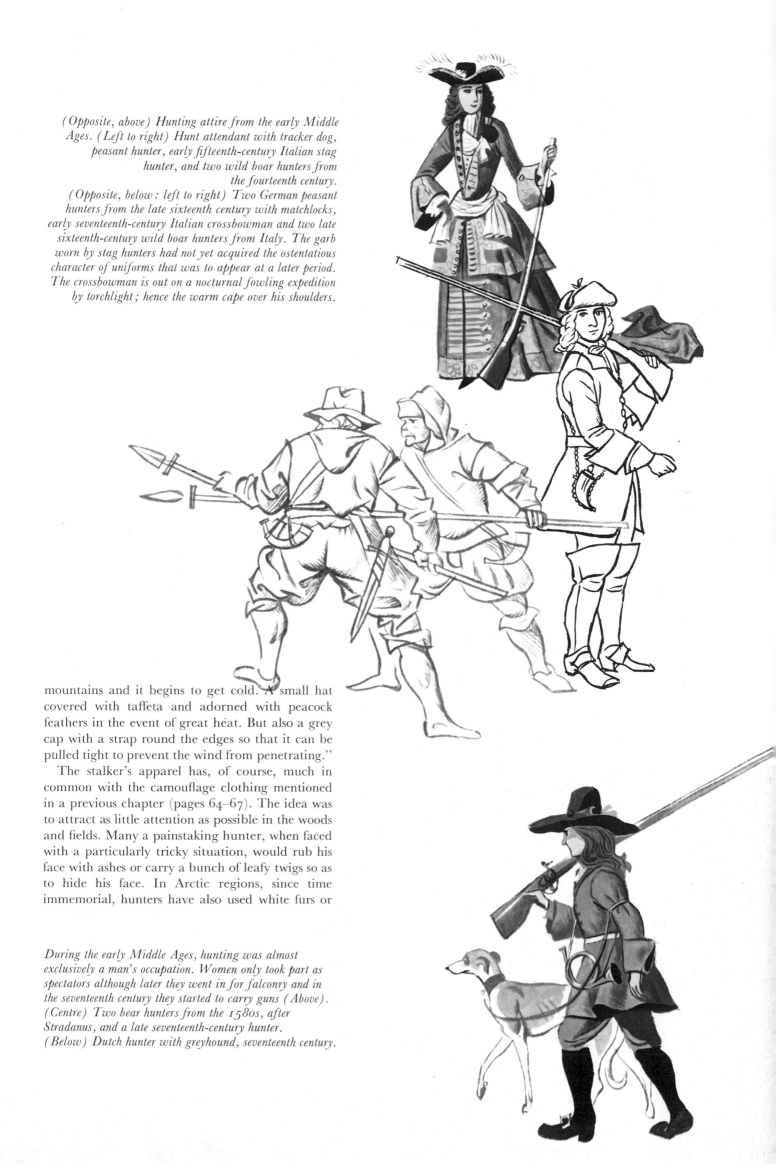

(Opposite, above) Hunting attire from the early Middle Ages. (Left to right) Hunt attendant with tracker dog, peasant hunter, early fifteenth-century Italian stag hunter, and two wild boar hunters from the fourteenth century.

(Opposite, below: left to right) Two German peasant hunters from the late sixteenth century with matchlocks, early seventeenth-century Italian crossbowman and two late sixteenth-century wild boar hunters from Italy. The garb worn by stag hunters had not yet acquired the ostentatious character of uniforms that was to appear at a later period. The crossbowman is out on a nocturnal fowling expedition by torchlight; hence the warm cape over his shoulders.

mountains and it begins to get cold. A small hat covered with taffeta and adorned with peacock feathers in the event of great heat. But also a grey cap with a strap round the edges so that it can be pulled tight to prevent the wind from penetrating.''

The stalker's apparel has, of course, much in common with the camouflage clothing mentioned in a previous chapter (pages 64–67). The idea was to attract as little attention as possible in the woods and fields. Many a painstaking hunter, when faced with a particularly tricky situation, would rub his face with ashes or carry a bunch of leafy twigs so as to hide his face. In Arctic regions, since time immemorial, hunters have also used white furs or

During the early Middle Ages, hunting was almost exclusively a man's occupation. Women only took part as spectators although later they went in for falcony and in the seventeenth century they started to carry guns (Above). (Centre) Two bear hunters from the 1580s, after Stradanus, and a late seventeenth-century hunter. (Below) Dutch hunter with greyhound, seventeenth century.

overclothes when hunting seal or sea birds early in the spring before the melting of the snow and ice.

During the seventeenth century not only royalty but also private persons of standing began to wear distinctive attire for the major meets. As a rule, people chose the colours of their family coat of arms, so that they could easily be recognised in the field from afar. It was above all in Germany that this interest in "hunting uniforms" developed; hunt attendants were attired according to rank and standing in exactly the same way as in army regiments.

(Above, left to right) Head piqueur's uniform—red—at the Electoral Court of Hessen-Darmstadt, 1780. The green uniform was introduced two years later for hunt attendants. The latter uniform was also used for small-scale drives. Kranichstein Castle.

The colours of the Wittelsbach family were worn at the court in Cologne in the eighteenth century: light blue and white, picked out with silver thread,

for hawking, grey and silver for wild boar hunting, green and yellow for the solitary stalker, and red and yellow when the hunting horn echoed down the avenues of the hunting reserve. There were carefully defined uniforms and accessories for every kind of hunt.

Women taking part in the chase were often dressed in male attire, but there are also plenty of examples of skilled horsewomen who found a side-saddle no hindrance to keeping up with the furious pace of the hunt — a great feat, indeed. In Scotland there is a rock painting from the eighth century showing a huntress on horseback using what is indisputably a side-saddle — incidentally, the oldest picture ever found of a side-saddle. As a rule, however, until the end of the Middle Ages, women attended hunts only as passive spectators.

An early eighteenth-century diary relates how the Bavarian electoral princess, Maria Amelia, was a very keen sportswoman who went hunting dressed in green male attire and a small white wig. Her ladies-in-waiting wore "Spanish clothes" and, according to the author of the diary, were hardly able to boast of beautiful complexions, since they always had to accompany the electoral princess in all weathers and therefore were weather-beaten like farm labourers.

After the French Revolution, the splendour of the chase in Europe diminished rapidly and hunting as a whole became a more plebeian sport. Simultaneously, fire-arms improved and it became possible to fire rapid shots at fleeing game. Instead of the electoral princes, viscounts and lords, to whom hunting had so long been synonymous with

(Above, right) A French count dressed for bird shooting towards the end of the eighteenth century. (After a painting by Alexandre Moitte.) (Centre) A South German peasant of the same period. Detail of a mural painting at Kranichstein Castle. (Right) English fowler dressed in the somewhat careless fashion of the Age of Revolution, clearly influenced by "Les Incroyables" of Paris — the Beatniks of the last years of the eighteenth century.

During the golden age of hunting there was no need for roomy game bags since the aristocratic hunters never concerned themselves with the spoils of the chase. Small bags of this type (left) were used for personal necessities such as ball-pouch, wheel lock key, and so forth. This bag is of deerskin, with a hunting scene and the monogram of Ludwig VIII of Hessen-Darmstadt embroidered in silk. Mid-eighteenth century. Kranichstein Castle.
(Below) "When out hunting, the huntsmen carry bags in which to put small game, powder and ammunition and some food. These bags vary in appearance, differing from district to district." (G. L. Hartig) 1861. Game bag of leather, plaited in part, and fitted with rings from which to hang any game birds shot. From the mid-nineteenth century.

stag hunting, it was now — if a slight generalisation be permitted — solitary woodland wanderers who went out with a fowling piece over their shoulders and a pointer on a lead.

As a result, hunting attire also began to change. It showed a tendency to become more practical. There suddenly arose a demand for stout leggings able to withstand the wet and also sharp thorns; in the large towns, shops were opened which catered solely for the modest hunter's equipment.

The first game bag was without doubt the falconer's originally simple bag in which he kept pieces of meat for the lure, live pigeons to use as decoys in training, jesses, bells and other essential items.

Together with an increasing demand among falconers for luxury and elegance, the design of the bag fairly soon corresponded better to the dictates of status. Falconer's bags from the Middle Ages until far into the eighteenth century were often wonderful specimens of craftsmanship — but occasionally they were also rather philistinic. As in so many other spheres, the distance between the sublime and the ridiculous is dangerously short. This is particularly noticeable when one looks at bejewelled, satiny falconer's bags, which were actually meant to contain bits of raw meat for the lure.

Otherwise, as a matter of fact, the game bag was uncommon, not to say non-existent, in the Middle Ages. The gentry never concerned themselves very much with the kill and the common man had far too much equipment on his shoulders to want to weigh himself down still more.

One of the earliest pictorial records of a game bag is in a drawing by Stradanus (see page 64) where it is carried by a partridge hunter. On the other hand, the bag in the picture is so small that it is hard to imagine that it was meant for the kill. It was more likely intended for bolts for his cross-bow or for his midday meal.

The game bags manufactured in the early eighteenth century were often of the same modest size and were probably mainly designed to hold the hunter's personal necessities.

It was not until the sportsman became a woodland wanderer and stalker in the late eighteenth century that more capacious game bags were called for. The new gunlocks also permitted fowling on a greater scale and the kill, easily damaged as it was, had to be kept somewhere, either carried dangling from loops or rings on the outside of the bag or bundled inside the latter. The hunter usually carried the bag on his left so that he could easily get at the contents with his right hand. If, however, it was necessary to have a *hirschfänger**, a small "stalking bag" was carried on the right so that it did not get entangled in the knife belt.

During the nineteenth century, game bags were normally made of calfskin or pigskin and decorated with patches of elkskin or badgerskin, from which the fur had not been removed. In some places game bags were also made from the incredibly tough and hard-wearing skin of the black-throated diver or of the grebe. The author of an old hunting book — Hartig — recommends, however, simple string bags as being the most hygienic. He believed that badgerskins and sealskins — which were also usual materials — did not dry quickly enough in rainy weather.

The game bag in its later versions may indeed have come to be associated with the solitary hunting practised by the common people, but it must be pointed out that the design of the hunting equipment of the old hunters of blue-blooded game indicated an almost defiant craving for luxury. The different knives were used for highly ceremonial purposes when the kill was dispatched and dismembered and they were indeed artistically decorated down to the smallest detail. In many cases the artistic excesses are almost a strain on the eye. Not one millimetre of the handle escapes the attention of the sculptor's knife, but the æsthetic qualities become apparent only if one takes the trouble to study the details under a magnifying glass. In a way, the tremendous futility of the efforts made by

* Translator's note: a long sword-like hunting knife.

Part of a set of hunting implements from the late seventeenth century. The bone handles are richly adorned with heraldic birds. Eagles, herons, swans, a crane, and pigeons are among the recognisable species of birds. Bayerisches Nationalmuseum, Munich.

the age of gold to achieve æsthetic perfection seems almost pathetic.

The sculptured handle of the hunting knife is rough to the touch and imparts the impression of a doomed era of culture.

99

(Left to right) Costume from the years around 1800, from Costume Français (Musée de Gien). French archer in Empire costume, 1811. German hunting attire, circa 1825. Woman's costume from the early 1830s. French suit with trouser legs reinforced with leather, 1840. French woman's costume, 1840 (Musée de Gien). French costume from the 1840s. English hunting attire, circa 1830. French uniform in fashion plate from 1855. Swedish hunting attire from the 1860s.

Nineteenth-century Hunting Costumes

The sportsman of the romantic nineteenth century was often a solitary woodland wanderer who carried Ossian's ballads or Schiller's poems in his game bag. He was dressed in the sombre colours worn by the peasant hunters of every century, but the cut of his clothes followed current fashions. The desire in the early nineteenth century to dress in

(Below) The hunter's hat, too, reflects the progress of fashion from elegance and luxury in the eighteenth century to the modest headgear of our day. However, in Scandinavia, at least, during the eighteenth century, a frequent sight was the extremely practical cap with flaps which could cover the ears or be tied across the crown of the head, depending on the vagaries of the weather.

the manner of woodmen was combined with almost comical concessions to bourgeois elegance, for example as regards the hat, which was the special characteristic of the immaculate gentleman.

It may seem a mystery to the hunter of today how a person could insist on balancing a top hat on his head at all times, whether it was for the strenuous business of stalking in scrub or for participating in a wild chase on horseback. It is true that contemporary handbooks recommended soft, round hunter's hats of a dark grey or green colour but they are very seldom found in old hunting prints or fashion plates. All in all, it may be said that the creators of the hunting attire of the Age of Romanticism apparently never went in for hunting or an open air life. They created elegant and tastefully patterned costumes which were often not even suitable for walking along a well-trodden footpath. There almost seems to have been a conscious effort to stress the social status of the hunting gentleman by making his attire as "distinguished" as possible. The idea was to be able to spot from afar that it was a gentleman who was approaching in the woods and not just some shabby stalker.

This was mainly true of week-end sportsmen, who dutifully complied with the demands of fashion designers. Doubtless, the real sportsman shocked his tailors with improvements and radical alterations. When G. L. Hartig described the "new" hunter's attire in his famous *Lehrbuch für Jäger, und die es werden wollen* in the 1820s, there was certainly no scope for foppishness or vanity. The colour of the costume was not allowed to be too dark a green or too much like the grey of a roe deer. All colours other than grey and green were unsuitable. The jacket was not permitted to be too short and the trousers were not allowed to fit too tightly. Naturally, all the metal buttons had to be covered with cloth so that they did not glitter. Heavy shoes and short grey leggings were the rule. The hunter of sea birds was advised to wear well-greased boots.

During the latter half of the nineteenth century, the hunting costume became more practical and there was less insistence on an elegant turnout. The hunter's worst worry was, however, the problem of keeping his feet dry — a problem common to all generations of hunters since the Stone Age. All the old handbooks abound with good advice on the subject. One writer, recommending an extra pair of thick socks to be kept in reserve, points out:

"Many a hunter feels that such a precaution ill becomes a hunting enthusiast. The majority of such people, however, when they grow old and are ridden by gout and rheumatism will no doubt regret having neglected to use this simple means of staving off a great many of the ailments of old age."

Next to gunpowder, the rubber boot is the most important invention in the history of hunting.

Cold Steel

For centuries, cold steel enjoyed the reputation of being the most "chivalrous" hunting weapon, and when the first gunshots began to be heard in the forests of central Europe there were many hunters who interpreted these sounds as the beginning of the decline of hunting. The use of fire-arms for hunting was long considered unsporting, at least as far as noble game such as red deer and wild boar were concerned, and many hunt masters forbade their people to use anything but the spear and sword for hunting of this kind. A Palatine prince commanded his hunters "to hunt well, but not shoot!"

The Emperor Maximilian of Austria, frequently mentioned in this book, was not unexpectedly one of those who had the most serious misgivings about future developments when fire-arms began to oust

(Above) Bear hunting with sword and spear. After Stradanus (c. 1580). (Left) Hirschfänger from the 1740s. By then, the hirschfänger had become somewhat smaller and gently curved towards the point of the blade (Bayerisches Nationalmuseum, Munich). (Below) Eighteenth-century belt for hirschfänger. Yellow deerskin with seams and patterns of white thread. Gilt buckle. (Musée de la Vénerie, Senlis.)

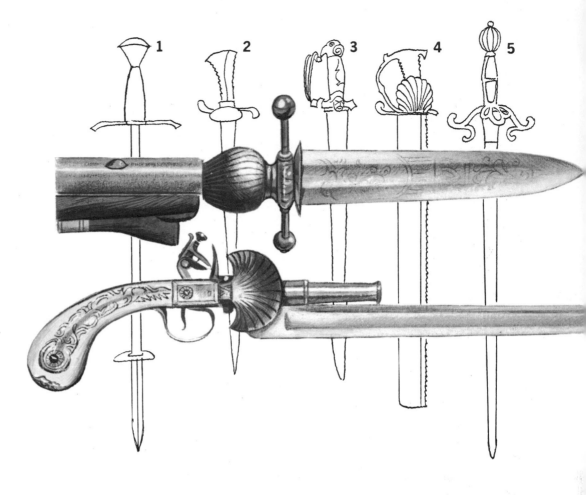

Different types of cold steel:
1. Wild boar sword with round blade merging into four-edged thrusting blade (Deutsches Jagdmuseum, Munich).
2. German hunting sable with deerhorn haft (Deutsches Jagdmuseum, Munich).
3. French hunting sword from 1780 (After Duchartre).
4. Heavy hunting knife with bone-saw on the blade, 1663. (Deutsches Jagdmuseum, Munich).
5. Hunting sword from c. 1580 (After Duchartre). In foreground: Combined cold steel and firearms. (Above) Hunting bayonet from the eighteenth century (Bayerisches National-museum, Munich) and (below) English hunting knife. The haft is a flintlock pistol (Deutsches Jagd-museum, Munich).

(Below) Richly sculptured eighteenth-century ebony hilt for hirschfänger (Bayerisches Nationalmuseum, Munich).

cold steel. He gloomily prophesied the imminent extermination of all game and appealed to all responsible huntsmen to continue to use the old well-tried methods. He himself set a good example by constructing a new wild boar spear (see page 141).

For the chase, the foot followers were mainly armed with spears or forks, while swords and short lances were used chiefly by the mounted huntsmen. For bear and wild boar hunting, both hands were used to wield the sword, as shown by the man in the picture (page 102, top left. Note the piece of leather to protect the left hand), so as to "serve" — the old French term was in fact *servir* — the quarry in the surest manner!

The wild boar's tusks and the stag's antlers inspired great respect, and, according to the *Roi Modus*, the wise hunter first threw stones to drive the stag into a thicket so as to be able to tackle it with greater ease. At the moment of dispatch, his hunting companions drew their hirschfängers two finger's breadths from the scabbard, a symbolic action of ancient date, intended to increase vigilance if the exhausted quarry were insolent enough to resist the noble huntsman.

The Stone Age dog, Canis familiaris palustris, *disappeared long ago from Europe but it survives in remote districts of Siberia. It is described as being long-haired and its colour is said to be grey with a tinge of black, rather like that of an elkhound. It has a white streak on its head and its belly is also white.*

The Dog

The Stone Age dog, pictured above, has been given the Latin name of *Canis familiaris palustris*. Perhaps the first dog that man took into his service resembled it somewhat. To judge from the only complete skeleton preserved, it seems to have had short legs like a fox, but also characteristics clearly reminiscent of both the jackal and the spitz of our day.

Most of the earliest history of the dog is shrouded in obscurity. For ages, scientists and scholars have carried on heated discussions in an attempt to throw some light on the matter. An account of all the arguments and counter-arguments which have been included in books on the origin of the hunting-dog does not fall within the scope of this work. All that can be said here is merely that the first dog known to have had dealings with man appeared somewhere on the dividing line between the Paleolithic and Neolithic ages, when man was still wholly a hunter. It is futile, of course, to speculate on what happened on the first occasion that man and dog kept each other company out hunting. Bearing in mind, however, that the jackal has been known to follow close on the heels of wandering nomad tribes in Africa, in order to sponge on refuse and other things, it is surely not going too far to presume that something similar happened in the case of the Stone Age dog at hunting stations of the Stone Age peoples in Europe.

Perhaps the first dogs, which lived near the cave dwellings, had tracked down and held some quarry at bay until the hunters arrived to kill it. Perhaps the hunters had then shared the spoils with their four-legged assistants and gradually this had led to confidence and co-operation. One would like to believe that human beings and dogs, each in their own way, became aware of the advantages of living together — a charming example of symbiosis.

Today no pure form of the dog remains in Europe, but an extremely closely related, perhaps identical breed, is to be found with some Siberian peoples. The picture shown above is based on a description in Edward C. Ash's monumental work, *Dogs: Their History and Development* (London, 1927).

Other European breeds of dog which are believed to have played a part in the development of sporting breeds included a species discovered in deposits in Austria and a powerful dog which lived during the Stone Age by Lake Ladoga. The latter is thought to have been a primitive form of the large spitzes.

When the outlines of the history of the dog family begin to become more distinct — above all thanks to the detailed accounts provided by ancient Greek and Roman authors — it is seen that there existed in Europe an astonishing number of breeds or perhaps, to put it more correctly, types of dog.

In early times, people did not worry about how they crossed different breeds with one another in their attempts to produce the best dogs possible. There were precise instructions on the best system to use. It is significant, as a matter of fact, that the word for bastard, *hybrida*, originally denoted, according to philologists, a dog that was a mixture of two different breeds.

The most sophisticated hunting enthusiasts used a different breed of dog for each type of hunting; one might almost say for each type of game. On the basis of extant descriptions in words and pictures, it is difficult to determine with exactitude what these dogs looked like in real life. On the whole, their approximate equivalents are represented in modern breeds of dog. (See Notes.)

We learn from the oldest laws that the lead dog and the tracker dog were the most prized for stag and wild boar hunting. Nothing definite, however, is known about their relationship to each other or whether they were possibly one and the same dog with merely two different functions. Be that as it may, the fines imposed for stealing or killing a dog of this kind were high compared with what it cost to commit a crime against other types of hunting-dog. The tracker or *Segusii* dog belonged to the

harrier group and was descended from the dog, mentioned above, whose fossil was found in Austria—*Canis familiaris intermedius*. Incidentally, the latter was the ancestor of pointers, *vorsteh* dogs, spaniels, setters and other tracker dogs with drooping ears.

Arrian describes in great detail the hunting-dogs of the Celts in the period around the beginning of our era. He mentions, for example, that the tracker dog often worked together with the coursers; in other words, in the same way in which the hunting of blue-blooded game was practised at a later date. When the tracker dog had found the quarry, the pack of coursing hounds were let loose and the chase began. The display of tracking by scent (the

The greyhound — vertagus — with a hare's head in its mouth served as the model for an oil lamp. Apulian bronze work from circa 300 B C. (The British Museum.)

(Right) Hunter with tracker dog.

(Centre) The hounds are released in pursuit of the startled hare. According to Arrian, the hounds should not be let loose immediately on the frightened hare. Instead, the latter "should be allowed to enjoy a respite and only after that should the hounds be released — if one does not want to ruin the show!"

(Bottom) Wild boars were pursued by large dogs, preferably mongrels.

We are told by Arrian how already in the days of antiquity people used both tracker dogs and coursers at the same time when hunting.

tracker dog) and hunting by sight (the courser) functioning in perfect unison was a much appreciated entertainment.

Arrian also writes about the *Segusii* dogs, which were just as skilful at tracking as the Cretan dogs, but which were especially trained for hare hunting. However, he deplores the fact that their looks cannot please even the most enthusiastic hunter, and "it is not worth while mentioning anything about their appearance, apart from saying merely that they are shaggy and ugly to behold; and indeed, those that are of the purest breed are the ugliest, so that he that likens them to beggars receives the greatest approval from the Celts. They also have mournful and whining voices, and during a drive their barking does not suggest that they are angry, but rather that they are complaining and begging."

The *Laconian* dogs played an important role as all-purpose dogs in classical times. They are described as being small, fierce and fox-like and were very popular in the Mediterranean countries. In Sparta they were kept as state-owned dogs which were always at the disposal of the citizens. When they were not in use, they were housed in large kennels.

Nevertheless, the most magnificent and most discussed of all the dog breeds of antiquity was the huge *Molassian dog*, which is thought to have been the ancestor of the bulldog, but whose origin is far from certain. It was used for the hunting of bears, aurochs, wild boars and other dangerous prey.

During the course of centuries, the dogs of our time were developed from the breeds of antiquity, with the retention of the main characteristics of the different breeds. We recognise the greyhound in the *vertagus*, the harrier in the *Segusii dog*, and in the huge boarhounds, in which the greyhound and the bulldog were combined, we see the Great Dane.

As regards bird-dogs, in the oldest documents they are mainly associated with a certain type of hawking; that is to say, the kind where the dog and the falcon, working together, make terrestrial birds squat so hard that the dog's master has no difficulty in throwing a tirasse net over the whole flock. In mediæval illustrations the spaniel is usually present on these occasions (see page 234). Later, spaniels — *hispaniolus* — occur again, especially as the companions of ladies of noble rank on hawking expeditions.

At a later period, when fowling came to be a gentleman's pastime, the spaniel and other bird-dogs rapidly gained in popularity.

The Scandinavian and other European mediæval statutes give us an idea of what breeds of dog existed, the different ways in which they were used and, not least, the esteem in which they were held. (See Notes.) The first known proper classification of the dog family, however, is John Caius's *De canibus Britanicis*, which was printed in London in 1570. The hunting-dogs presented on the next page were taken from his list. (See Notes.)

Nevertheless, the dogs which for a long time played by far the most important role in the history of hunting were the "running" hounds which were used for "hunting at force".

During the Middle Ages, interest in this form of

TERRARIUS
Dog that penetrated lairs and burrows, the ancestor of the terrier breeds of our time. Specialised in foxes and badgers.

LEVERARIUS
A small dog of the harrier type used for hare drives. Like the preceding and following breeds, it was a dog that ran by scent.

SANGUINARIUS
A tracker dog of the harrier or bloodhound type which has been held in high esteem since the days of antiquity; its popularity is apparent in no small degree from mediaeval statutes.

AGASAEUS
Gazehound. A large courser, which ran on sight. The gazehound was a cross between different types of greyhound, Great Dane and shepherd dog.

LEPORARIUS
Large greyhound, which was used for the "hunting at force" of foxes, red deer, roe deer and hares. Later became popular in England, where it was used for coursing.

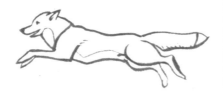

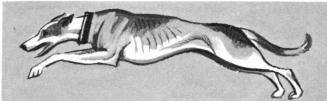

LEVINARIUS
Limer. A heavy courser which was used for close combat with wild boars, stags, wolves and other large game.

VERTAGUS
Tumbler. This was the dog Arrian had in mind when he wrote: "In my opinion, therefore, a true thoroughbred dog is a precious possession which does not come the way of the hunter without the favour of some god."

HISPANIOLUS
Spaniel. Bird-dog which seeks out the quarry but does not kill it. It was used for catching partridges with tirasse nets (see page 234).

INDEX
Setter-type dog. The name means informer; the dog indicates to the hunter the whereabouts of the squatting bird.

AQUATICUS
A water spaniel. Popular in the Middle Ages in England, where it was introduced from Spain.

sport grew and grew, and royalty all over Europe spent immense sums of money on their packs and kennels. It was not uncommon for private persons to maintain several hundred dogs; in some cases as many as a thousand or more — Gaston de Foix is said to have kept no fewer than 1,600 stag-hounds.

These large packs were naturally divided up into several smaller units, which were then stationed in different parts of the country, so as to be available when the master paid a visit and wanted to hunt. A very popular stag-hound in mediæval times was the St Hubert, and for a fairly long time the royal packs were mostly composed of this breed. During the time of that very keen hunter Louis XIV, an effort was made to produce the very largest and swiftest dogs possible in the group of "running" breeds. This resulted in hounds that were apparently able to halt a stag after half-an-hour or forty-five minutes.

When the king grew old and began to have difficulty in keeping up with the pace of stag-hunting, he issued an order for slower dogs to be bred. This was in fact done, by means of cross-breeding with other breeds that were not of such a high class!

In England, there has always been a great interest in fox and hare hunting. Since the seventeenth century, the foxhound, which is descended from the bloodhound, has been mainly used for this type of hunting; more about its use will be found on a later page in this book, in the chapter on the red fox and fox-hunting.

In the Scandinavian countries the opportunities for "hunting at force" or coursing have not been as great as in the rest of Europe. Nevertheless, these forms of hunting occurred in the royal hunting reserves on the island of Öland or in Djurgården, on the outskirts of Stockholm, and also occasionally, perhaps, on large private estates.

Duke Frederick, Gustavus III's brother, had experience of the somewhat special problems facing stag-hunters in Sweden. At the end of the eighteenth century, he tried to hunt with a pack of thirty hounds, which were a present from Germany, but according to the royal gamekeeper, J. L. von. Greiff, the hunt ran into considerable trouble through the hounds, "which were unaccustomed to fences and made a terrible noise every time they arrived at a fence!"

Coursing was arranged to provide a form of entertainment in which wolves, which had been captured in nets, served as the quarry. In Charles XI's diaries, mention is made in several places of this kind of coursing, which was generally arranged on the ice on Lake Mälaren. In order to give the blood-drenched spectacle added attraction, the wolf was starved for some days before the fight was due to take place, but it is not known whether the dogs were given the same treatment. To judge from the dramatic coursing paintings executed by the court painter, David Klöker Ehrenstrahl, at the end of the seventeenth century, bloodthirstiness seems to have been equally distributed between the combatants.

As John Bernström pointed out, the large *shepherd dogs* that were used for coursing in the Middle Ages began to be replaced during the seventeenth century by the large foreign coursers.

Harriers are mentioned for the first time in 1526 by Gustavus Vasa, in a letter in which the king asks the addressee to purchase "a good pair of harriers", but it is impossible to say whether these dogs bore any resemblance to the modern harrier or whether this was merely the name applied to a good tracker dog. Charles XI relates in his diary that he hunted hares and foxes together with his son, Charles XII. It was not until the last century, however, that a start was made in earnest to breed pure forms of the various local types of harrier that had existed in Sweden for centuries.

I

With the establishment of hunting on a more organised basis at the European courts during the early Middle Ages, as a result of various laws and regulations, game gradually fell into two groups.

One group, frequently referred to as royal game, was, as the name suggests, reserved for the king and those upon whom he had bestowed this privilege, while the second group was more or less open to everyone. The species belonging to the category of royal game have varied a good deal at different periods, but red deer and fallow deer have always been automatically included under this heading. In addition, the wild boar, bison and aurochs were usually considered to be members of the group.

As a rule, the bear has also been classed as royal game, although already in the *Sachsenspiegel* and other mediaeval treatises it was at the same time included among the outlawed animals which each and every man was under an obligation to kill. Since the elk had all but disappeared from central Europe in the Middle Ages, it did not feature in the list of royal or noble game. In Scandinavia, however, it was included in this group. The same state of affairs applied to the wild reindeer.

The chamois, ibex and mouflon were not originally classed as royal game, but despite the loud protests of the Alpine population, were transferred to this group, thanks partly to the Emperor Maximilian's interest in Alpine hunting. This was also the case with the marmot.

Among the birds which since olden times had automatically belonged to the ranks of royal game were the swan, bustard, heron and capercailzie. Over the centuries, many writers of hunting books have extended the list to cover several other species, including the black grouse, pheasant, hazel hen, eagle and eagle owl, crane, bittern, and many others.

The roe deer and wolf have occupied a special half-way position. In France, *la Louveterie* was to some extent the sport of the privileged classes, and it was considered a great feat even in royal circles to have killed a wolf. In common with the bear, however, the wolf was at the same time an outlawed animal which one and all were allowed to kill.

In Sweden, the roe deer was classified as royal game during the Middle Ages, probably because red deer were to be found almost solely in the

hunting reserves and were consequently of no importance as game that could be freely hunted. As regards the standing and composition of the group of blue-blooded game, many status factors, which are difficult to understand nowadays, must be taken into account.

In addition, during the eighteenth century a number of borderline cases were placed in a somewhat vague intermediate category. Apart from the wolf and roe deer, this group included a number of huntable species of game birds which were regarded as being slightly too "good" to belong to the game available to all and sundry. The intermediate group generally embraced the grouse, black grouse, ptarmigan and hazel hen.

All other game were classified as falling within the common man's sphere, and as a rule were of no interest to the hunting gentry of the Middle Ages. The reason for the indifference shown by the latter class of society will be dealt with on another page, but to put it briefly, owing to the lack of good fire-arms, shooting birds and small game was not a very entertaining pastime. A striking reversal of the social position of game belonging to the lowest group was indeed to take place when fire-arms had developed so much that rapid wing shots were possible. During the Middle Ages and far into the seventeenth century, trapping and stalking were considered to be hardly becoming for a gentleman. It was really not until the eighteenth century that

bird shooting, for example, began to be regarded as suitable even for the aristocracy.

The principal, and in the eyes of many people, the only noble game was the stag: the European red deer. Naturally, the fallow deer also belonged to the category of noble game but was regarded as a stranger, despite its having been hunted in several parts of central Europe during the Stone Age.

After having disappeared from Europe already in prehistoric times, it was reintroduced from Asia and kept in *vivaria* in Roman times. It is found on painted vases with hunting motifs from Mycenaean times in Greece and was regarded there as the symbol of night and darkness, owing to the star-studded sky of white patches on its coat. Byzantines and Moors also introduced the fallow deer as game in various parts of the Mediterranean countries in the early Middle Ages, but it never acquired the same importance for the chase as that enjoyed by the swift and temperamental stag.

As already mentioned in the chapter on the hunting horn, the Merovingians were great hunters, but not until the advent of the Franks and Carolingians is it possible to declare that organised hunting in central Europe had come to stay. The credit for this achievement was due above all to Charlemagne, who in addition to his many other activities, found time to cultivate a passionate interest in everything connected with hunting. He appointed a whole host of officials, whose sole function was to be responsible

"As I have already told you before, the stag should be big and his coat should be dark or light brown. He should have a rather bulging belly, large tufts of hair underneath. He should be broad across the shoulders, have thick and lofty hind quarters, high and plump flanks, white rump, called a looking-glass, short tail and thick neck with plenty of flesh round the breast. It is extremely pleasant to hear stories about such stags" (King Modus).

Hunting with decoy stags in the rutting season was practised above all in classical times by the Romans. This, however, was not a method found in the Middle Ages or later.

for hunting and game preservation. He gave his head gamekeepers such authority and standing that the organisation of hunting all at once became one of the most important offices at the imperial court. Hunting on land, hunting on water, falconry, stag-hunting, and all the other sub-divisions of hunting, were allotted specially trained personnel who devoted themselves exclusively to their own particular spheres.

It was under Charlemagne that stag-hunting began to be associated with the magnificent splendour that was to develop uninterruptedly towards ever-increasing luxury for the next thousand years. His personal friend, the poet and abbot Angilbert, wrote a very graphic poem in which he describes in great detail the Emperor's hunts at Brühl.

It resembles a tapestry woven in words and is just as vivid and naïve. We see the hunt attendants and grooms in the palace yard getting ready for the

Fencing off enclosures with canvas screens was an important part of hunting at force. Hunting cloth from Kranichstein Castle.

hunt; we see the Emperor riding out at the head of a splendid assembly of princes and important persons, followed by trumpeters, hound-men, net-carriers and other people on foot. Noble ladies of wondrous beauty and high birth accompany the procession on horseback as spectators — women did not take an active part in hunting until the late Middle Ages.

The hounds are unleashed, and to the sound of barking, shouting and deafening blasts on horns, the hunt moves off at a wild gallop through the shady groves of the hunting reserve and across broad fields and open glades. These hunts were not well planned, for on the whole, anything was killed that happened to get in the way of the hounds, whether it was a pregnant hind or newborn fawns. After the hunt, the company gathered in tents or leafy bowers and refreshed themselves with Falernian wine until sunset.

Charlemagne's son, Louis the Pious, is described as having been an even more passionate hunter than his famous father, and it seems incredible that he had any time at all to do anything else but hunt. He hunted the stag until the start of the wild boar season and went hawking when there was nothing else to do; he was constantly on the move, from one end of his kingdom to the other, in search of as much variety as possible.

The growing interest in stag-hunting — or, to put it more correctly, the hunting of noble game, the sport of kings, which also included the wild boar — rapidly led to advances and improvements in hunting methods. From having been a fairly barbarous slaughter of every living thing that people were able to lay their hands on, detailed rules were now worked out as to how hunting was to be practised. There also arose an extensive terminology, which every nobleman had to master completely in order not to run the risk of dishonour.

In different parts of Europe, experienced hunters devoted themselves to the writing of handbooks on hunting techniques and ethics. As a matter of fact, several of these books have been made accessible, thanks to translations and commentaries by the leading living authority on mediaeval hunting literature, Professor Gunnar Tilander. One of the

When the dead stag was disembowelled, the entrails and the blood were mixed with bread and distributed to the pack. Detail of "The hunting tapestry", 1425–50. (The Victoria and Albert Museum, London.)

most famous of these mediaeval hunting handbooks is *The Hunting-book of King Modus and Queen Ratio*, the original title of which is *Lě livre des deduis du roi Modus et de la Reine Ratio*.

It was written in the 1370s by the Norman noble Henri de Ferrières, and devotes a lot of space to stag-hunting, which is described in detail in twelve chapters. The reader is instructed how to talk about stag-hunting, how to recognise stag tracks, how to search for the stag, how to track it down with a tracker dog and release the pack of hounds after it. In addition, the reader is instructed on the correct way to use the hunting horn, sword and hunting knife as well as how the entrails should be distributed among the hounds. (See Notes.)

De Ferrières's book came to be used as a basis for other mediaeval hunting handbooks, not least for one of the most highly praised of all, Gaston de Foix's *Livre de Chasse*, which was completed some twenty years later. Its style is easier and less dry than its predecessor, on which it is nonetheless largely based.

The ever-increasing interest in hunting during the Renaissance was accompanied by greater demands for luxury and splendour. The hunting of noble game required large expanses of country, rich in game, where leafy woods alternated with open fields and meadows.

In order to meet the demands for hunting grounds of this kind, kings began in the early Middle Ages to appropriate large areas of land for use solely for hunting purposes. In addition, they curtailed the rights of the landowners and peasants with but a scant measure of consideration for the latter's interests. Game was protected in every way between the hunting seasons and the result of this uninhibited "game preservation" was, of course, that blue-blooded game increased enormously in and near royal hunting grounds.

The chapter on the wild boar includes an account of how much the country people suffered through the ruthless hunting passion of the feudal lords.

In some areas, however, the repercussions of the damage done by game to growing crops began to be felt by the hunting lords themselves, since it sometimes proved difficult to wring taxes from the impoverished people, even by means of old, well-tried methods. When the lords saw that all this was a potential danger to their own economy, they realised that the time had come at last to do some rethinking. Already Louis XI of France (1423–1483), a passionate hunter, understood that it was both more convenient from a huntsman's point of view and best for the country's economy for the game to be collected together in enclosed hunting reserves, where it was then possible to indulge to one's heart's content in drives, hunting at force or solitary stalking in the midst of a multitude of animals.

With this end in view, large numbers of stags were rounded up in the neighbourhood of the hunting reserves and transferred to the enclosed area. In this way, the hunters were spared the eternal moans and groans of the peasants.

Nets, of course, were more necessary for stag and

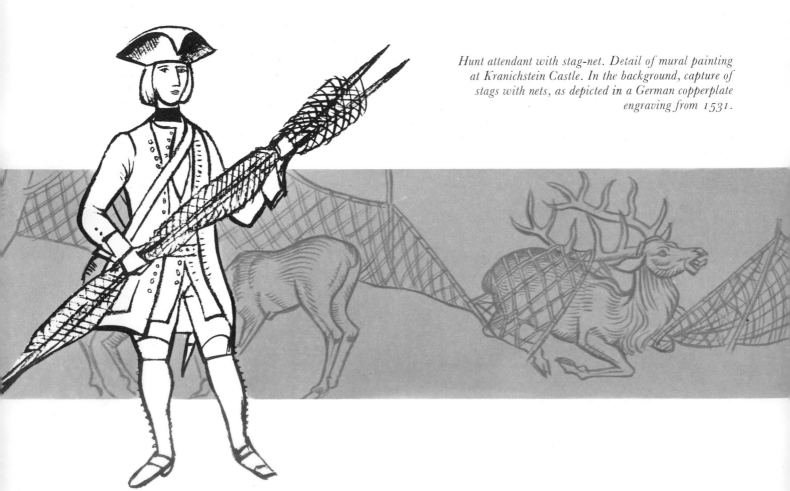

Hunt attendant with stag-net. Detail of mural painting at Kranichstein Castle. In the background, capture of stags with nets, as depicted in a German copperplate engraving from 1531.

Hunting screens often bore the owner's monogram. They were so bulky that three screens alone constituted a full waggonload.

wild boar hunting before the appearance of fire-arms. Later, nets were used mainly for the purpose of capturing the animals alive. In the course of the seventeenth century, the nets employed in the big drives began to be superseded by huge canvas screens with which the hunters shut in the animals they wished to hunt. For reasons easily understood, the use of these screens for hunting involved enormous expense and required a large number of servants. As a rule, the screens were three or four yards high and ten yards or more wide; they were so heavy that three screens constituted a full waggonload. They were hung from thick ropes and joined closely together. Sometimes, however, the canvas screens were replaced by permanent palings or fences in order to simplify matters.

When the screens were in position so that they formed a square, with one wall open for the drive, the hunting area was sealed off and guards were posted, whose task it was to prevent the animals from breaking out. A cordon was carefully thrown round the game and gradually the circle diminished in size, so that in the end the animals were crowded together in a small space. After this, they were driven into the screened-off area, which was then closed completely and the participants in the hunt — if the word can be used in this context — moved in for the kill.

It is no exaggeration to maintain that this type of "hunt" was one of the first signs of the decadence that was to find its most repulsive expression in the seventeenth and eighteenth centuries in various forms of "super hunts". Hunting was transformed into a vulgar type of entertainment in which people cast aside their inhibitions in the most perverse blood-spilling orgies. The brutality that was the order of the day makes it fully apparent to us that the animals were regarded as being "soulless".

A pavilion was generally built in the middle of the animal enclosure. Here, pleasantly shielded from the sun and with fortifying drinks within easy reach, the hunters were able to shoot at random into the midst of the harried herd of deer, which as a final insult were slowed down in front of the guns by row upon row of obstacles.

It is with the most naïve delight that an author of hunting books like von Fleming describes how "*die*

Herrschaften" should make large-scale massacres as entertaining as possible. He dwells particularly on the amusement caused by the ladies present, when they talk about stags without a mastery of the correct terminology. If the stag-hunter is guilty of a linguistic blunder, he is in fact punished with blows from the flat of the knife in a suitable place. The waggish author adds that, as regards ladies, this form of punishment can easily be given an interesting twist.

Even at the time of the worst depravities, therefore, there was a strict observance of the mediaeval ritual for stag-hunting, and woe betide anyone who was guilty of a breach of etiquette. He was forced to lie across the slain stag and was administered a fixed number of heavy blows with the hunting knife. In addition, he had to put up with a lot of insults from his hunting companions. (See Notes.)

Hunting at force was sometimes arranged in woodland areas that had been cordoned off. This was in fact absolutely necessary when the hunt happened to take place in huge tracts of continuous forests, as in eastern Europe, for example. In France, the home of hunting at force, special arrangements were made in the hunting reserves, even in the early days, for the convenience of the hunters. Broad avenues were cut through the woods in different directions, thereby making it easy to follow the course of events during the chase. In suitable spots, clearings were made where the hunters could assemble or stop for a break. In such country, canvas screens were unnecessary and it was up to the head *piqueur* — the leader of the hunt — to see that the hunt did not stray too far.

During the seventeenth century, thanks above all to Louis XIV, hunting at force developed into a well-organised sport, with strict rules for every stage of the hunt. Overleaf I have tried to illustrate, in words and pictures, the most important phases of an eighteenth-century stag-hunt, as run at Compiègne, Fontainebleau, Chantilly, or any of the other famous hunting reserves outside Paris.

Louis XIV not only introduced the term "*la Curée*" into stag-hunting. Unfortunately, he also had many other grotesque ideas about adding a bit of colour to hunting. In 1697 he held a nocturnal hunt at Chantilly, when the whole forest was lit

VALET DE LIMIER. FAISANT LE BOIS

Using a skilful tracker dog, the head *piqueur* locates the stag he intends to hunt. He is very careful not to frighten it; he merely wishes to make sure where it is, as well as note the size of the antlers and anything else that might assist the hunters.

LE RENDEZ-VOUS OU L'ASSEMBLÉE

Meanwhile, the hunters plan the attack and what is to happen when the stag makes off. The hounds are still on the leash and everyone is waiting for the signal from the head *piqueur*.

LES BRISSÉES

The head *piqueur* has marked the stag's tracks with the aid of twigs and the first fanfare is sounded on the hunting horn. With a cry of: *"Volez! Volez! Mes chiens! Après! Après! Mes valets! Mes amis!"* the hounds are released on the hot scent and so the hunt proper begins.

L'ATTAQUE

The hunt moves through the forest at a furious pace; signals are heard the whole time from the horns of the hunting company, and as soon as it has been ascertained that the hounds are chasing the right stag, a cry of *"bonne chasse"* — good hunting — comes from all directions. The moment a horseman sees the stag he sounds *"la vue"*. There is a different signal for each phase of the chase.

LE DÉBUCHÉ

Should the stag happen to leave the hunting ground in panic, the head *piqueur* must immediately gallop off with the whole pack of hounds, sounding his trumpet constantly, in order to stop the stag if possible and force it to return.

LE CHANGE

If things go wrong and there is a great abundance of game in the hunting ground, the hounds may easily pick up the scent of another animal and the pack may disperse. It is up to the *piqueurs* to stop any breakaway movements and make sure that the hounds return to the right track.

LE RELAIS

Some of the hounds rest in the forest at a strategic point from which the *piqueur* can easily see when it is time for them to join the chase. There are broad clearings through the hunting ground so that the *piqueur* can see at once when the stag passes.

LE CERF À L'EAU

As a rule the hunted stag tires after $2–2\frac{1}{2}$ hours of the chase and then if possible plunges into some lake to cool off. The *piqueurs* sound the signal *"Bat de l'eau"* before this aesthetic climax of stag hunting.

L'HALLALI

The stag is exhausted and stands at bay. Some "hunters" then creep up from behind and cut its Achilles' tendons so that it cannot hurt the hounds. The head *piqueur* or the master of the hunt rushes forward and gives the stag the *coup de grace* with his *hirschfänger*.

LA CURÉE

The final magnificent phase of the stag-hunt was introduced by Louis XIV. A loud blast on the horns proclaims the successful end of the hunt. The pack of hounds fight for the entrails, the tracker dog is allowed to get its teeth into the stag's head, and one of the *piqueurs* displays the trophy.

By keeping a watchful eye on breeding and by shooting on a carefully planned basis, the eighteenth-century hunting gentry were able to produce stags with antlers of a size that scarcely occurs any more. Shown here is the famous 32-pointer "Battenberg Stag" from 1765 (see Notes). (Kranichstein Castle).

(Below) Stag-hunting even influenced the design of hunting carriages. The drawings are based on the sketches of the carriage-makers. (Left) Voiture de Chasse, from the early eighteenth century. (Right) Voiture de Chasse, built in 1789 for use as a four-in-hand. Both are at the Musée de la Vénerie, Senlis.

up with torches and cressets; a whim that was described as being typical of the revered "Sun King".

All in all, the hunting of blue-blooded game tended in some cases to be transformed into nothing but a spectacle, on account of the craving for new and more sophisticated forms of sport. The most extraordinary masked hunts were held; the participants appeared in clothes of varying degrees of strangeness; they were particularly fond of ancient Greek and Roman costumes. A colossal hunt was arranged for the wedding of the Margrave Ernest von Brandenburg and Princess Sophia zu Dresden in 1662. It was led by the Elector John George III of Saxony, incidentally a gentleman descended from great hunters — his father and grandfather headed the central European lists of kills during the seventeenth century.

Among a huge company of hunters who set out for the woods there were, for example, two giants dressed up as savages, four satyrs with shepherd's pipes (on a hill), three nymphs, His Electoral Highness himself, in the guise of Diana riding a white stag, three persons dressed as lion-tamers in green livery and two bagpipers attired as savages. In addition, the company included bear-trainers, Lapps with dogs and reindeer, hunt attendants with English bloodhounds, bird-hunters with dogs, other trappers carrying tridents and cages with captured otters, falconers, a hunt attendant carrying a cage with squirrels and hamsters, gamekeepers with wild boars, lynxes, rabbits, wild cats and other animals in cages, etc. All in all, an impressive and at the same time curious collection of people out together on the same hunting expedition.

This hunt, however, was on a fairly modest scale in comparison with the magnificent stag and wild

boar hunts arranged by other electoral princes. Since the moment of the stag's plunging into a river or lake and the sounding of the signal *"Bat de l'eau"* were looked upon as being the highlights of hunting at force, it was the custom simply to dig huge pools, into which all the deer in the drive were compelled to plunge, so as to present a colourful sight as they fell to the hunters' bullets. The pavilions developed into huge constructions with terraces and balconies. Orchestras played sweet music and all around sweet-scented flowers and beautiful fruit hung from the trees and bushes, presumably as a means of somewhat softening the effect of the terrible bloodbath.

Wide staircases and lofty arches also helped to provide as magnificent a setting as possible for the spectacle.

One of the most lavish stag-hunts ever held was arranged by the Elector of the Palatinate in honour of his counterpart in Mainz on August 13, 1764. Thanks to the fact that a diary was kept by one of the guests, a Roman Catholic prelate, we have a detailed description of the whole entertainment, which was held in the Neckar valley.

The actual hunting grounds lay on the banks of the river, where all the trees on a high hill had been cut down. An ornamental garden with arabesques composed of varicoloured types of earth had been laid out on the slopes. The hill was surmounted by a huge leafy arch, through which an army of huntsmen in green costumes, picked out with silver thread, were to drive the deer. The latter had been rounded up in advance.

On the other side of the river, a large building had been specially constructed for the occasion. It was designed like a palace with terraces and an enormous staircase. At either end of the building there was in addition a small pavilion with balustrades, where the musicians were placed. Moored in the middle of the river was a large raft, most luxuriously decked out with brilliantly coloured ornaments and statues.

The spectators, estimated by the diarist at some 10,000 persons, stood on the slopes round the hunting enclosure.

When the Elector gave the signal for the hunt to begin the stags were driven in flocks of twelve, fifteen and twenty animals through the archway on the hill and down the slope, towards the building where the hunters were waiting with their guns at the ready. The moment the stags plunged into the water, a violent barrage opened up. Immediately a stag was killed, hunt attendants rowed out and hauled the kill up into a barge.

104 stags were killed in the course of an hour or so, and the hunt was then terminated, probably because there were no game left; to use the words of Corneille, *"Et le combat cessa faute de combattants"*, the battle ended for want of combatants.

The Germans seem to have excelled in the art of arranging super hunts; the various minor princes tried to surpass one another as regards extraordinary ideas, and there does not appear to have been any particular sense of good taste.

The Elector of Bavaria built magnificent hunting ships, reminiscent of a Venetian Doge's vessel, from which to shoot stags that had been driven down into the water from a hunting reserve in the neighbourhood of a lake.

It is difficult to understand how even real hunters could sometimes stoop so low as to take part in, or arrange, this kind of spectacle. Even that renowned lover of the chase Ludwig VIII of Hessen-Darmstadt, as a break from "ordinary" hunts at his lodge at Kranichstein, deigned to indulge in the most extraordinary hunting frolics, which included not only animals wearing clothes but also other frightful devices.

It would be unjust, however, to describe these spectacles as really common phenomena; in a way, they were probably the equivalent of hunts that might be arranged nowadays for visiting VIPs.

On the other hand, at all the royal courts of Europe hunters were to be found with a sense of responsibility, who showed great zeal, a sort of

The shooting of stags in an area enclosed by canvas screens first took place in the seventeenth century. This innovation may be said to mark the beginning of the degeneration of hunting. It was a particularly cold-blooded form of the chase, warmly recommended by the writers of hunting handbooks until the late eighteenth century, and it still occurred during the last century!

religious fervour almost, in maintaining their stag populations and in ensuring that hunting was done in a decent manner. By means of careful planning and by controlling breeding it was possible, in certain principalities, to produce first-class stags of a size whose equivalent we scarcely ever see nowadays. Stags with particularly fine antler buds were captured in the autumn, so as to make sure of obtaining the antlers when they were shed. This is what happened in the case of Ludwig VIII's famous trophies, the "Battenberg Stags". The largest pair of antlers belonging to these stags is shown on page 118. It may be said to have thirty-two points, as long as one follows the example of the keeper of the hunting-lodge by applying the term "point" to every excrescence big enough to hang a key on.

During the eighteenth century, interest in stag-hunting reached its climax in various parts of Europe, not least in Germany, where a number of princes won renown as stag-hunters. Ludwig VIII spent large sums of money on hunting and the old castle at Kranichstein became a centre of stag-hunting in this area of Germany. A careful record

was kept of the trophies, and portraits of the best stags were painted by court artists specially employed for the purpose. On the wall of one of the staircases there is a life-size painting of a stag. The picture commemorates an unusual occasion, when the hunted stag rushed into the castle yard and through the open door. A special turret-room was built at one end of the building, from which the hunters were able to shoot stags that were driven from the neighbouring castle park.

No less famous a stag-hunter was the Elector Leopold von Dessau, who hunted with a pack of 150 hounds. In contrast to the majority of other hunters, he was in the habit of releasing the whole pack *at the same time*. The idea was to give the hounds and the stag an equal chance. Usually the hounds were released in relays, so that there were always rested hounds in reserve, but this custom did not appeal to the fair-minded Leopold.

His frequently commended sense of fair play as far as game were concerned seems somewhat doubtful, however, when one learns elsewhere that on one occasion he pursued a particularly stubborn stag over a distance of some sixty miles, and that in so doing he is said to have ridden eight horses to death!

Hunting at force was regarded more as a field sport than anything else and the kill was of secondary importance. Various methods, some less pleasant than others, were used in an attempt to prolong the pursuit as much as possible, in order to enjoy all the more the performance of the pack — *la muete* — on the scent. The training of the tracker dogs and hounds was very carefully planned to ensure an impeccable hunt. It was of great importance for

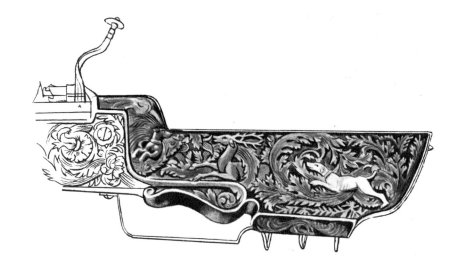

the pack to be led by a capable hound, which the others followed.

Gradually, it became increasingly difficult to hold stag-hunts anywhere other than in enclosed hunting reserves and interest switched instead to fox-hunting, which, in spite of strong opposition from various quarters, still occurs in many parts of England, and to rabbit and hare coursing with greyhounds. The brown hare is also hunted with large packs of beagles and harriers; the hunters follow behind on foot. It is presumably mainly thanks to the huge, park-like areas of private land that hunts with horsemen and hounds have managed to survive so long in the United Kingdom.

In Scotland, where there are large numbers of red deer, the importance of stag-hunting has obviously been quite another matter than in southern England. Deer-stalking, in particular, has enjoyed a reputation as a very fine sport. Some connoisseurs occasionally recognise two forms of deer-stalking. There is real stalking, which takes place in uninhabited country, where deer, guaranteed wild, are the quarry, and artificial stalking. The latter occurs on private land, where the owner puts out food for his deer and keeps an eye on them. According to the experts, artificial deer-stalking is a miserable imitation of the real thing. Deer-stalking is a most exhausting form of hunting, requiring great physical strength and the fitness of

an athlete. It may be added that the terminology that has grown up around stag-hunting in England has never achieved any success in the Scottish Highlands where, in fact, stag-hunting has not been surrounded by so much pomp and circumstance as on the continent.

Interest in the hunting of blue-blooded game as a sport awoke considerably later in Sweden than in central Europe and can hardly be said to have occurred until well into the sixteenth century. In Denmark, however, hunting at force was practised at least two hundred years earlier. It was above all the sons of Gustavus Vasa who began to hunt for pleasure on a scale comparable with continental courts.

One of the reasons why hunting at force or large-scale drives with canvas screens never became popular in Scandinavia was the lack of suitable country for hunting in the grand style. Besides, the supply of red deer was not good enough for large hunts. To remedy this state of affairs, John III established hunting reserves in various parts of the country, so that he could indulge in the sport. The largest of the royal hunting reserves was Öland; the king turned a large portion of the island into his private hunting ground. He apparently had arrangements to obtain the Öland estates of noblemen on an exchange basis, so as not to run the risk of having his hunting upset by the privileges of the nobility!

John III's dictatorial attitude in this matter is best illustrated by the ruthless hunting regulations he introduced into Öland. No dogs were allowed on the island unless one of their forelegs had been mutilated, and the islanders were even denied the right to kill hares and squirrels. The penalty for

French piqueur uniforms for hunting at force. The uniform on the extreme left is from 1813, while the remainder date from the last golden age of hunting at force in the days of Napoleon III. (Right) Dog whip of bone from the same period. (Musée de la Vénerie, Senlis.)

breaking the regulations was naturally severe, and if the offence was repeated, the peasant lost his head and the nobleman his home and lands.

Öland was admirably suited to hunting at force on account of its wide open spaces with comparatively few trees. The huge reserve was a favourite hunting ground for the court for a long time. When Carolus Linnaeus travelled through Öland in 1741, he made a number of entries in his diary criticising the fact that the court maintained red deer on the island. The latter caused great damage to the crops of the impoverished peasants — who were forbidden, incidentally, to use firearms — and Linnaeus would have liked to see the deer replaced by sheep. However, he refrained from expatiating on these views in the official report on his journey! (See Notes.)

More than forty years were to pass before conditions in Europe changed in the direction so discreetly hinted at by Linnaeus in the diary of his Öland journey. With the advent of the French Revolution of 1789, the system of hunting was completely transformed, not only in France but also in several other European countries, where the monarchs apprehensively paid heed to the signs of a democratic wind of change. (See Notes.) Gone were the days of the magnificent super hunts; the large packs of well-trained stag-hounds were disbanded, the silver-threaded hunting uniforms in the colours of the different noble families lost their splendour, and indeed, many of the great aristocratic hunters lost their heads under the busy guillotine.

"Twenty years of devastation and misery have wiped out practically every trace of hunting traditions," as Desgravier sadly remarks in his *Du parfait Chasseur* (1812). The few members of the gentry who tried to the last to keep the memory of the grand hunt alive, naturally at a safe distance from Paris, were most reminiscent of faithful attendants in some forgotten museum. All around them the stud-farms, kennels and hunting reserves, beautiful as the landscape in a tapestry, fell into decay.

The grand hunt, and above all the stag-hunt, were to enjoy an unexpected and rapid new lease of life, however, under Napoleon I, who understood the status value of the super hunt. In his memoirs, Metternich describes a stag-hunt in the company of Napoleon in 1807 at Fontainebleau, where the Emperor had introduced a number of German red deer to replace those slaughtered during the Revolution.

Court painters such as Carle Vernet showed that as regards elegance, the hunts of the Napoleonic age in the woods near Paris were not really inferior to those of the Sun King. On the other hand, a striking decline became noticeable during the reign of Louis Philippe. During the many years of unrest, the revolutionaries had run riot in the imperial hunting reserves at Versailles, Marly, Saint-Germain and elsewhere. They had more or less wiped out everything in the way of red deer, roe deer and pheasants. The "Bourgeois King" did nothing to repair the damage; on the contrary, hunting suffered under his rule.

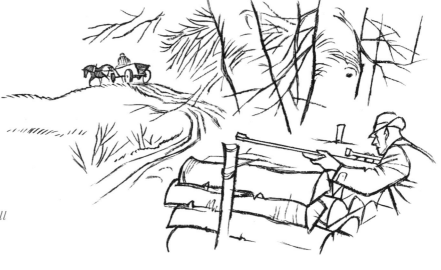

"*It is better still, however, to use a cart to which new wheels have been fitted, so that they grind against the axle. The deer will stop when they hear the cart and will show no fear, since they are used to wood being transported in carts through the forest.*" (*Roi Modus.*)

It was not until a quarter of a century later that the grand hunt — "*la vénerie imperial*" — was to enjoy yet another golden age under Napoleon III; but despite the elegant turn-out and the splendid uniforms, stag-hunting was nevertheless a mere shadow of its former self.

The French Revolution — and improved fire-arms — indirectly increased interest in stalking or ambushing red deer and other large game throughout Europe. Following the many years of war and unrest, the red deer population had diminished considerably in most places, and hunters were indeed obliged to resort to an intensive programme of wild-life conservation if large game were not to disappear completely from their lands.

Many of the mediaeval methods of hunting red deer, so warmly recommended by King Modus and his colleagues in cynegetic literature, were once again in frequent use. Methods which in former times had been employed only by poachers were now accepted by the gentry. As a result, an entirely new attitude to hunting began to appear; people spoke highly of hunting ethics and did not pay as much attention to the "heroic" aspect of the hunter's life as in olden times, when Olaus Magnus and kindred spirits considered that "Noble is the bag obtained by hunting; acquired by trickery it is despicable".

When Olaus Magnus spoke about "hunting" he was, of course, referring to the noble chase on horseback, which the writers of antiquity regarded as the warrior's best school!

The red deer has always played an important role in folklore, magic and superstitions. Under mediaeval hunting laws anyone was allowed to pick up discarded stag antlers, if they were found in the woods. The regulations show that deer antlers were coveted possessions, and the reason is easily understood. Since time immemorial, deer antlers have held an important position in the pharmacopœia, and as recently as the late seventeenth century people spoke of "the genuine deer apothecary", where practically every disease could be cured with the aid of secret deer preparations. (See Notes.)

The red deer has always had the reputation of being the noblest of all blue-blooded game, and no animal could be better suited to carry the crucifix and halo of the legend of St Hubert. The origin of the legend is vague and originally concerned Saint Eustace, although it was later transferred to Hubert, whose feast-day on November 3rd is still celebrated in many countries with stag-hunts and other hunting events. (See Notes.)

The woodcut in the eighteenth book of the History of the Scandinavian Peoples *by Olaus Magnus, 1555, is one of the very earliest pictures of an elk. The* alces *described by Caesar is on the right. From "Caesar, Commentarii", edited by Aldus Manutius, 1575.*

THE ELK

In prehistoric times the elk was widely distributed in Europe; it followed close on the heels of the extension of the pine-tree's range towards the south and south-west after the end of the ice age. When, however, the pine was gradually forced back by deciduous trees at the time of the subsequent climatic change, the elk moved northwards with it. In Britain and Denmark the elk had disappeared already by prehistoric times, but it remained for a long time in the enormous tracts of wild country which stretched right across central Europe and which the writers of antiquity called the Hercynian Forest. There were still elks in the western parts of France in the early Middle Ages. It may be deduced from the Nibelungenlied and from several imperial hunting laws that elks were hunted in the regions close to the Rhine in the twelfth century, in Bohemia in the sixteenth century and in Silesia, Galicia and Hungary during the seventeenth and eighteenth centuries. By that time man can be singled out as being directly responsible for the rapid decline which, particularly during the period after the Thirty Years' War when roving bands of soldiers shot at everything edible, constituted a serious depletion of the number of elk on the continent.

In Germany there are still several place-names which recall the times when elks were still to be found there. One of the best known is the monastery of Ellwangen, which was founded by two knights in the ninth century to commemorate a successful elk hunt. According to an old chronicle, a bull elk had been found in the rugged Virgunna Forest and had then been pursued in a hunt of long duration until it met its fate at a place which was christened Elchenfang (later Ellwangen). The elk's antlers were hung up in a place of honour in the monastery that was founded at the spot and, after various adventures, they ended up in the chapel of Amboise Château where Charles VIII fastened them with an iron chain. They were destroyed there during an enemy attack, but an order for a replica was placed with the famous goldsmith Benvenuto Cellini. That, too, was destroyed and a copy of the copy was made. The latter was on view at a hunting lodge outside Berlin just prior to the Second World War. By this time, however, the copy of the trophy was as far removed from the original as can be imagined, and had been transformed into a monstrous set of stag antlers three metres long.

The story of the Elchenfang elk is significant in several respects; firstly, in that the slaying of an elk

Distribution of the elk in prehistoric and in modern times. It became extinct in France in the early Middle Ages. It existed in Flanders in the tenth century and was probably exterminated in the twelfth century or thereabouts in the southern and western parts of Germany. In Bohemia there were still elks in the fourteenth century. The last elk was shot in Saxony in 1746, in Silesia in 1776, in Galicia in 1760 and in the western areas of Prussia in 1830.

was such a remarkable event as early as the ninth century; and secondly because already two or three centuries later people had such a poor idea of what elk antlers looked like in reality.

When the naturalists of antiquity had to describe the elk, this animal had long since disappeared from northern Italy and the Balkans, and the descriptions were therefore based entirely on hearsay. The late Hellenic author Pausanias maintained that the elk occurred in the land of the Celts and that it was so extremely shy and fleet of foot that it could not be tracked down and slain by human beings. In order to capture an elk it was necessary to surround huge tracts of forest. This was why the elk was such a rare animal in the Roman arenas where it was counted as a great celebrity on a par with the giraffe and the tiger.

This, in its turn, is why the elk appeared so very seldom in ancient Greek and Roman art and in mediaeval art on the continent. It also explains why the examples mentioned in literature are nearly all open to doubt.

The pictures in old zoological works show what a vague idea continental scholars had about the appearance of the elk. The shape and position of the antlers are indeed still a problem for many painters of the elk. Here we see how the question was solved in the Theatrum universale omnium Animalum quadropedum *of Johannes Jonstonis, as recently as an edition from 1755.*

When the earliest naturalists were faced with the task of describing these rare animals, the results were indeed curious. The first to venture to tackle the subject was Julius Caesar who, in his famous history of the Gallic wars, described the many remarkable animals that frequented the Hercynian Forest and here mentioned *alces* for the first time. He informs the reader that this animal is similar in shape and colour to the deer, and gives a strange account of its way of life.

"The elk has no antlers and is entirely lacking in joints in its legs, for which reason it is unable to lie down to sleep. Instead, it is obliged to lean against a suitable tree trunk when it wants to rest. The wily Germanic hunters take advantage of this fact by cutting through the roots of suitable sleeping trees without allowing them to fall. When an elk later on leans against one of these trees, both the tree and the animal crash to the ground and the hunter has only to go up to the helpless quarry and kill it."

This strange method of hunting is based on fables and hunting stories which especially flourish in regard to animals in the border region between fact and fiction. It may be added that the Greek geographer Strabo, who lived at about the same time as Caesar, mentions a people called the "elephant eaters", in the neighbourhood of the town of Sheba in Arabia, who trapped elephants by felling their sleeping trees. *Physiologus*, which was written about A.D. 370, contains the same information about elephants, but the account ends on a gently moralising note.

125

The descriptions of the elk which were written by authors after Caesar hardly helped to make the picture more credible. Pliny confused the matter still further by sub-dividing the elk into two species, namely the elk and the "elk-like animal", *echlis*, which was not only stiff-legged as in Caesar but also had to walk backwards when eating so as not to be impeded by its upper lip which drooped considerably. Similar characteristics were shared by other types of mammals according to ancient writers; for example, it was said that the reindeer had to eat with its head on one side so that its antlers would not get caught in the ground vegetation! As in the case of the jointless legs, it is a question here of ancient fables which stubbornly lingered on and were applied to hitherto unfamiliar animals.

Mediaeval writers added their share to the hunting stories by declaring that not only was the elk the only animal which human beings were unable to track down but also that, at close quarters, it was one of the most dangerous beasts in this part of the world. Both Barthelomeus Anglicus and Gesner maintained that the elk stored water in a large skin bag under its chin. They stated further that the water got hot if the animal was being chased and that the latter defended itself successfully by squirting the hot water at both hunter and hounds "which then bark most terribly and are covered with burns". This unpleasant characteristic of the elk was ingenuously recorded as recently as 1764 in *The Sportsman's Dictionary* — striking evidence of how long fantastic stories about this game animal, half-mythical in the eyes of the people of central Europe, took to die.

The *Encyclopedée de la Chasse*, 1769, also stressed vigorously how dangerous the elk was: it is extremely difficult to kill with fire-arms, since the hide is so strong and tough; furthermore, the hunter is warned against its quick legs, for with a single blow of its forelegs the elk can easily kill a man. Hunting at force is the main method recommended in this French handbook; it must indeed have been an exacting sport. We know that the nobles of Courland hunted elk in this manner and that Frederick I of Prussia arranged a magnificent hunt for Peter the Great when "several hundred elk were killed with the cross-bow". The latter occasion must have been, however, an example of a drive on the grand scale.

In view of the great respect shown for the elk, it is

perhaps not out of place to say a few words about its magic properties. In central Europe the hooves were thought to be of great medicinal importance for curing epilepsy, and when the elk in time became extinct on the continent, it was an easy matter to use ordinary cattle hooves to deceive patients. According to popular belief, the wearing of elk-hoof amulets was also a cure for cramp and ordinary headaches.

Of the other parts of the elk with magic properties, the hide was the most important. It was sometimes considered to be impossible to pierce and, according to Olaus Magnus, it was worn by fierce Scythian forest dwellers during the early Middle Ages. In winter the hides were first dipped in water so that they became hard as armour plating. During the seventeenth century a short elkskin jacket became a common item of military equipment and in some measure ousted the uncomfortable iron and steel cuirass worn by cavalry when in action. A short extract from Schiller's *Wallenstein* shows that the

magic properties of elkskin were well known even much later:

Was wollt ihr da für Wunder bringen
Er trägt ein Koller von Elends Haut
Dass keine Klinge kann durchdringen!

It is not beyond the realm of possibility that this fashion in uniforms had a catastrophic effect on the number of elk in the north-eastern parts of central Europe. According to Olaus Magnus, many thousands of elkhides were shipped annually from Scandinavia and hides were also included in the skin-tax which the Lapps had to pay during the sixteenth and seventeenth centuries. In Poland there was a sharp decline in the number of elk, partly as a result of the Emperor Paul's decree that the Polish cavalry were only to wear trousers of elkskin. In Sweden a gloomy future would certainly have been in store for the elks if all the cavalry regiments had followed the example of the Östgöta Cavalry, whose standard uniform included the elkskin jacket long into the nineteenth century.

Far into the Middle Ages, Scandinavia was for the most part one large area of elk country and, as was mentioned on an earlier page, the earliest inhabitants of northern Europe hunted elks a lot, employing various methods. Above all, they pursued elks on crust snow. In addition, they used pitfalls and *älgled*.* A few examples have also been found of hunting on a more organised basis, where pitfalls and the driving of elks over precipices were combined with extensive fencing similar to the type prepared by the stone age hunters in western Europe for aurochs and horses.

There is a good deal of evidence that the elk was

* Translator's note: *älgled* (pl. — *älgled*) was a trap for elks. A self-releasing spear was placed close to a track used by the animals.

an important game. Countless fragments of elk antlers have been found in "the black soil" in the Viking settlement of Birka in central Sweden and the elk often figures in the first provincial laws from the early Middle Ages. In the West Göta statutes elk hunting was allowed in the same manner as that prescribed for the large beasts of prey, and this may possibly indicate that the elk was regarded as vermin. In the middle of the fourteenth century, however, the first restrictions on elk hunting were introduced — it was forbidden between Lent and the feast of St Olof — a fact that may possibly be construed as a sign that the elk was becoming less numerous in farming country.

Gustavus Vasa occasionally sent warning letters to the inhabitants of the provinces of Dalarna, Värmland and Sörmland, since many of them did nothing but roam about in the woods hunting "elk animals", with the consequent danger that the latter might soon die out. When threats were of no avail, it was time to include the elk among "the king's protected animals" and elk hunting was put in the hands of royal officials and the nobility. Originally, only the roe deer had been counted as royal game; the turn of the red deer came later and, finally, it was the turn of the elk. One of the reasons for according the elk such a privileged position was doubtless to save it from extinction as a result of the unrestricted hunting that went on, particularly in the early spring. There is much to suggest that the elk would never have survived in Europe without special legislation for its protection.

After having been regarded almost as an outlawed and destructive animal in the oldest provincial laws, the elk, in the space of two or three centuries, had joined the select company of noble game. Quite a record. There may have been many reasons for this.

Many thousands of elks died in order to supply the European armies with hides for uniforms. The hide was believed to contain magic properties and to be impossible to pierce. When Gustavus II Adolphus rode out to the battle of Lützen wearing, despite warnings, an elkskin jacket instead of a suit of armour, he did so on account of a gunshot wound in his shoulder received at Dirschau. (The Royal Armoury, Stockholm.)

Since the Swedish nobles tried hard to imitate the customs of foreign courts, it is perhaps not so strange that the elk was not originally included among those animals in Sweden deemed to be noble game. It was, after all, practically unknown as game on the continent and consequently not worth the attention of courtiers. But when Olaus Magnus, thanks to his major work on the Scandinavian peoples in the mid-sixteenth century, spread the fame of such exotic phenomena as the elk abroad, it gained the recognition of the Swedish king and was proclaimed a royal animal.

John III appears to have shown particular interest in the elk. In letters to his sheriffs in 1587, he mentions the elk *first* among those animals which "We absolutely wish to have protected in every corner of this kingdom", and some years later he started, at Flottsund, the country's first and presumably only elk reserve. Perhaps his object was to copy foreign practice and arrange elk hunts there under easy conditions.

Hitherto, the civilised world's knowledge of the elk had been influenced by the writings of the authors of ancient Greece and Rome, but in the second half of the sixteenth century this tradition was broken to some extent by, for instance, two writers with Swedish connections. One of them was Olaus Magnus, who has already been mentioned, and the other was Apollonius Menabenus. The latter was, for some years, John III's physician. His impression of Sweden was not altogether favour-

able, and it was with undisguised joy that he soon returned to southern climes from the "inhospitable and wild regions" whose inhabitants possessed, he felt, an intellectual blindness exceeding that of all other people. However, the elk so dear to John III seems to have made an indelible impression on this learned Italian, and in 1581 he published in Vienna a small work on the elk, *Tractatus de magno animali*,* which apparently aroused great interest, since three editions appeared in one year.

It is true that the book was mainly concerned with the large animal's use for medicinal purposes, but it also gives us glimpses of the elk as seen by an unbiassed eyewitness. Menabenus mentions that elks shed their antlers every year, which shows that they belong to the deer family. The antler is not so long nor has it so many branches as is the case with stags; it is more like "the wing of a large bird". Elks occur in small flocks and in the winter they very cunningly walk one behind the other so as to prevent their pursuers from being able to count their number. In the autumn, winter and spring, it is the custom of the Swedes to hunt the elk with "small hand mortars", whatever he may have meant by that. Menabenus's respect for the scholars of antiquity does not prevent him from clearly dissociating himself from the half-mythical *alces* which tottered about on stiff legs in the Germanian forests, but he is careful to point out that the elk of the Scandinavians, "the large animal", had nothing in common with that of Caesar, Pliny and the other writers.

For two or three hundred years, the elk continued to be reserved for the king and the nobility, and the law provided severe penalties for anyone caught poaching. The first publication referring solely to hunting conditions in Finland is, characteristically enough, a stern letter addressed by Gustavus II

The provincial arms of Jämtland from 1660 show an elk being attacked simultaneously by a dog and a bird of prey. The picture certainly bears an obvious resemblance to the scene on page 41.

* In translation, the full title was: *Treatise on the large animal, called Alces by some, but which the Germans call Eland, and on the medicinal properties of its various parts.*

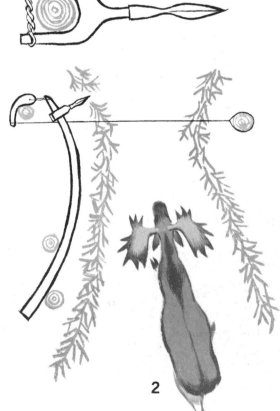

Pursuing elks in open country must have been an exacting sport. It is apparent from a picture in Olaus Magnus that elks were captured by combining pursuit with the use of nets. (Right) an elk pitfall from Härjedalen. The poles placed crosswise served to guide the falling animal on to the spear in the middle. (Alongside) Elk trapping ground with eight pits with fencing between each one. (After Widén.)

Adolphus to the inhabitants of the Aland Islands reminding them of the strict ban on elk hunting. Anyone who killed an elk ran the risk of incurring the death sentence or, if he was lucky, of being banished for life to the wilds of Ingermanland. Anyone scaring off an elk which might, for instance, be feasting off the meagre crops in the oatfields was heavily fined. The death sentence was apparently never carried out, but on two occasions poachers were deported to America as a punishment for killing elk. Generally, however, the penalty was restricted to running the gauntlet, work on fortifications or a fine of six oxen.

Elk appear to have been still in good supply at the beginning of the eighteenth century, and there are many descriptions of successful elk chases; for example, those arranged by A. Schönberg for

Frederick I in Uppland and Bergslagen, where it was not unknown for fifteen elks to be killed in one day in addition to all the other game. There are descriptions from Dalarna of a somewhat unusual method of hunting which was occasionally practised. The elk were driven out on to stretches of ice where they are said to have been an easy prey for the hunters. It is not very clear how this form of hunting was done, but it is possible that it took place when the ice was free of snow, for then elks were apt to slip and fall, whereupon they were quite helpless.

Some time in the mid-eighteenth century the elk appears to have become rarer all of a sudden. For example, Linnæus, in spite of a great amount of travelling in the provinces of Scandinavia, never managed to see a wild elk, and he describes it as rare. Matters really looked bad for the elk when Gustavus III signed, in 1789, the famous decree according to which every commoner who owned taxed land was also given the right to hunt on his property. This was, of course, very praiseworthy from a democratic point of view, but it spelled disaster for the elk. The cruel crust-snow hunts, in

An älgled *could be constructed in several ways. (1)* Älgled *from Jämtland. A dry fir or aspen branch (a) is bent backwards and placed along the ground so that the narrow end reaches a thick length of wood (b) along which the spear (c) rests, pointing upwards at an angle. The spear is released when the elk touches the trip wire. (2) Another Jämtland* älgled *seen from above. In this case the spearpoint is attached to the tautened bow itself. (3) Side view of the spearhead fastening device. (After Ekman.)*

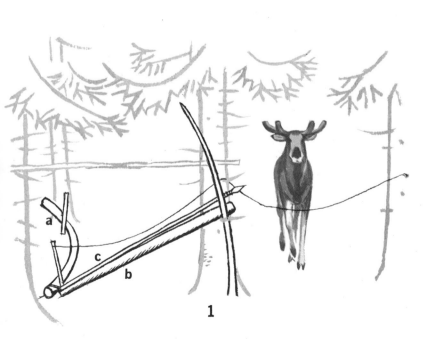

1

2

3

particular, became immensely popular, and hordes of people would ski day and night until they caught up with the exhausted elks, which by this time were often lacerated to the bone by ice and snow crust.

The occasional hunter who took the trouble to think soon realised that this state of affairs could not go on for very long before the elk was exterminated in Sweden. However, the first person who really did something about the matter was the legendary bear hunter, Herman Falk of Värmland, who, after a lot of opposition on the part of the authorities, managed in 1825 to bring about a total ban on elk hunting for ten years. Despite frequent poaching during this period of protection, the position of the elk really began to improve gradually but, when the ten years had come to an end, a veritable war started against the creature, and out in the countryside the slaughter acquired ridiculous proportions.

Thanks to Falk's further intervention, the laws were speedily revised, and as early as 1836 elk hunting was restricted to the period between August 1st and the end of November. The terrible days of winter hunting were over at last.

But it was not until the large animals of prey had been exterminated in the south of Sweden in the latter half of the nineteenth century that the elk really began to become more numerous. It also started to spread in the northern provinces of Sweden where for more than a century it had been driven out by beasts of prey and by human beings. It is rather amusing to note that, in certain parishes in northern Sweden, they were just as unfamiliar with the long-legged fairy-tale animal which suddenly appeared as the writers of antiquity were in their day; and, like the latter, they actually described the elk as an animal without joints in its legs. Sven Ekman wondered whether this legend was the relic of some ancient Germanic myth, or if it had reached the country people through those classes of society with a knowledge of Latin.

The pitfall and the *älgled* were among the most widespread and most frequently used of the many trapping methods in existence. Both were extremely cruel and, for reasons easily understood, they were just as dangerous for people wandering around in the woods as for the animal for which they were intended. Already in the earliest provincial laws, there are strict decrees regarding the use of *älgled* and fairly soon they were permitted only in the least densely populated areas of the kingdom. Pits were dug in northern Sweden as recently as the 1820s but the *älgled* persisted for a longer time and apparently still occurred in the 1890s. The *älgled* was so designed that the animal itself released the spear, which sometimes was replaced by a set gun. It was prepared at the intersections of routes known to be taken by the animals. By adjusting the tension of the trip wires it was possible to decide in advance what part of the animal's side the spear should hit. If the wires were sufficiently slack, this led to the shot being aimed behind any person who might, by mischance, walk through the *älgled* and this, of course, was a good thing.

When the pit and the *älgled* gradually passed out of use — both were prohibited by the hunting by-laws of 1864 — the snare came into its own in some areas of northern Sweden. A certain technique was required for snaring which was done most successfully by specialists of great renown.

Various types of elk hunting have been practised in Scandinavia, but the oldest and most difficult method is stalking, or the still hunt as it is also called. If this type of hunting is to be successful, woodcraft and a deep knowledge of the nature and behaviour of the elk are necessary. The stalker should move about as silently as possible and the whole time make sure that he is moving against the wind; he should be as sensitive as a seismograph to every sound and movement. It is a kind of hunting which may be just as rewarding if the person concerned is armed with a gun, camera or a pair of binoculars, or if he is simply curious about nature in general. It is the method employed by the solitary elk hunter.

Lying in ambush, for example on the German *hochsitz*, or shooting platform, close to the grazing grounds of the elks is a very common variant of the still hunt; in the north of Sweden, at least in former times, it was often done at the rutting places of the

bull elks. On the other hand, the use of calls to deceive the animals during the rutting season was never particularly widespread in Sweden in the past, in contrast with North America, where some hunters achieved extraordinary skill in the use of birch-bark horns to deceive the bulls into coming right up to them. The distinguished naturalist, C. U. Ekström, had only heard of one person who possessed this ability and "on account of this skill he was believed to be a magician".

L. Lloyd recorded a rather curious kind of hunting from Dalarna that comes under a sub-section of calling. Various fiddlers are said to have called elks successfully by playing their instruments. A fiddler from Venjan is said to have been so badly knocked about by the music-loving elks in 1851, when they discovered his deceit, that he was confined to bed for a whole month. There is unfortunately nothing to prove the truth of this story, but, in view of the love that certain animals clearly have for music, it is not altogether beyond the realm of possibility.

The use of dogs for hunting elks in Scandinavia has also a long history, above all in the northern areas. There are two main kinds: hunting with wide-ranging dogs or with lead dogs. With the first kind the dog is released on a fresh scent and keeps the elk at bay, barking loudly to guide the hunter to the spot.

In brief, the aim of hunting with a lead dog is for the dog to use its power of scent against the wind to lead the huntsman to the elk. This method of hunting makes great demands on the dog and on the hunter, in that order. The dog must move about in as unexcited and quiet a manner as possible and, by its behaviour and reactions indicate the right direction to the huntsman; this means that there must be perfect co-operation between man and hound if the whole thing is to be successful.

The beating method to hunt elk is practised notably in the southern parts of Sweden, where the elk is common and when the main object is to shoot a predetermined number of animals. The guns are posted in a row and a chain of beaters drive the elk towards them. The hunter must, above all, be an excellent shot, but only the master of the hunt need have a thorough knowledge of the habits and habitat of the elk.

Formerly it was also to some extent the practice to hold large-scale beats, organised almost like a military operation, in which whole parishes took part; the kill might then be quite impressive. This manner of hunting will be described in greater detail in the section on the bear.

It might be said that the history of the elk in Scandinavia is that of its hunters. Over the centuries the ups and downs of this animal have been influenced by the hunters and the laws that the latter have introduced. The Västgöta law stated laconically that "he that kills the elk owns him". In those days it was still hunted as vermin and was the enemy of any peasant making a clearing in the forest. Then, suddenly, it was promoted to the rank of a royal animal and became a favourite quarry for the entertainment of the noble and the powerful; while in more remote country districts its hide went to make uniforms, through the imposition of heavy skin taxes. Perhaps the elk's darkest hour occurred in the first half of the last century when, apart from experiencing a shortage of the vegetation on which it depended for its food, as a result of grazing by domestic animals, it was subjected to great pressure by large numbers of wolves and bears, and by hunting-mad peasants with good fire-arms and fast skis. When the hour of recovery came at last, the bears and wolves, as well as the *älgled* and crust-snow hunters had suddenly disappeared from the scene. Within less than a century, this large game animal, once doomed to die, was found in greater numbers, presumably, than in prehistoric times.

In 1888 the official number of elks shot in Sweden was 1,966. At the present time, the annual kill is about 35,000.

But the very great increase in the numbers of elks in Scandinavia, which started sometime in the mid-nineteenth century, must not be interpreted as resulting solely from a relaxation of pressure on the part of hunters or from the decline of predatory animals, even if these factors were of great importance. Ingemar Ahlén, in his survey of the

ecology of the deer family, showed what far-reaching effects cattle-raising has had on the family's nutritional habits. After occurring only in a fairly limited area of central Sweden in the eighteenth century, the elk spread over the whole of the Scandinavian peninsula — with the exception of parts of western Norway, southernmost Sweden and the highest mountain regions — in the space of scarcely a hundred years. This was the greatest faunal change in recent years and can to a large extent be attributed to an increase in the supply of food for elks owing to changes in the timber industry, agriculture and cattle-breeding.

Following the redistribution of agricultural land, which started in the late eighteenth century in southern Skåne and slowly spread to other parts of Sweden, the countryside changed very noticeably. One not insignificant result was that pastures shrunk while more land came under the plough.

In the past, the woods had been full of cattle and herdsmen, so that elks met with considerable competition in their search for food. As a result of the land reforms, however, cattle began to be brought together in enclosed pastures. In several of the areas studied by Ahlén there has been an increase, in some cases as much as tenfold, in the elk's winter food — wild berries, lichens and shoots of deciduous trees and bushes. In former times, there was no winter food at all for the elk in some areas.

Simultaneously with the end of cattle grazing in the woods, sylviculture increased considerably. This greatly aided the elk population, thanks to the appearance of clearings with a rich supply of nourishment. In Dalarna, a ten per cent increase

has been noted in the availability of food for the elk since the turn of the century, owing to modern methods of sylviculture.

It seems that developments are now at the stage when the supply of elks has reached its optimum. Large areas of woods with an excessive number of elks are overgrazed and, according to Ahlén, this means that the Swedish deer population (red deer, elks and roe deer) is not likely to increase.

Already in the Middle Ages, many areas were as rich in cattle as in the nineteenth century. Consequently, there is reason to suppose that for many years the elk's range was comparatively limited and that the animal was rare in many places, above all in Norrland.

The elk is a good example of the high degree to which man can influence an animal's environment and prospects of survival. The Swedish elk population has been very sensitive, both to technological advances in agriculture and sylviculture, with all that this has meant to the supply of food, and to hunting; that is to say shooting and trapping, or the depredations of large animals of prey.

The elk population which we have in Sweden today is the result of many contributory factors, but it is first and foremost a product of civilisation. In historical times the elk population has certainly never been larger than it is now. The elk's natural enemies — the wolf and the bear — no longer exist and the only balancing factor remaining —

In Scandinavia the use of dogs for elk hunting is an ancient tradition. (Left) Hunting with a wide-ranging dog which has brought the elk to bay. (Right) hunting with a lead dog.

apart from "overpopulation" with disease in its wake — is the hunter.

Hunters on the continent look upon the elk almost as a mythical animal, and those who visit Scandinavia never cease to wonder at the fact that this denizen of the forests is in such lively and intimate contact with people and built-up areas.

In some places, elks wandering into gardens in the outskirts of towns may occasionally be a nuisance to the local population who are unable to chase them away; elks often visit the suburbs of Stockholm and have been known to cause traffic jams. Nearly every year one or two enterprising elks wander about in the very heart of the Swedish capital, and on a recent occasion an elk was seen in Riddar-holmen in the heart of the mediaeval Old Town! The terrifyingly large number of road accidents occurring where new arterial roads cut straight across well-trodden elk crossing-points bear witness to the fact that elks are also a danger to traffic.

In many parts of central Sweden the elk is by no means an unusual feature of the countryside. When motoring through one of the districts where elks are particularly abundant — northern Upp-land, for instance — it is not uncommon to see ten elks or more in the oatfields by the main road in the space of two or three hours on a summer evening! The elk is an animal that is never far from people's thoughts in Sweden. The Swedish naturalist, Sven Rosendahl, once said that "there is a kind of dialogue being carried on between the elk and the Swede". He was referring to the mutual curiosity which is a feature of the relationship between human beings and the mysterious long-legged animal of the forests.

However much study and research may be devoted to the elk, it is nonetheless a constant topic for discussion. A final pronouncement on its character and behaviour is never possible. Nearly every encounter with an elk provides the interested observer with new ideas and opens up new per-spectives. Take, for example, the way in which the elk's coat varies in colour according to the light; the variations in its pattern of movements; the differences between immature animals of both sexes or between dissimilar types of elks as regards the shape of the body or its markings — just as a distinction is made between palmated and branched elk antlers, so it would be possible to distinguish between asthenic and athletic elks! — the rich variety of different sounds, and so forth.

The elk is an animal that never ceases to fascinate and to stimulate curiosity; it is an animal that always has something new to offer.

THE AUROCHS AND THE BISON

The aurochs and the bison still occurred in large areas of Europe at the beginning of the Middle Ages. They were hunted with dogs and with the bow and arrow by the Merovingians in France, slain with the lance at close quarters by Charlemagne at Aix-la-Chapelle (Aachen), killed, together with elks and other wild animals, by the heroes in the *Niebelungenlied,* trapped in pits by Poles, Hungarians, Lithuanians and Northmen. The aurochs and the bison were part and parcel of the European landscape of the early Middle Ages with its extensive tracts of wild country. More or less simultaneously with the end of the Dark Ages and the incipient stabilisation of political and social conditions, there began the decline of the aurochs and the bison.

The connection is obvious but should not be interpreted as the only explanation possible. The reason for the extermination of the aurochs and the almost complete destruction of the bison is doubtless to be found in a combination of various factors. Their natural habitat, the untouched virgin forests, shrank to a minimum at the same time as persecution by the hunters was intensified and made more efficient as a result of improved weapons and trapping techniques. In view of the fact that vigorous measures were taken to protect both species as royal game in those areas where they still occurred, it would be strange if the hunters alone were responsible for the way matters turned out.

Now it is only to be regretted that the aurochs were not given the same respite as the bison. If that had happened, it would perhaps also have been possible to save this magnificent species of wild game from destruction. Curiously enough, the aurochs was, as a matter of fact, considerably more common than the bison during the early Middle Ages, according to what the distinguished authority on both these species, B. Szalay, has been able to establish thanks, for instance, to a study of place-names. A more detailed account of the sad end of the aurochs will be found in the chapter on hunting horns (page 71). The existence of engravings and paintings of the aurochs from the middle of the eighteenth century has led to the theory that scattered specimens may have survived a century after its "official" demise, but there is no evidence that the artist used live models for his work.

During the late Middle Ages, the aurochs and the bison had been obliged to retire to the eastern parts of Europe, chiefly to the great forests in the border areas between Lithuania, Poland and Russia, where they were also held captive in royal preserves. Olaus Magnus, for example, was able to note this fact on the occasion of a visit in 1528. It was also in this part of the continent that the bison managed to survive the longest, following the death in 1627 of apparently the last aurochs. It was mainly in the Bialowieza Forest in the province of Grodno that the large prehistoric animals had their haunts, but there were also isolated occurrences in Silesia, Lithuania and the Caucasus. In the last-mentioned

area the bison became extinct as recently as 1925 but was reintroduced in 1954.

In his account of the Gallic wars, Julius Caesar writes about the huge bisons and aurochs which lived in the Hercynian Forest. "They are hunted with great enthusiasm; they are trapped in pitfalls and killed. By feats such as these, young men harden themselves and by means of this method of hunting they improve their skill; those who have killed the largest number of animals win great renown, once the horns have been publicly displayed as proof.

"It is impossible, however, to accustom these beasts to the presence of human beings and to tame them, even if they are caught young."

The word "bison" is probably derived from the Sanskrit *visana*, meaning "the horned one". The name is also found in a number of place-names — an indication of the bison's former range in Europe. Visontium in northern Spain and Besançon in France are two examples. Visnaholm Manor in the Swedish province of Västergötland is perhaps yet another instance.

The bisons in the Bialowieza Forest were protected as royal game by strict decrees; poachers were punished more or less mercilessly. The result of this drastic form of game protection was very satisfactory and, as recently as the nineteenth century, there was a plentiful supply of bison in the district. The hunts which were arranged by the Polish kings also achieved wide fame. When Augustus III of Poland held a hunt on September 27, 1752, in one day, for example, forty-two bison, twenty elk and two roe deer were killed.

Naturally, these royal hunting entertainments were carefully prepared in advance. In good time before the hunt, the attendants collected a large number of bison by driving them into a particular area which was then enclosed with nets, fencing and fires. Next, tents and pavilions for the shooters were erected in a suitable glade nearby. When the hunters had gathered, the bison were driven past within easy range and it was merely a question of firing away into the midst of the woolly brown monsters. Every time a bison fell, a fanfare was sounded, and when evening came torches lit the

(Left) Sixteenth-century picture of the bison. From Rerum Moscoviticarum.

135

scene of the slaughter and the huge quantity of dead game.

In spite of the strict protective regulations, the numbers of bison decreased considerably during the eighteenth century. 1755 is mentioned as the year in which the last animal was shot in Prussia. By 1790 the bison had disappeared from Hungary, where earlier it had been well-established. In Poland, too, there was an unfortunate drop in its numbers towards the end of the century. Nonetheless, as recently as the 1780s, King Stanislaus-Augustus, at the head of a colourful court of courtesans, generals, cavaliers, officers, Uhlans, Cossacks and horseguards, mowed down bison from a magnificent three-storey pavilion which had been built, especially for the occasion, in the middle of the woods. It was the last time that a grand hunt in the old style was held in the Bialowieza Forest and, in 1803, when the area became part of Russia, a total ban on bison hunting was introduced. Permission to shoot bison was then given only by the Czar personally and solely for scientific purposes.

In October 1860, however, the peace of the bison's woods was brought to an end once again. Czar Alexander II arranged a great hunting festival for an impressive number of kings and princes from neighbouring countries. Two thousand peasants from the neighbourhood were pressed into service with the chains of beaters, and each and every man received a glass of wine in addition to his day's pay. This sounds like surprisingly humane treatment. It may be added that the following year the Czar officially abolished serfdom in Russia.

Compared with Augustus's hunt a hundred years earlier, this one was, however, considerably less impressive: two days' hunting resulted in twenty-eight bison, two elk, ten fallow deer, eleven wild boar, sixteen lynxes, sixteen roe deer, seven foxes, four badgers, and two hares.

A colossal royal hunt took place in the Bialowieza Forest in 1890 when, in the course of a fortnight's constant hunting, the kill included forty-two bison, thirty-six elk and 138 wild boar. During the next few imperial hunts the number of bison shot diminished appreciably, but in spite of the obvious trend of matters, a toll was taken of the remnants of the herds until the First World War. In the chaotic conditions created by the war and the subsequent Russian revolution, the Polish bison received their final deathblow, and in 1921 the last animals were shot by a poacher. By this time the only bison left alive in a wild state were the Caucasian herds, and they, as has already been mentioned, were doomed.

At the beginning of the 1920s, a society was founded for the preservation of the bison. A count was carried out of the bison in the zoological gardens of Europe, and the appearance of a herd book enabled a careful watch to be kept on breeding. The Skansen Zoo in Stockholm came to play a significant part in saving the bison from extinction, since the zoo there possessed excellent breeding animals.

It was indeed Sweden that became the chief supplier of the bison which have now been given a new chance in the Bialowieza Forest. In 1960 there were about 400 bison in the whole world and now there are good prospects of the species being able to survive.

The hunting of the bison in the Middle Ages was often done on horseback and with the use of large packs of hounds. However, what was considered the most heroic method was that adopted by Siegfried and Charlemagne who engaged the huge beast on foot with a spear or lance as the only weapon. This form of hunting was feasible only in a dense wood of large trees. The huntsman selected a suitable tree behind which to take refuge and when the monster came rushing along — pursued by hounds and

This ostentatious statue was erected in commemoration of one of Czar Alexander II's bison hunts in the Bialowieza Forest. The names of the most distinguished huntsmen present on the occasion are engraved on the plinth. There was a time when it looked as if the statue would also become a mausoleum of the European bison in its last refuge — the last "free" bison was shot during the Russian Revolution — but, as a result of foreign zoos sending new animals to Poland, the bisons have been given a new chance in their old surroundings.

136

The Polish hunter met the bison armed solely with a spear and a sword — exactly like the heroes of antiquity.

beaters — the huntsman struck it with his sword or spear. The huntsman then had to hurl himself quickly behind the tree in time to escape the enraged animal, which then drove its horns into the tree. By repeating these tactics a few times the bison was exhausted and eventually defeated.

People had great respect for the strength and dangerous nature of the bison. It was not only the horns that were considered dangerous but also other parts of its body, which looked harmless. As early a writer as Oppianus maintained that its tongue was so rough that the animal was able to tear skin to shreds by licking it; and serious descriptions from the end of the nineteenth-century state that the bison used its tongue to get a grip on the hunter's clothes and throw him to the ground, whereupon it killed him with its hoofs. People were even warned about its tail with which it was said to be able to deal dreadful blows to any careless person.

Just as with red deer and reindeer, bison hunting was also done with the aid of stalking cows during the rutting season. However, by far the most usual, and most disastrous, decimation of the European bison occurred with the help of pits or by stampeding the animals over precipices. According to Pausanias, bison were caught by driving them towards a deep gorge or pit on the edges of which hides, covered in blood or thoroughly smeared with oil, had been spread out so that the animals would lose their foothold. In his chapter on the aurochs, Olaus Magnus gives a variant form of this method, according to which a fatty substance was rubbed into the ground to make it slippery. His description ends as follows: "Thus they are caught, rendered helpless through their fall."

Gunstock of South German type from seventeenth century with bone inlay decoration. Wild boar hunt on foot with spear and hounds. One of the hounds is wearing a protective coat. (Leger- en Wapenmuseum, Leyden.)

THE WILD BOAR

By the time that hunting had begun to develop into a refined pastime for the privileged classes, in the early Middle Ages, the bison, aurochs and bear had already been chased away from large areas of the continent. "Heroic hunting", in which the huntsman pitted himself against a fierce opponent, had consequently become restricted to combat with wild boar, an animal which, since olden times, popular belief had associated, and sometimes confused, with the above-mentioned animals. After the beginning of the Middle Ages, they were often grouped together under the general heading of "black game".

The fact that wild boar hunting was called "heroic", and was reserved for royalty at an early period in history, was also because the wild boar was regarded as the personification of evil. It is apparent, from many examples in mythological literature, that it was possible to interpret the knight's combat with the wild boar as a kind of allegorical picture of the struggle of righteousness against the devil; for example, Meleager's combat with the Calydonian boar (see page 35). In Konrad von Megenberg's *Buch der Natur* — written in the fourteenth century and held to be the first book about nature in the German language — the wild boar is depicted as symbolising the wicked man who refuses to repent and, instead, remains for ever in his state of black and midnight sin. Its tusks are curved inwards, towards each other, so that it injures itself first when it attempts to injure others.

For centuries, this somewhat unscientific approach set its stamp on the attitude of hunters to the wild boar and may to some extent explain the cruelty and ferocity which sometimes characterised wild boar hunting. (See Notes.)

Together with stag hunting, boar hunting is certainly the most frequent hunting subject for ornamental purposes. Wild boar hunts are depicted on painted vases from classical antiquity, on powder-horns, sword-hilts, gun-stocks, musket locks, dagger-blades, cross-bows and elsewhere. Two main groups of hunting occur in this connection. Firstly, the chase on horseback with sword, lance or spear, and secondly, the more usual combat on foot between the hunter, armed with a spear, and the boar, held at bay by a pack of hounds, two of which have seized the beast by the ears. Naturally enough, fighting a wild boar at close quarters in this manner was accorded most honour, and since the method is still practised today by a number of hunters on the continent, it may be said to be one of the oldest extant forms of European hunting.

The hunt proceeded in the following way: the boar was first located by a tracker dog and then the pack of large hounds was let loose. These hounds are mentioned already in the Salic law (A.D. 500) and a distinction was made there between *veltrus porcarius*, boarhound, and *veltrus leporarius*, harrier. They were considered to be very valuable and heavy fines were imposed for killing or stealing these hounds. By crossing greyhounds and mastiffs, a heavy, long-legged and swift-footed race of the great dane type was produced, well fitted for engaging the wild boar in battle. For a long time, however, it retained the main characteristics of the greyhound.

In order to protect the valuable hounds against the sharp tusks of the wild boar, they were sometimes provided with protective coats of iron mail. This fashion appears to have been most common during the Middle Ages but held its ground until well into the eighteenth century, above all in Spain. It can scarcely have been comfortable for the hounds to run in the heavy coats, and it was probably only the most highly-prized animals that wore them.

In mediaeval times, when the stag hunting season finished at the end of October, it was generally followed by boar hunting. Consequently, the latter sport came to symbolise the months of November and December. In the magnificent tapestry series *"Belles Chasses de l'Empereur Maximilien"*, woven about 1530, the two most beautiful compositions are, in fact, devoted to wild boar hunting in November and December. In the latter composition the Emperor engages the boar, brought to bay by the hounds, with a short wild boar sword. He is wearing a short red jacket with gold galloons and a white fur collar, with a red toque on his head.

The wild boar sword, which the Emperor is carrying in the December tapestry, is not without interest as far as the history of hunting goes. (See illustration on page 141). It was introduced by the enthusiastic hunter, Maximilian I, primarily as a weapon against wild boar, designed for hunters on horseback, but for some reason or other it never

Spear and forks intended for wild boar hunting. (From left) Spear from eighteenth century (Kranichstein, Darmstadt), "Saufänger", sixteenth century (The Electoral Armoury, Munich). Halberd c. 1580, (after Duchartre), "Saufänger", sixteenth century (Bavarian Museum, Munich.)

Boarhounds wearing protective coats of padding and mail. (Spain and Germany.)

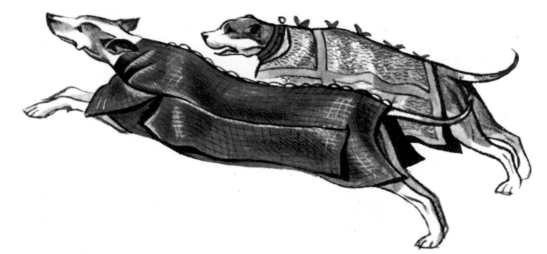

Wild boar tusks were used as ornaments already by the Stone Age peoples. In olden times they were also believed to be capable of curing a stitch or a sore throat. They have been popular trophies since time immemorial. This is how they should be mounted, according to a modern hunting handbook.

Hound attacking wild boar while the huntsman waits for an opportunity to use his spear and sword (limestone frieze in the choir of Basel Cathedral. Twelfth century).

managed to oust the older types of weapons. Already, a few decades after the Emperor's death in 1519, people had as a rule gone back to spears and forks of various kinds.

By that time, too, the construction of a spear-cum-fire-arm had begun: the broad blade of the spear was fitted with one or two short barrels as well as a wheel lock. As is apparent, the demand for valour at a wild boar hunt had diminished considerably since the days of Heracles and Meleager.

Other leading methods of hunting wild boar included the use of beaters combined with the net technique, mentioned by the *Roi Modus* under the heading of "the royal manner of boar hunting", and shooting from platforms erected close to the water holes frequented by these animals. Wild boar were also trapped by the use of pits, but in the *Roi Modus* this was considered a pastime for the poor.

This brings us to the question of the legal ways in which the poor might obtain a joint of wild boar for food. Opportunities for this were probably almost non-existent even as early as the fourteenth century, when the *Roi Modus* discoursed on hunting sense in his famous book.

Already, at the beginning of the Middle Ages, kings and princes had begun zealously to guard their unlimited right to hunting noble game. There are numerous contemporary laws containing drastic examples of the punishment meted out to those who usurped this privilege. It was not only poaching that the authorities clamped down on but often also the clumsy attempts on the part of the unfortunate peasants to persuade the wild boar not to invade

their fields and vineyards. The attitude of sovereigns in this matter was characterised by the most distressing egoism and indifference to the fate of their subjects.

In the sixteenth century, John III of Sweden transformed the entire island of Öland in the Baltic into one large hunting reserve, where the wild boar were allowed to roam at will, and the punishment for anyone who was impudent enough to kill noble game was death. Since dogs might frighten the quarry away, the peasants were allowed to keep dogs only if they maimed one leg of each animal. Conditions were similar on the continent and, as a result of this ludicrous "game protection", and in combination with a drop in the numbers of the large beasts of prey, the wild boar increased enormously. During the sixteenth century they began to appear in numbers which today are beyond our powers of imagination.

The lengths to which the European princes were prepared to go to satisfy their craving for hunting wild boar may well be called one of the darkest chapters in the history of hunting. In many areas the peasants were forbidden to fence their fields and, if they were allowed to do so in some generous cases, it was on the explicit condition that the pales were not made so high or pointed that the animals might injure themselves when they jumped over. With the increase in population and cultivated land, the damage done by game finally became almost disastrous for the farming community: this once caused Martin Luther to preach a fiery sermon about the hunting-mad princes who forbade

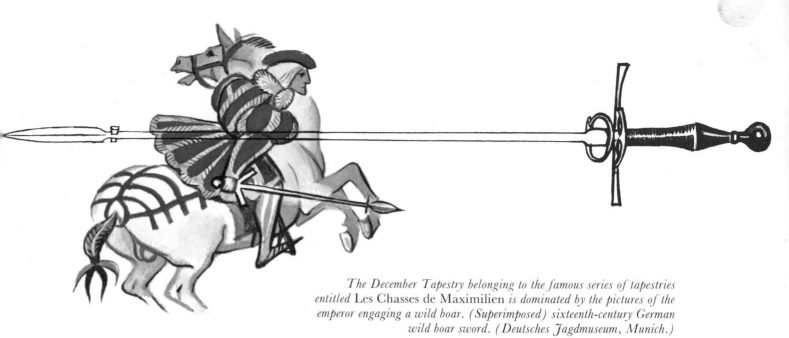

The December Tapestry belonging to the famous series of tapestries entitled Les Chasses de Maximilien *is dominated by the pictures of the emperor engaging a wild boar. (Superimposed) sixteenth-century German wild boar sword. (Deutsches Jagdmuseum, Munich.)*

the peasants to protect their property against destructive animals, without a thought of providing compensation for the losses.

Complaints and appeals for compassion were now to be heard from all quarters. Pathetic petitions were drawn up and submitted with a multitude of excuses amid the threatening growls of monarchs and landowners.

"Although people have with toil and trouble and fences enclosed and protected the vineyards both day and night, this has not helped at all," writes the Burgomaster of Stuttgart to the ruling duke in 1543. He describes how wild boar had begun to appear even within the town walls in broad daylight, and in numbers "which no man can believe possible". They were so impudent and tame that they feared neither shouts nor scarecrows and it was hardly possible even to drive them from one vineyard to the next. When the fields were empty in the autumn, the peasants were afraid that the wild boar would come to disturb the seed so that everything would have to be re-sown, as had happened in previous years. "Although we should much prefer to continue to show patience in this matter, we were unable to abstain from bringing these justified complaints to the attention of Your Highness." So ends the burgomaster's letter.

At first, these appeals were dismissed with a wave of the hand. Nevertheless, the princes did what they could themselves to cut down the numbers of wild boar, even if this was scarcely done out of concern for the people's wishes, but rather to satisfy a passion for hunting which in time became more and more depraved.

In some cases it became a sort of pathological bloodthirst: it was no longer a question of hunting but of slaughter. In 1737, King Augustus II by his own hand killed more than 400 wild boar in the course of a single hunt in Saxony, a region rich beyond measure in wild game. Still worse figures are given in Johannes Tänzer's work *Der Dianen hohe und niederz Jagdgeheimnüss* (Koppenhagen, 1632) in which are published the lists of the kill made by two distinguished hunters. We are told there that the Elector John George I of Saxony, in the course of forty-four years of enthusiastic hunting, killed 31,902 wild boars (116,906 mammals of different kinds in all), and his activities were continued with impressive energy by his son, John George II, who in twenty-four years managed to slay 22,298 wild boars (in all, 111,141 animals). In other words, during the time that he was active as a hunter, John George II succeeded in killing 2·6 wild boars a day, in addition to a considerable number of other

(Below) During the sixteenth century, the wild boar spear was used mainly by the people on foot, while the sword was intended chiefly for the mounted huntsman.

game. Seen as a purely physical achievement this commands respect and one certainly wonders how he had time to spare for other occupations.

These bloodbaths were the beginning of the degeneration of the hunting of noble game. They later increased in popularity, mainly under French influence, and were also enthusiastically adopted by royal courts all over Europe. It is really beyond the scope of this book to give an account of the barbarous spectacles which are usually classed under the heading of "grand hunts" or "hunting entertainments". However, as an illustration of the decadence of hunting, it may perhaps be of interest to give some indication of the miserable state of affairs.

In order to vary the monotonous slaughter of the enormous quantities of game which accumulated in central Europe as a result of feudal legislation, various entertainments in conjunction with the hunts began to make their appearance. Love of the theatrical and the artificial was characteristic of the times, and left its mark on these spectacles too, which were often staged in conjunction with weddings, christenings and on other solemn occasions. Large numbers of game were collected together in enclosed preserved or palace grounds, after which they were set upon with every available weapon. In order to give a more festive air to the proceedings, rockets and fireworks were tied to the

wretched animals, and rockets or burning arrows were fired at them; other forms of cruelty are best not mentioned. At a wild boar hunt arranged at a court in the Palatine Electorate, an enormous flight of steps was built, leading up to an artificial hill. Huge herds of wild boar were driven there, to be mown down by hunters who were posted in galleries along the steps. The dreadful cries of the boars were drowned by an orchestra which played throughout the firing. Close on 1,000 boars were killed on this occasion. (See Notes.)

Nevertheless, these magnificent shoots did little to limit the damage done by the hordes of wild boar. Gradually, one prince after another was obliged, willy-nilly, to give in to the demands of his people, and outlaw the boar. It was not until the end of the eighteenth century that the boar began to be regarded as vermin to be killed as soon as it left the sanctuary of the game preserves.

In prehistoric times the range of the wild boar extended as far north as central Sweden and southern Norway. In the Scandinavian peninsula, however, it occurred mainly in the southernmost parts, where fossil remains have been found here and there. The wild boars which Eric XIV hunted in his game preserve on the island of Öland in the Baltic are believed, on fairly safe grounds, to have been the remnants of the original wild stock. At the end of the seventeenth century, however, the last

animals seem to have disappeared, since that very enthusiastic hunter, Frederick I, introduced a number of wild boars from Germany in 1723. They appear to have acclimatised themselves well since, a mere twenty years later, they were reported to have caused an incredible amount of damage to fields and meadows. In 1752 the long-suffering peasants managed to obtain permission from parliament to exterminate the animals; twenty years were to pass, however, before the wild boars on Öland had disappeared for good. It was not only because they ran riot in the cornfields that the islanders wanted to get rid of the boars. As Linnæus points out in his *Journey in Oland and Gotland* (1741), it was also because they mated "with the farmyard pigs and breeding gets more or less out of hand".

It must be mentioned that the primitive domestic species of pig, which originally came from the wild boar, was so shaggy and dark in colour that in the heat of the moment it was not always very easy to distinguish between wild and tame animals.

In Denmark the peasants complained that, in the autumn, the wild boars ate up the beechmast intended for the farmyard pigs and that they had to drive their pigs back to the sties when the autumn hunting started, since such a large number of them were killed by mistake by the eager wild boar hunters.

In Jutland, for a long time the last Danish stronghold of the boars after they had been wiped out in the islands in the sixteenth century, there was a stubborn struggle between the Court and the peasants as to whether the animals were to be allowed to live or not. It was not until the early nineteenth century that the last native Danish boars were shot at Silkeborg and Meilgaard. The boars which appeared in southern Jutland at a later date had crossed the frontier from northern Germany.

Since time immemorial, the interest shown by hunters in hunting wild boars has been fostered by the ferocity of the animal, as well as by the fact that many ways of hunting have been possible at nearly any time of the year. A very extensive vocabulary of terms relating to such hunting has arisen in every language on the continent and, on the whole, the majority of methods employed have survived to the present day; stalking, hunting by moonlight, the use of shooting platforms, keeping vigil by water-

The use of a platform or tower close to some suitable water-hole is just as popular a method of boar hunting to-day as it was in the Middle Ages. The Roi Modus recommends a platform two feet high (nowadays they are considerably higher) since then the wild boar is unable to catch the hunter's scent. "Keep your eyes open and take a look right round. Then you will have a pleasant time, for animals of all kinds are fond of going to an oft-frequented water-hole of this kind and the wild boar delights in rolling about in the mud."

holes, small- and large-scale drives, are all practised in more or less the same way that the *Roi Modus* once recommended. Even the wild boar spear, swathed in leather straps, is still manufactured, although it is no longer used for heroic single combat but mainly for dealing with animals with gunshot wounds.

It is perhaps regarding the role of the dogs that the greatest changes have taken place. Gone are the days when the howling pack of huge wild boar hounds hurled themselves at the boar and held it until the hunter reached the spot. The barking of these dogs caused the Nimrods of old to sigh with happiness.

Experts consider that a dog that is noisy and not too fast, a dachshund or similar dog, for example, is the most suitable for wild boar hunts at the present time.

THE CHAMOIS AND THE IBEX

When the bitter climate of the ice age had its effect on the fauna of the continent, chamois and ibex were widely distributed and frequented the same habitat as the woolly rhinoceros, musk ox, mammoth, lemming and other Arctic animals. When the ice-cap receded, the chamois and ibex retreated up into the mountains, since the warm climate in the lowlands did not suit them. In time, they adapted themselves remarkably well to their Alpine environment.

Many prehistoric rock paintings and engravings, particularly in caves and on rocks in southern France and Spain, bear witness to these animals having been a favourite quarry of the Ice Age hunters. If one may venture to draw some conclusions from this art as to the hunting methods employed, it seems that spears and, in the case of southern Spain, bows and arrows were the most usual weapons. A remarkably vivid painting at Cueva de la Arana shows a whole herd of ibex being attacked by a dozen archers.

There are considerably fewer records of chamois and ibex hunting after these animals began to withdraw to the Alpine regions, and remains of their bones have been found remarkably seldom in the villages of the Swiss lake-dwellers. The fact that these bones occur there at all is taken to indicate that the hunters went on expeditions up into the mountains during the Neolithic Ages.

The chamois and the ibex were well-known to the writers of antiquity, and Pliny, who recommends a mixture of chamois suet and milk as an excellent remedy for dizziness, was amazed at the unbelievable swiftness of the ibex, which does not seem to be impeded by its huge recurved horns. According to Pliny, the latter were used as a kind of lever, thanks to which the ibex was able to negotiate rocky crags or chasms with ease.

Mention is made of chamois hunting in manuscripts from the twelfth and thirteenth centuries, but its acceptance in earnest as a game animal was due to the Emperor Maximilian I, who, it is true, was very active as a soldier and politician, but whose greatest passion, by far, was hunting in all its forms. We saw on an earlier page how he introduced new weapons for wild boar hunting and how he showed great interest in this sport, but dearest to his heart was the hunting of Alpine game. This required boldness, strength and unusual patience, all of them qualities which were high in the estimation of "the last knight". To judge from contemporary writers, Maximilian must have been very close to the ideal of a mediaeval hunter. The demands he made on the capabilities of his hunting companions are also mentioned in some awe — in fact, no fewer than two of his three wives died hunting, which goes to show that he did not even spare his dearest ones.

Like a modern athlete, he was constantly in training and we are told that, to limber up for a coming Alpine hunt, he climbed the tower of Ulm cathedral and stood on one leg on a frieze near the top.

He hunted chamois in various ways. Usually he went out stalking on his own with a cross-bow which, according to eyewitnesses, he was able to use with astounding accuracy; he himself stated that on

several occasions he had shot wild duck in flight with a crossbow, which is an indication of his marksmanship. Nevertheless, in addition to hunting by himself, he organised large-scale hunts with beaters, to which he invited visiting princes.

The procedure at these chamois hunts was that the animal tracks in a chamois territory were blocked with nets or other obstacles, after which hounds and beaters drove the quarry down from the snow-fields towards the valley. When the chamois found their tracks blocked, they were obliged to find new and unknown paths across the crevices. The master of the hunt used his knowledge of the locality and his experience to lead the quarry to rocky pinnacles or ledges where, in the end, all ways of retreat were cut off. The hunters were armed with one or two special chamois spears which, in some cases, might be more than eighteen feet long and which were used simply to push the cornered chamois over the precipice. It was out of the question to throw the spears since they would then be lost in ravines and crevices.

A good chamois spear was treated as a precious possession and, in the intervals between hunts, was wrapped in linen cloths and stored in a box to avoid damage by damp or sunlight. Curiously enough, there are no perfect specimens of chamois spears in museums. Moreover, there are only a few pictorial records in existence of this cruel and strange form of hunting which apparently lost its popularity as soon as fire-arms became available. But in Caspar Rordorf's *Der Schweizer Jäger*, published in 1835, we find that hunting with the chamois spear still occurred in several places

"You must wear grey and green clothes; partly grey, partly green. Those are the best colours for stags and chamois." (From Maximilian I's Haimlich Gejaidt Puech.*)*

The equipment of the chamois hunter must be light and handy. The man kneeling and fastening steel spikes to his shoes is armed with a matchlock (After Jost Amman, 1580) while the eighteenth-century huntsman is carrying the short and heavy musket, used by hunters in the Alps, which was first manufactured about 1700 in Bavaria and which could kill a chamois or a bear at a distance of up to 200 yards. The gun shown above is an Austrian wheel lock musket from the first half of the seventeenth century. (After Held.)

mentioned by name, which since time immemorial had been famous as suitable *Gemsenklemmen*.

The protection of game organised by Maximilian in his domains was exemplary, and an impressive number of gamekeepers made sure that poaching was kept within reasonable limits in the enormous hunting preserves, which were difficult to guard. In addition, the hunt attendants included a large number of specialists such as marmot masters, trackers, otter spearers, masters of hounds, chamois hunters, chamois hunt servants, and so forth. All these people constituted a small army of attendants which must have cost the hunting-mad emperor a pretty penny every year.

In winters when there was a lot of snow, he fed wild animals with hay and, by putting out rock salt for the chamois, he managed to make them remain in their territories. Letters that have been preserved show that he never allowed affairs of state to prevent him seeing to the protection of game, or chastising gamekeepers who had been guilty of negligence in this matter. Naturally enough, the results were excellent and the mountains were full of game.

Following Maximilian's death in 1519, a rumour spread among his people that on his deathbed the Emperor had made over to the peasants in the mountain districts the right to hunt chamois, ibex, red deer and other large game. These tidings naturally led to ruthless and uninhibited hunting, and soon all the fruits of Maximilian's successful efforts to protect game were completely destroyed.

Contemporary chroniclers relate that it was not only the menfolk who hunted but also old people and children who could hardly stand. Even peasant women went off hunting as soon as they had a moment to spare. "No laws were of any avail against that kind of hunting craze," as one writer sadly sums up the situation.

The chamois was valued not only for its meat. According to popular belief, many parts of its body also had magic or medicinal properties which might make the strenuous business of hunting worth the effort.

In the eyes of the superstitious mountain people the chamois was a demon. The devil himself had created the chamois, attaching his goat's beard to its chin, and it was only with the devil's kind assistance that a person could become a successful chamois hunter. The legend still survives in Austria about the devil who took refuge in a huge male chamois with silver horns.

The milk and blood of the chamois cured dizziness, its hair and hooves gave strength, smoke from its burnt horns helped against epilepsy, and if one tied its severed tongue to one's waist, it was possible to see equally well by day and by night.

More important than anything else in the chamois were, however, the so-called chamois stones, bezoars, which were sometimes found in the stomach of chamois and ibex and which were regarded as a remedy for all conceivable complaints. They were a protection against aches and pains, they increased the virility of the old and the decrepit, eased childbirth and many other things. If a small amount of a bezoar were scraped off and placed in a musket charge, the shot never missed the target.

Shortly after Maximilian's death, the shots from the first fire-arms started to echo in the Alpine valleys, and the chamois, previously so difficult to hunt, at once became a considerably easier quarry. Rordorf, who was mentioned on a previous page, is the source of one of the most detailed descriptions of chamois hunting in earlier days. According to him, only the simplest equipment imaginable was required: a little food, a rope, a game bag, an alpenstock and, preferably, two guns. According to his own account, he introduced chamois hunting with tracker dogs. In the beginning, he had to put up with a lot of insults from the mountain people as a result. In the long run, however, drives using dogs proved unsuitable, since the timid chamois fled from their mountains for good when the ravines began to echo to the sound of barking dogs.

Nowadays, drives with dogs are forbidden in many places. A "quiet" drive is the best, using great stealth to shepherd, as it were, the chamois in the right direction.

Nevertheless, as in Maximilian's day, stalking is still the correct method of hunting chamois. Here, the hunter's experience as an alpinist, marksman, and expert on game continues to be decisive for the outcome of the hunt and those who go in for it find it difficult to imagine that any other form of hunting can offer such sublime æsthetic pleasures.

Stalking may be said to include the use of decoy-calls during the rut when the hunter uses a mussel to make the bleating noises which are music to the ears of the male animal. Hunting is also done with the aid of a "chamois hood": the hunter conceals himself under a dark cloak on which are fastened a pair of chamois horns. In Berger's view, the second method is dangerous in areas where there are several hunters using such hoods. There have been cases of people shooting each other by mistake on such occasions. On a so-called "staff of office" from the Stone Age, which was found in Dordogne, there are human figures clothed in chamois hoods, but it is uncertain whether they represent ritual dancers or camouflaged hunters.

Despite illegal hunting and persecution, the chamois has never been so badly affected as the ibex, a species which has miraculously managed to survive until the present day in the Swiss and Italian Alps. The fact that this animal has not been exterminated is entirely due to feudalism, though that may be a dirty word in these democratic days. Whichever way one looks at it, the truth of the matter is that, in spite of everything, the European nobility, with their strict hunting privileges, have in fact only one kind of big game on their conscience — the wild ox — while the other four continents can produce a lamentable list of extinct species.

Was it perhaps Maximilian's severe protective laws which saved the pitiable remnants of the ibex still to be found in the Alps during the Middle Ages? Even a century before his time, however, the ibex was fairly rare in Switzerland and the Tyrol, and it became extinct in several cantons as early as the sixteenth century, despite the most rigorous laws against hunting. The ibex was still fairly widespread in antiquity and occurred frequently and in large numbers in the Roman arenas, which usually provide a reasonable indication of the amount of large game in central Europe.

Evidence that the ibex was becoming rare at the beginning of the seventeenth century is provided by the severe corporal punishment imposed for poaching, and by the fact that the Archbishop of Salzburg had these rare animals protected at the request of the princes who owned hunting preserves. But not even the support of the Church was sufficient to save the ibex in the Austrian and Swiss Alps. The last of the original stock of ibex were wiped out during the nineteenth century. The encouragingly large number of ibex which are to be seen leaping about in the Swiss and Austrian Alps

Camouflage has been used for chamois hunting but it is considered to be a dangerous method. There was a case of a man shooting his father by mistake; the latter, wearing a chamois hood, was moving about stealthily. It cannot be said with certainty whether the chamois masks drawn on the wall of a cave in Dordogne were used for ritual dances or as camouflage for hunting. (After Breuil.)

today are the result of a successful reintroduction in recent years.

The true Alpine ibex managed to survive in Piedmont, where it was saved by the commendable efforts of Victor Emmanuel III. It is thanks to this monarch, popular on account of his sympathy with the Italian liberation movement, and not least on account of many notorious gallant adventures — to use the language of the reference books — that we still have in the Alps a stock of the original wild ibex. The Spanish ibex, which is a subspecies, has had better luck and occurs in several places in the mountain regions of Spain.

It is no exaggeration to maintain that the deplorable fate of the Alpine ibex was due entirely to man's ignorance and susceptibility to superstitious beliefs.

The ibex had the misfortune to be regarded as a walking pharmacy, a black magic laboratory. Every part of its body contained valuable medicinal properties, according to popular belief, and there were certain organs which were worth their weight in gold. The so-called "heart crosses" were in particular demand. They were leaflike ossifications in the partition walls of the ventricles and in some rare cases might be shaped like a cross. They were framed in gold and used as amulets to counteract every conceivable thing.

It was therefore not surprising that the ibex became such a popular quarry in the Alps that neither laws nor decrees were able to stop its slaughter. At the end of the seventeenth century and beginning of the eighteenth century the struggle between the peasant hunters and the feudal gamekeepers became so fierce that the Prince-Bishop John Ernest of Salzburg felt obliged to have the ibex exterminated in order to bring the bloody and, above all, costly disputes to an end! Ibex which, at that time, were in royal game preserves, were thoughtlessly crossed with domestic goats and in that way spoilt from the genetic point of view. Those that have now been reintroduced into the Swiss Alps all originate, however, from the genuine stock which was preserved in Piedmont.

In comparison with ibex-hunting, chamois hunting is considered by experienced Alpine hunters to be sheer child's play. The ibex hunter must reckon with having to stay out in the mountains several days on end, in difficult cases, before he manages to kill his quarry. Naturally, if he is lucky, it might not take so long. In fact, one of the ibex's characteristics is its extreme curiosity. This is especially true of the old males, which sometimes wander about on their own. They are fond of jumping on to a rock, from which to survey their pursuer with innocent frankness and with great

During the Ice Age, the ibex, in common with the chamois, was widely distributed in Europe. Numerous cave paintings in southern France and in Spain show that the hunters of those times hunted the ibex mainly with the throwing-spear and the bow. This ibex from a cave at Niaux shows clearly that it is the ancestor of the Spanish subspecies. (After Breuil.)

It is entirely thanks to the strict conservation of game which King Victor Emmanuel organised in Piedmont from 1863 onwards that the Alpine ibex was saved for posterity. Poaching was punishable by a maximum of five years' imprisonment, and some fifty gamekeepers enforced the laws. There are estimated to be about 4,000 ibex in Piedmont at the present time and it is from this race that ibex have been introduced to other parts of the Alps.

generosity, in view of the fine target they then present.

Several subspecies of the ibex occur in the Mediterranean countries and in some places they have been crossed with domestic goats which have returned to a wild state, and this in a most bewildering manner. It is therefore very difficult to draw a dividing line between the different groups based merely on the shape of the horns and the colour of the coat, indeed, from the genetic point of view the difference between the races is considered to be insignificant. The Spanish ibex differs from the Alpine ibex by, for instance, its smaller size and its curved lyre-shaped horns. It has been threatened with extinction for a long time — it disappeared from northern Portugal in the 1890s — but nowadays it is a permanent resident in various places in mountainous areas of Spain.

The ibex which occur in the Greek archipelago have been crossed with domesticated goats in a number of cases, but the famous bezoar goat, which today is to be found only in the White Mountains of western Crete, is believed to be completely genuine.

Information about the number of these animals still left in the White Mountains is very unreliable, but the figure is somewhere between fifty and 300. At present, the authorities are doing their utmost to save the remnants from poachers and from being crossed with domesticated animals. One reason for this is the wish to make the bezoar goat the national animal of the island. This symbol is a good choice, for the bezoar goat is a classical beast with deep roots in the mythology and ancient history of Crete. It was once worshipped as the goddess Artemis; it was the animal which adorned Cretan coins and was celebrated by Homer as the ruler of the highest mountain peaks; a magnificent animal, strong and, at the same time, agile, loved by human beings.

In classical times, the holy bezoar goat was protected by strict laws. Aristotle tells us that if the animal was wounded, it cured itself by eating a plant which grows only in Crete.

The southern European ibex has been almost as close to extinction as the bison once was, but it has recovered more rapidly and at present the future seems fairly bright for the ibex in Spain and in the Alps. This is a result of careful wild life preservation, combined with a better information service on these matters. Fortunately, bezoar stones and heart crosses have lost their value in Europe.

(Below) The ancient coin depicting the ibex is from Crete where there is still a small colony of genuine bezoar goats in the White Mountains in the western part of the island. (After Keller.)

THE MOUFLON

Mountain game also includes the wild sheep — the mouflon — a magnificent beast with curving horns. Owing to relentless persecution, it must be considered to be one of the rarest animals in the Mediterranean countries. It moves about nimbly among rocks and ravines with the agility of the ibex and the chamois. It is as sensitive as a seismograph to sounds and scents of a suspicious kind. There is something "dry" and granite-like about the mouflon's appearance; its colour is that of the sun-bleached and weather-beaten rocks and it blends extremely well with its environment.

Mouflon hunting was considered to be one of the most specialised kinds of hunting in mountainous country. This unbelievably shy animal required from its hunter both great experience and physical strength. Hunting the mouflon was scarcely a social occasion, such as stag hunting, suitable for a company of huntsmen bent on an easy day's sport.

It was impossible to encircle the mouflon and guide it in a particular direction, as was the practice when hunting ordinary noble game. The mouflon was even afraid of the praiseworthy attempts of gamekeepers to feed it in the winter.

One method of hunting this animal was for beaters to descend very cautiously through passes and gorges towards the waiting guns. Naturally, the most sporting technique was to steal up within range of the animal; the best day for this method was when there was a strong wind to cover up any accidental noise that the huntsman might make.

In areas with a resident population of mouflons, flocks of up to fifty of the animals, always led by an old, experienced ewe, sometimes occur.

In spite of the difficulties involved in capturing the mouflon, this beautiful wild sheep has been successfully introduced in mountainous regions of central Europe. Mouflons are to be found today in many areas of Germany and Czechoslovakia and their importance as game seems to be on the increase.

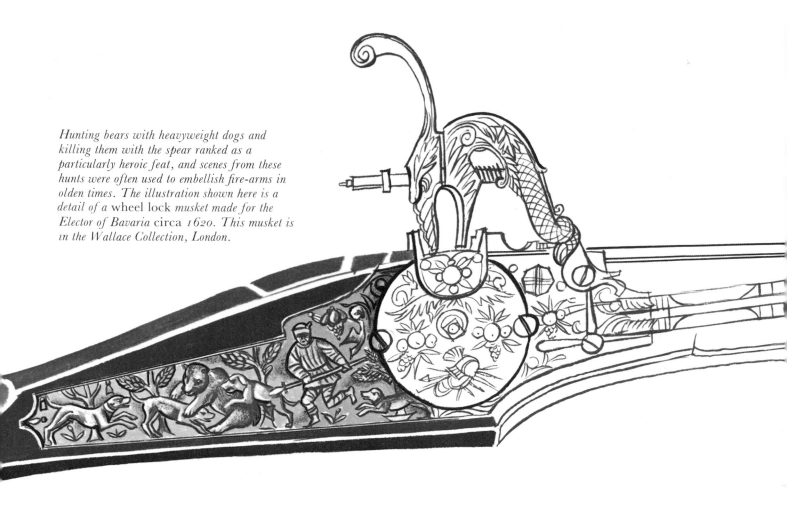

*Hunting bears with heavyweight dogs and
killing them with the spear ranked as a
particularly heroic feat, and scenes from these
hunts were often used to embellish fire-arms in
olden times. The illustration shown here is a
detail of a* wheel lock *musket made for the
Elector of Bavaria circa 1620. This musket is
in the Wallace Collection, London.*

THE BEAR

The bear was never the victim of the same un-
reasoning hatred as the wolf; at any rate, the hatred
was of a different nature. The wolf was considered
to be wily and ferocious, always hostile to man and
ready to ambush him and his livestock in a cowardly
manner. "This harmful, ungrateful, greedy and
untamable animal has always been hated by
human beings," to quote the eighteenth-century
French naturalist, Buffon. The bear, on the other
hand, has often been described as an enemy in the
same class as man; it has sometimes served as a
symbol of strength and wisdom. Furthermore, the
bear is also the animal which in physical structure
was considered more than any other to *resemble* a
human being. A skinned bear is almost uncannily
like a broad-limbed man.

The "human" and "divine" characteristics,
ascribed since time immemorial to the bear, have
given it a special position among beasts of prey. It
has even been worshipped in many places. The
belief that there was sexual intercourse between
male bears and women is widespread in various
cultures. This belief is indeed said to be one of the
many reasons for the bear festivals that were held
by, for example, the Lapps.

The emperors of the ancient world were keen on
owning bears for various purposes, both for inclusion
in the animal exhibitions at the Circus Maximus
and as domestic animals. We are told that
Valentian had two favourite tame bears, "Goldi-
locks" and "Innocence", which were fed on human
flesh. On one occasion, after "Innocence" had
devoured an unusually large number of persons, the
generous Emperor had her released into the woods,
by way of a reward for her feat. The office of
bear-keeper was for a long time a coveted and
respected post at the Imperial Roman court.

The pagan feast arranged by Julius Capitolinus,
at which 1,000 bears were said to have been on
display, before the majority of them were killed by
the delighted spectators, is surely an unbeatable
record as far as exhibitions go.

One may, of course, feel sceptical about this high
figure, but there are many indications that the
bear really was extremely common everywhere in
the European forests in the days of antiquity.
Xenophon tells us how the bear was either killed
with poisoned carcasses, or was captured in pits
with the aid of a tethered goat as bait. Oppian
gives a detailed description of bear-hunting with
feathered ropes — a predecessor of the canvas
cloth of later times — and nets. Shouting and

151

Presumably, bear coursing occurred mostly in enclosed game preserves during the Middle Ages. This typical South German gun stock bears the signature of the same team of master craftsmen as the weapon on the previous page. Daniel Sadeler made the lock and Hieronymus Borstorffer fashioned the stock. 1620s. (After Held.)

blowing horns, the beaters drove the bear towards the net. As soon as the bear touched the net, the attendants rushed forward and wound the net around the animal.

The killing of a bear was regarded as an incomparable test of virility and was celebrated according to a person's means and station. There is a story about a certain Emperor Hadrian, who was so proud of a successful bear hunt in Mysia that he built a town — Hadrianutheræ — on the spot where the bear had been slain!

In central Europe, the bear was generally considered to fall within the sphere of blue-blooded hunting, but at the same time, of course, it was an outlawed animal which all able-bodied men were obliged to kill as soon as an opportunity presented itself.

During the Middle Ages, when the abundance of bears was a problem in large areas of Europe, strict laws were enforced to keep the bear in check. When the summons to a bear-hunt was issued, every household that was able to do so had to send a brave and full-grown man with a stout spear in his fist. Anyone who was content to send a callow youth had to pay a fine. Any person who came across a bear during the hunt and was too cowardly to attack the beast, or help his comrades already engaged in combat with it, was not only fined but

also incurred the displeasure of his master. In some areas, the villages were also required to maintain packs of bear-hounds.

The bear was a valuable prize, and even if rulers encouraged people to hunt it freely, they nevertheless passed laws to ensure that they obtained the most valuable parts of the animal. If, for example, a poor man killed a bear that had torn his cattle to pieces, the paws, head, skin, and the much-coveted fat, went to the ruling prince. On the other hand, bear-hunting privileges for the aristocracy were rare. As far as I have been able to ascertain, only the illustrious von Reidel family of Hesse enjoyed what were termed "rights extraordinary for bear-hunting" in the principality. Unfortunately, I have no information as to the age of these rights, but we may assume that they originated in the seventeenth century, when the bear had begun to become so uncommon in central Europe that it was no longer a major problem for the rural population.

We now come to the question of the bear's distribution. In spite of an exceedingly intense persecution, it is still surprisingly widespread in our part of the world. Needless to say, the bear disappeared a long time ago from farming country — in Germany, the last bear of the original population is believed to have been killed at Ruhpolding in 1835 — but in sparsely-populated mountain areas

Stradanus's bear-hunters of the 1570s relied on the spear as a matter of course, as did the owner of the halberd (inset), which was used at the bear-drive on August 17th, 1842, in Dalarna. (The Nordic Museum. Stockholm.)

The bear's present range in Europe, according to Haglund, Couturier and van den Brink.

it has succeeded in maintaining a stubborn foothold. According to Haglund (1964), bears are thriving locally in Spain, France, Italy, Yugoslavia, Albania, Greece, Rumania, Bulgaria, Hungary, Czechoslovakia, Poland, the Soviet Union, Finland, Sweden and Norway. To anyone regarding the bear as a typical animal of the wilds it might seem rather strange that there are wild bears padding about a dozen miles or so from the fashionable beaches of Biarritz, or some fifty miles from the Via Veneto in Rome.

Nowhere, however, is the bear really common except in certain areas of the Balkans. In spite of its relatively wide range, it has for the most part become a rare animal in the uninhabited tracts of Europe. This is particularly apparent from a study of figures from eastern Siberia and Kamchatka, where bears have occurred up to the present day on a scale comparable perhaps to the state of affairs in Europe in prehistoric times. There are accounts of veritable herds of over a hundred bears being seen on one and the same occasion. One of the first travellers to visit these regions, Steller, describes how the local population picked wild berries unmolested by bears on the same errand.

The hunting techniques employed on the Continent when bears were abundant differed somewhat from those used in Arctic regions. If contemporary engravings are to be believed, coursing with hounds was very common, but one explanation may indeed be that coursing was a good subject to portray. For a long time meeting a bear with cold steel was considered to be the "most honourable" method. When the Swedish warrior-king, Charles XII,

organised his famous bear-hunts at Kungsör in central Sweden, in the early eighteenth century, none of the people taking part in the hunt was allowed to carry fire-arms. To tell the truth, coarse-meshed nets were usually put up between the spear-carrying hunters and the bear. Unfortunately, Charles XII gave a poor display of sportsmanship when he afterwards forced the captured bears to hobble along on two legs, from the place where they were caught to his camp in Kungsör.

It is obvious that this type of bear-hunting was extremely popular and quite a few princes established bear-reserves near their castles, so as to be able to arrange exciting bloodbaths on suitable occasions. To be on the safe side, the present author will not mention how many of the 477 bears killed by John George I of Saxony, and his equally hunting-mad son, over a seven-year period were really "wild" and not living in enclosures, but nevertheless, in view of their other kills, this figure is a surprisingly modest one. The hunting of the cooped-up bears involved the use of every conceivable cruelty, and the distinguished German writer of hunting handbooks, H. F. Fleming, very obligingly suggests (1724) a variety of ingenious methods of being beastly in an amusing way.

Although beyond the scope of this book, it may be added that the bear, more than any other animal, has been trained for games or used for various kinds of show. Bears were matched against other animals in the ancient manner in Paris as recently as the 1830s. Dancing bears are still to be seen today, stumbling about in Balkan villages, suffering from lack of food and the heat of the sun, to the great delight of the local population and tourists. So there

153

is no reason for us to pride ourselves on being any better than the people of past generations, who tied rockets to their captive bears to give an extra special touch to the killing after supper.

The aura of glory surrounding an "eye for an eye and a tooth for a tooth" encounter with a bear found expression in a variety of strange ways. A copper engraving by Stradanus, an illustrator of hunting scenes, shows hunters wearing armour, enabling them to tackle with ease bears coaxed out of their winter dens. I do not know whether this picture is based on fact. It was, perhaps, merely a form of wishful thinking in harmony with the age of chivalry. Other kinds of close combat between hunter and bear exist here and there in Europe. Berger assures us that in the Pyrenees the *oseros*, members of the corps of bear-hunters, were armed with a double-edged, pronged knife in their left hand and a heavy hunting-dagger in their right when they were dressed up for bear-hunting. The left hand was swathed in thick rags, as a protection against the bear's bite when the hunter was wrestling with the bear. The wrestling is the real *raison d'être* of the hunt. To describe this, as Berger does, as the "finest" form of hunting bears is certainly an understatement.

Another method, equally or more heroic, was employed in Sweden, as a matter of fact, as recently as the 1830s. It is noted in the first periodical of the Swedish Sportsmen's Association as a new means of defence for bear-hunters in Jämtland. The hunter's arm was covered with stout metal plates studded with thick spikes, and he then thrust his arm into the mouth of the bear when it advanced on him. When the bear sank its teeth into the metal plating, the hunter pulled his arm away, and had time to

kill the bear in the momentary confusion that was reckoned to occur as a result. There is also a similar description from the province of Härjedalen, but this unusually fierce kind of hunting does not appear to have been particularly popular.

In southern Europe, autumn was frequently the season for drives, when the bears made their way down to the oak-woods to feast on the acorns. In addition to this, the animals were also stalked, or shot from platforms which had carrion placed near them.

One of the most original methods of capturing bears was the use of the so-called bear cudgel, in the Baltic countries and in Russia. It was a cross between a means of protection and a trapping device, and was used to protect the wild-honey harvest on cultivated land against raids by bears. A picture of the ingenious bear cudgel in action is presented as a typical feature of Lithuania in Olaus Magnus's *Carta Marina*. Harvesting wild honey is an ancient and very important industry in a number of eastern European countries. It is understandable that the beekeepers had trouble in keeping the sweet-toothed bears away from the honey-trees.

The bear cudgel was nothing more than a heavy wooden log, which was fastened to a rope so that it hung right in front of the hole used by the bees. The idea was that the bear, irritated by this obstacle, would knock the club to one side. The weight of the latter, however, caused it to swing back at the bear. As the bear got more and more annoyed, the blows dealt by the cudgel increased in strength. With a bit of luck, the cudgel might in the end strike the bear a fatal blow and knock it down.

This clever device was often supplemented by the "bear cradle". The latter was a square platform

"Never retreat a single step from a bear with which you have come to grips." Hans Orre, bear-hunter, Lima, Dalarna.

Bear-spear with reindeer-horn sheath to trick an attacking bear. (The Nordic Museum, Stockholm.)

which hung by four ropes from one end of a crossbar, fastened to the honey-tree in such a way that the platform was level with the bees' entrance hole. It was fastened to the tree by an attachment that readily came undone. When the bear sat on the platform in order to steal the honey in greater comfort, the attachment came loose. Whereupon the pole, which had a counterpoise at the other end, swung out, with the bear on the platform attached to it, some distance away from the tree trunk. The only means of escape for the trapped animal was to jump down to the ground. To deter the bear from choosing this way out, a number of pointed stakes were driven into the ground under the tree.

The numerous illustrations of these ingenious trapping devices show that they were successful and much used in Lithuania and neighbouring areas of Russia. In other words, in the very area where Olaus Magnus believed that the bear cudgel was the most characteristic phenomenon.

"Everyone must hunt the bear because he is a symbol of superior power," to quote the words of the mediaeval Östgöta law. The Hälsinge law stipulates the following: *"Bears and wolves and gluttons are the property of the man who kills them. They are not to be allowed to go in peace anywhere."*

In Scandinavia, as in other parts of Europe, bear-hunting was an ancient social duty laid down by law, but it was not until the first hunting statute of 1647 that regulations came into force regarding the payment of bounty-money to those who killed animals of prey. "For every adult bear, four dalers: for every bear cub, one daler." Gradually the bounty-money proved to be of great significance in the final banishment of the bear from southern and central Sweden in about the middle of the nineteenth century. The fifty crowns which constituted the sum paid in the 1860s — during the period of bad harvests — was a real fortune to the poor peasants, and the intensified hunting brought about such a great decline in the number of bears that, already in 1893, the Swedish parliament withdrew bounty-money in an effort to save the bear from total extinction.

Although the war against the bear in Sweden was just as thorough as that waged against the wolf, it was not, however, aimed at the total extermination of the species. Not even the most fanatic hater of predatory animals has wanted, in his heart of hearts, to see the bear removed for ever from the list of Sweden's fauna; it is much too valuable for that. Besides, even the most intractable have had to admit that the majority of bears are harmless plant- and berry-eaters, who prefer to stain themselves with bilberry juice rather than with blood.

In his detailed study of the brown bear's habits, Bertil Haglund shows how much this animal lives on vegetable matter and red ants, even in areas where reindeer and elk are available. As a matter of fact, he even quotes cases of bears plodding straight through herds of reindeer, which had panicked and scattered, without reacting and attacking the reindeer. As regards the meat diet, it has indeed been noted that bears show greater aggressiveness towards elk than towards reindeer. Generally speaking, however, it may be said that the bear is popularly believed to be more ferocious and bloodthirsty than it is in reality. This reputation is to a large extent the work of the press and other news media. You cannot sell newspapers with headlines about small, berry-eating bears: they must be big, ferocious and dangerous.

It is not clear, of course, whether Frederick I was prompted by a desire for nature conservancy or anxiety about the well-being of an excellent game animal, when he exhorted his head gamekeeper, Anders Schönberg, "to moderate his hunting so that the race did not die out". But when the leading nineteenth-century bear-hunter, the legendary royal gamekeeper Hermann Falk, wrote a hundred years later: "Whatever may be said about the damage done by the bear and its insatiable appetite, I do not want to see it exterminated, however, nor do I wish it to disappear completely from the Swedish

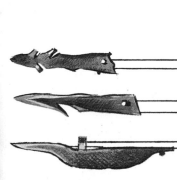
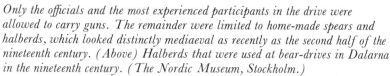

Only the officials and the most experienced participants in the drive were allowed to carry guns. The remainder were limited to home-made spears and halberds, which looked distinctly mediaeval as recently as the second half of the nineteenth century. (Above) Halberds that were used at bear-drives in Dalarna in the nineteenth century. (The Nordic Museum, Stockholm.)

hunting scene", we realise that he regarded the bear as a precious part of Sweden's countryside.

The common people hunted the bear chiefly when it was asleep in its den, since this method was regarded as the most efficient, and yet the least hazardous. By following the bear's tracks in fresh snow in the late winter, the experienced hunter could work out roughly where the bear was hibernating — the position of the bear was pinpointed. As a rule, care was taken not to disturb the bear while its position was being pinpointed. Instead, the hunters waited for a heavy fall of snow before starting to drive it out. Sometimes, however, they would block the exit to the den in order to be sure that the bear did not slip away. The main advantage of a thick layer of snow on the ground was that the bear's mobility was reduced; quite a point in view of the primitive hunting weapons of former times. There was also another reason for waiting. Bearing in mind that bounty-money of one daler was paid for a bear-cub, it was indeed worth while delaying matters; there might be a female bear in the den!

Driving a bear from its den was by no means without its hazards, even if scarred bear-hunters took the necessary precautions. Many unknown factors were involved in the operation; a spear might break, a foot slip, or a gun misfire. As a rule, several men were organised into a team to help one another during the hunt. Two men drove a couple of poles crosswise into the ground in front of the opening, while others used various methods of getting the bear to wake up and look out. Sometimes everything happened so surprisingly quickly that the poles were thrust aside and the bear,

"Waterlocked" bear-drives were held in the summer. An isthmus between two lakes was beaten while the shores were often watched by hunters in boats. The chain of beaters kept in line and halted once or twice to straighten out. Every tenth man acted as a marker. The leader remained either in the centre of the chain of beaters or in the middle of the line of guns.

uttering a roar, hurled itself at the man who happened to be nearest. Sometimes, on the other hand, the bear might stubbornly refuse to show itself, so that in the end everyone began to think that the den was deserted. There are fantastic stories — fully authenticated, however — of hunters who, in their desire to find out what was happening, crawled into the narrow den, carrying a torch or a spear. If they were lucky, they were able to make short work of the bear in the hole inside.

Our knowledge of bear-hunting in Sweden during the first half of the nineteenth century, a period when predatory animals were abundant, has been greatly enriched by a Welshman, Llewellyn Lloyd, who settled in the province of Värmland in western Sweden in the 1820s. He spent the rest of his life there, indulging in the pleasures of the hunt, particularly bear-hunting. He wrote several large works on hunting in Scandinavia, which are of inestimable value from a historical point of view. Lloyd was a wealthy man and his appetite for adventures with bears insatiable. This state of affairs soon became known to the common people all over the country. As soon as a bear-den had been located, a message was sent to Lloyd. The latter set off immediately and shot the "monster". As a rule, no real adventures occurred when a bear was bearded in its den. On those occasions — to quote a latter-day bear-hunter in Norrland — "dealing with the bear was as easy as killing a pig".

The most serious accidents during the clearing of a den naturally occurred when for some reason or other the bear refused to flee, and instead preferred to put up a fight. As a rule, it attacks on all fours and does not stand up on its hind legs until the time comes to leap at the hunter. That was the moment when the latter had to have his spear at the ready.

It was common knowledge that the bear's reflexes are extraordinarily quick at this particular moment, and that it can thrust the spear aside, as quick as lightning, with one sweep of its paw. Sven

157

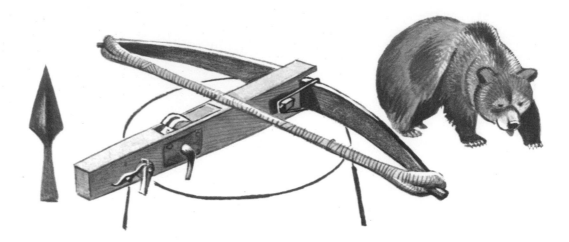

Ekman, who met many of the Norrland bear-hunters of former times, heard accounts of several different ways of parrying the bear's attack at the critical moment.

A feint attack was made to confuse the animal or, alternatively, the rear end of the spear was rested on the ground so that the weapon pointed obliquely at the bear. When the latter attacked, it impaled itself on the spear. This technique was also employed in other parts of Sweden. At Esplunda manor in Närke, the method is depicted in the work of a peasant artist.

Even greater cunning was used in northern Jämtland. There, the head of the spear was protected by a reindeer-horn sheath. The latter came off easily enough, but remained on the spear when the bear rushed out of its den. The bear was meant to get its teeth into the sheath, thinking that it was a human hand, and pull it off the spearhead. As a result, it would be bewildered for just that fraction of a second necessary for the spear to be thrust in at the right spot (See Notes).

In the early and mid-nineteenth century, when bears were numerous, there were some champion hunters who were able to boast of having killed thirty or perhaps even forty bears in their lifetime. These figures were considered to be impressive. There were exceptional cases of peasant hunters killing as many as fifty or more bears. Any figures higher than this, however, should be treated with a certain amount of reserve. Naturally enough, the kills bagged by the hunting gentry were bigger, but the latter bought surrounded dens or participated, as guns, in large-scale drives. By the age of sixty, Llewellyn Lloyd, mentioned above, had been present at the killing of 102 bears. He declared, with a modesty which is a little hard to accept, that in later years he could not be bothered to keep count of them. He was beaten by two by the great

bear-hunter Hermann Falk (See Notes), but the majority of these were in all probability shot during drives.

Be that as it may, real records were set up by the Finnish bear-hunters of the early and mid-nineteenth century. Mårten Kitunen, whose active hunting life occurred at the end of the eighteenth century, personally killed 193 large bears, "in addition to an even greater number of youngsters", and his somewhat younger colleague, a captain of engineers by the name of Berndt Höök, took second place with 134 kills.

When bears and wolves became excessively audacious at shepherd's huts and other remote dwellings, large beats were arranged on an organised basis in order to reduce their numbers. Many people were required for these beats if they were to be successful, and this fact explains why they occurred solely in the more densely populated areas of southern and central Sweden. Large-scale hunts were organised on Frederick I's behalf by his head gamekeeper, Anders Schönberg, usually in the form of beats in the summer. No effort was spared in the arranging of these enormous hunts. Already a year before the hunt was scheduled to take place, the vast hunting ground was marked out and lanes for the beaters cut through the woods. In addition, the local gamekeepers had orders to keep a watchful eye on the animals in the area, to see that they did not slip away.

Next, the gamekeeper humbly submitted his report to the king, and the hunt was duly scheduled for the coming summer.

Hermann Falk, who was active a century later, simplified Schönberg's beating system and made it more adaptable — not for nothing was he an experienced officer and an unusually talented organiser! Falk used two kinds of beats, the straightforward drive and the "closed circle" beat.

(Left) Steel crossbow for use as a missile-trap for bears. It was loaded with broad-bladed arrows and was set on a tree-stump. The line attached to the trigger was fastened to carrion. (The Nordic Museum, Stockholm.)
(Right) Method of setting a bear deadfall. (After Nils Keyland, The Nordic Museum, Stockholm.)
(Below) The heavy, bear jaw-trap was generally chained to a log, to prevent the bear from making off with it. (The Nordic Museum.)

In the first case, the chain of beaters moved towards the guns, while in the second type, the beaters linked up to form a complete circle round the area where the bears were believed to be. The summer drive was held for preference on an isthmus between two lakes, when the beat was described as being "waterlocked". Falk also arranged drives in the early spring, when the bear was about to leave its winter den. The bear was particularly shy then and the "closed circle" type of beat was the surest way of capturing it.

Falk summarised his knowledge of bear-hunting in a little pamphlet entitled *Information about the bear-beat as practised in Värmland* (1819), typically enough, in the form of an army order, with bluntly-worded sections dealing with the duties of the master of the hunt and the beaters during the drive. In the populous parishes in the neighbourhood of Lake Siljan in the province of Dalarna, famous beats were organised on a large scale on several occasions at the beginning of the nineteenth century. The bags varied between eighteen bears and one bear, despite close on two thousand persons taking part on each occasion. In the mid-1850s, the number of bears increased once again, and the parish councils then decided that the time had come at last to get rid of these predatory animals. This resulted in a mammoth hunt that was arranged around midsummer 1856, in which no fewer than 4,000 or so persons took part. It passed into hunting history under the name of "The Great Mora Bear Drive" and was the largest hunt ever held in Scandinavia — presumably also in Europe. The actual stationing of the miles-long chains of beaters lasted two whole days and nights. That is to say, they spent two nights in the woods and lit large bonfires to keep the bears inside the area being beaten. It was not until the evening of the third day that the whole beat encircled the clearing, which had been made near the shores of Lake Vansjön.

Curiously enough, there are only a few eyewitness accounts of this last and most spectacular version of the old Scandinavian peasant drives, and it is a great pity that it took place beyond the reach of film cameras. (See Notes.)

The result of the hunt was satisfactory. The kill was the largest recorded in Sweden at a single hunt — twenty-three bears, nine elks, two or three wolves and one lynx. There were good reasons for suspecting that several other bears had been wounded by shots or had died after breaking through the chain of beaters. It may be presumed that, in addition, one or two elks had been secretly killed in order to eke out the food supply in some impoverished village.

Apart from the den-hunts and the large-scale beats, a variety of trapping equipment was also used against the bear. This consisted mainly of sturdy jaw-traps. In some places, indeed, the latter were the only types of equipment used. There were innumerable ways of planting and setting a jaw-trap. It was hidden at bears' crossing-points, in ant-hills, in water springs or near some slaughtered cattle. The jaw-trap was attached to a heavy log, to prevent the bear from going very far after it had been caught. Incredible stories exist, however, about its strength on such occasions. There are accounts of how a bear climbed high up into a tree with the log hanging from its foot, or of how it

simply tore off its foot if the log happened to get caught between two trees.

According to a passage in the old Västgöta law, "if a man treads on a bear-spear and dies as a result, the owner of the bear-spear must pay a fine of three marks". From Jämtland also comes a description furnished by Nordholm (1749) of trapping with the aid of bear-spears of the same kind as the *älgled*,* but not as high as the latter. Hillerström (1750) gives a very detailed description of how the *björnled** was set in his native Västmanland village, where it appears to have been placed as a rule in the immediate neighbourhood of an animal which the bear had killed but had not had time to devour. The carcass was enclosed in a small pen with an entrance where the spear was put in position. It is doubtful whether this trapping method was really permitted in central Sweden. Be that as it may, the *älgled* had long been forbidden in the densely-populated parts of the country. In the thoroughly revised version of the old hunting statutes, which was presented in 1755 by a committee of experts headed by Anders Schönberg, a complete prohibition of spring-guns and the *björnled* was proposed.

Deadfalls have also been used for catching bears. On account of their bulkiness, however, they were considered impractical and were only used in rare cases. According to an old popular belief, Lapps in the neighbourhood of Gällivare, some time in the early eighteenth century, tricked some roving Russians into going under a huge bear deadfall and killed them in this fashion. This story provides an indication of the size of these traps. (See Notes.)

* Translator's note: See chapter on the elk.
* Translator's note: A method of killing bears. Compare "*älgled*" in the chapter on the elk.

Although at times matters may perhaps have seemed somewhat black for the future existence of the bear in those parts of Europe from which it had retreated after the intense persecution of the eighteenth and nineteenth centuries, there does not seem to be any immediate danger for the present; that is, if we are to believe the experts who have been carrying out a count of bears in different parts of the European continent. Aided by Couturier's figures, as well as by other sources, Bertil Haglund has estimated the number of bears in Europe (outside the large Russian bear territory) at somewhere in the region of 3,000 animals. The majority of this extremely scattered population is not in the northernmost part of Scandinavia, as many people might imagine, but in the Balkans, above all in the mountainous and wild country of Bulgaria, which is reputed to harbour 1,200 bears! The bear is tolerated in this area and has increased enormously in recent decades.

Although insignificant, an increase has nevertheless been observed in Sweden, as well as an extremely cautious incipient expansion in a north-westerly direction. Some people believe that in the future the bear may very well gradually begin to recapture the old areas from which it was once driven by enormous chains of beaters and through constant persecution. As a result of the abandonment of every other small farm in the interests of streamlining agriculture, the "wilds" will return to southern regions of Sweden, naturally in the form of trim pulp-woods where once there were billowing fields of corn, but also as sparsely populated country with undisturbed haunts for animals. The odd bear would certainly not have anything to complain about in the districts of Sweden abounding in elks and roe deer.

The first known picture of a great bustard, displaying, is to be found in a cave-painting in Andalusia, Spain, an area still abundant in bustards. (After Breuil.)

THE BUSTARD

There was a time when the bustard — the great bustard — was distributed fairly widely over Europe, but, like the majority of a number of other large birds, it is sensitive to changes in its environment and, of course, to persecution on the part of man. It was still found in the eighteenth century in suitable places in England, France, Holland and Sweden, and in western areas of Germany, but in the first half of the last century it disappeared as a nesting species from these countries. Nowadays, it is found regularly only in southern Spain, on the Pomeranian plains and in the neighbourhood of Berlin, as well as in suitable places in eastern Europe. Wherever it is found, it clings to what remains of sparsely-populated steppes and open plains with few trees and bushes.

The reasons for the rapid decline were many, but one of the most important were the changes in the bustard's biotope as a result of developments in farming techniques and an increase in the amount of cultivated land. The extensive heathlands have been transformed in many places into farmland, where ploughs and harrows have been at work. In addition, of course, hunting weapons improved and — at any rate, as far as England is concerned — the growing interest in natural history collections at the beginning of the nineteenth century resulted in high prices for the eggs of rare birds.

It is a strange fact that every century has surrounded the bustard with an aura of mystery. It is strange, too, to note the ease with which it became a legendary bird, almost a fabulous creature. One of the contributory causes of this was the uncertainty about the bird's appearance and behaviour which prevailed among the old zoologists. If one is to believe the various sources, it was both a nocturnal and a diurnal bird, both a bird of the mountains and a bird of the valleys, a water- and a land-bird, a plant- and meat-eater, etc. As a rule, people agreed on one point — that it was an enormous bird; it is indeed. It is the biggest of all European birds — not even excepting the mute swan — and a fully-grown, old male bustard has been known to weigh up to 53 pounds (the record for the swan is $49\frac{1}{2}$).

There is a greater difference between the sexes

as regards weight than is the case with any other species of bird. If the average weight of a male is between 26 and 33 pounds, the corresponding figures for the female birds are between 9 and 13 pounds. (See Notes.)

In the late eighteenth century, the bustard was a nesting species on several of the sandy plains in southern and north-western Skåne — above all in the neighbourhood of Åhus and Ljungby, as well as near Trelleborg, in the Cimmerred area. A veil of secrecy, however, has descended on this large bird's habits in Sweden, despite the eye-witness accounts of such a distinguished expert as Sven Nilsson. Its disappearance from its nesting places in Skåne must have happened very quickly and gone relatively unnoticed, since a young zoologist by the name of C. J. Sundevall, in spite of searching the area in question as early as the 1830s, was unable to find a single eye-witness of the bustard's existence there only a few decades earlier. With all due respect to the great Sven Nilsson, he even doubts whether any permanent colony had in fact existed in the above-mentioned places.

Nevertheless, there are several descriptions of the methods employed in Skåne to hunt the bustard. In addition, eggs originating from Skåne, and still in existence, show that Sundevall's scepticism was probably unjustified. The last area where the bustard was resident was near Åhus. The fact that it was also driven away from there was attributed to land reforms, which changed farming methods and increased the acreage of cultivated land at the expense of the formerly deserted sandy plains.

Hunting the shy bustards required a great deal of knowledge concerning their habits and behaviour. There are descriptions from Skåne of how they were hunted with the aid of greyhounds, which were transported in a covered waggon as close to the birds as possible before being released. Since the heavy bustard, in common with the swan, was obliged to run a yard or two into the wind, so as to get air under its wings, the dogs sometimes managed to overtake the bird before it had time to take off. It was more usual to creep up within range with the help of a stalking-horse or disguised as a harmless peasant-woman.

There are illustrations in many old hunting books showing people hunting bustards on horseback, with the aid of greyhounds. Several writers have described these pictures as sheer imagination. Under certain conditions this method is nevertheless feasible. In particular, it was practised on the steppes of southern Russia in freezing rain, when ice on the bustards' feathers prevented them from taking off. However, since this type of weather is not common, this method of hunting can hardly have been used very regularly. The German bustard expert Wolfgang Gewalt, who described "ice hunting" in Hungary and the Danube area, stresses that ice on the ground is all that is required, since the bustards when fleeing are then unable to get a foothold with their comparatively small feet. The use of greyhounds for hunting bustards is also mentioned in descriptions from several parts of Spain, France and England — Newmarket heath and Salisbury plain in the 1660s.

In Spain, where the bustard is still fairly common in certain areas — in Andalusia, for example — waggons concealing the guns were still in use at the end of the nineteenth century. Abel Chapman, the source of this information, was present when sixty-two bustards were shot in one season in this fashion.

Chapman, who had had a lot of experience of bustard hunting, believed that by far the most

The use of greyhounds for bustard-hunting was successful only in winter, in freezing rain or when there was ice on the ground.
The mediaeval two-wheeled stalking-barrow, camouflaged with branches, gradually developed into the large, covered bustard-hunting waggon (below), generally disguised as a load of hay, in order to deceive the timid birds. (After Jagdbuch des Herzogs Johann Casimir von Sachsen, *1639.)*

reliable method was for the solitary hunter to outwit the wary birds, with the aid of two beaters. A happy combination of luck and strategic skill was the prerequisite for a successful hunt. Once a flock of bustards — a *bandada* — had been spotted with binoculars, the beaters carried out a wide pincer movement and met at a carefully calculated distance from the birds. The aim was to force the bustards up-wind and make them fly over the gun. In the meantime, the latter had wormed his way as close as possible to the flock. A fair measure of caution was required for this stealthy advance; for as Chapman says, it is undoubtedly a good thing for the hunter to camouflage himself in green clothes, but it is even more important for his movements to be as inconspicuous as possible.

In Spain, a large number of bustards are still shot by poachers each year. The latter, however, naturally use more subversive methods than those mentioned above. During the dry season in the summer, water-holes in the plains are visited at dusk by the flocks of bustards, which make a relatively easy target for the gun, who prepares his ambush in good time. The poachers also use a very ancient method. This is employed at night, once the bustards' roosting-places have been located out in the fields. Two men are required for this method of hunting; in addition to the hunter with his gun, there is an assistant armed with a powerful electric torch and an ordinary cow-bell tied to his ankle, so that it tinkles regularly during the advance in the dark. The bustards are used to the tinkling of cattle-bells and show no reaction when two shadowy figures move about close to them in the dark. When the men reach the roosting-place, they switch on the torch and paralyse the bustards with

the bright light. In Chapman's day, bright oil-lamps were used. They remained alight during the whole of the men's advance, and the idea of fleeing never entered the heads of the dazzled birds.

This form of hunting occurred mainly in the winter, when bustards assemble in large flocks.

In central Europe, particularly in the small German principalities, where hunting was very much a sport for the gentry, a special type of beating was practised. These beats were somewhat similar in character to the so-called "closed circle" drives for beasts of prey in Scandinavia. A lot of people were required, and they formed a wide circle round the bustards. When the birds could see no way of retreat whatsoever, their consternation was so great that they did not think of taking off before the hunters were within easy gun range.

The bustard, like the crane, bittern and whooper swan, is an extremely vulnerable bird of the wilds. Its future in Europe in our time depends entirely on man's goodwill. It quickly disappears from those places where it is exposed to constant attack, but on the other hand, it obviously learns fairly rapidly to protect itself against the various wiles of hunters. In East Germany, where the European bustard has one of its firmest strongholds, it is, fortunately enough, completely protected. The same is true of at least twenty-one regions in the Soviet Union, where no one is allowed to hunt it (1959). The bustard is a hopelessly old-fashioned bird. It has no desire at all to adapt itself to agricultural progress. In populated areas of Europe, its main need at the present time is to be left in peace — not only by poachers but at least equally as much by photographers, inspired with the hope of making a scoop out of Europe's largest and shyest bird.

During the Middle Ages, the still unfledged young herons were captured with the aid of poles with hooks on the end, or were taken from the nests by specially trained climbers whose equipment of rope, hooks, baskets etc, is to be found carefully noted in account books.

THE HERON

One of the reasons why the heron came to belong to "blue-blooded hunting" was its suitability for hawking. The food value of the heron, however, was also largely responsible for the privileged classes reserving it for their pleasure. In contrast to the view of later centuries, the heron in fact enjoyed a very good gastronomical reputation and was seldom missing from feasts in olden times. At the famous banquet given on the occasion of the

No birds in recent times have been the victims of such uninhibited persecution as that suffered by the great white heron when the dictates of fashion required ornamental feathers in ladies' hats. The slaughter took place only during the mating season and the number of birds sacrificed on the altar of fashion could be counted in millions. After nearly three million little egrets in the United States had been almost wiped out, it was the turn of those birds in South America. In 1898, 1,583,733 egret skins were shipped from Venezuela alone, but a mere ten years later it was difficult to reach a total of 257,916. This picture was drawn in the extreme south of Andalusia where the little egrets still find sanctuary. (Extreme right) Two cattle egrets. (Centre) A solitary heron.

Archbishop of York's taking up office in 1465, the food served to the guests included 400 herons. (See Notes.)

As a matter of fact it was not only in mediaeval times but also much later in history that the heron had a place of honour in aristocratic homes. It was larded with bacon fat before roasting and was served with preserved ginger or wild strawberries. A German writer tells us enthusiastically that heron tastes like venison. The young birds, in particular, were in great demand and they were caught, at least in England, by heron-catchers who used long hooks to pull down the still unfledged birds from nests or branches. Some of the captured birds were then put in *aviaries* of the Roman type, where they were fattened for the banquet table, while others were reared for use in training falcons.

The strict regulations which existed for the protection of heron colonies give a clear indication of the high esteem in which the heron was held. It may be added that the heron, apart from its importance as a delicacy and its popularity for falconry, also played a leading role in folk medicine and black magic. There is evidence from many areas of Europe that various parts of the heron were supposed to possess magic powers for fishing, and this fact no doubt helped to increase its value still further in the Middle Ages. People believed that a heron's foot in one's pocket would ensure a successful fishing expedition. It was, however, considered to be even better to grease the bait or the fishing-line with the bird's fat or with the oil formed in the decomposing corpse of a heron. (See Notes.)

Motionless as a lizard, the heron stands by the river bank, staring down into the water, and seizes a fish with a mechanical movement of its thin neck, swallowing its catch with spasmodic twitches, and an absolutely expressionless gaze in its cold metallic eyes. Was it possible that there was warm blood in this bird, that its body functioned in the same manner as that of normal birds? It was formerly a common belief that the heron possessed only one intestine, through which the captured fish was often able to pass without any trouble at all. The heron was believed to be able to swallow the same fish two or three times in succession before the catch remained in its stomach for good.

The Greek writer, Oppianus, declared that the people of antiquity loved the heron and held it in high esteem, but in the middle of the nineteenth century the German Lenz made a very laconic comment on this statement: "*Jetzt verhasst*" — "now hated". This provides an indication of how the attitude of different eras and civilisations towards the heron has varied. Despite the occasionally ruthless persecution suffered by the heron in various countries — perhaps above all in Germany and France — its numbers seem, on the whole, to have remained fairly constant in Europe since the Middle Ages.

Of course, the heron is one of the easiest species of birds to count since, as a rule, it nests in colonies in well-defined areas. There are fairly reliable figures available from the middle of the nineteenth century onwards. They show that the number of herons has even tended to increase in recent years. This was the case in France (where the decrease has otherwise been very noticeable) during the Second World

It was mainly in its capacity as quarry for the sport of falconry that the heron acquired its position as noble game. If the downed heron was uninjured, it was usually released at once, after a ring had been placed on one of its legs.

War, and the connection between this fact and the ban on hunting weapons in force at the time is very striking. Numbers dropped again rapidly after the War, and the famous heron colony at Champigneul (Marne), where more than 200 pairs nested at the turn of the century, was considered, at least a decade ago, to be completely abandoned. This colony is marked on a map from 1668 and mentioned in documents as early as 1388, which goes to show how very ancient heronries may sometimes be.

The other species of herons which mainly occur in the marshes of the Mediterranean countries and eastern Europe are no longer of any importance as regards hunting, but in the years at the turn of the century two of them — the little egret and the great white heron — were subjected to an unprecedented persecution on account of the demand for ornamental feathers for ladies' hats. The great white heron survived almost by a miracle and the north-western limits of its range in Europe are now in Austria.

Cranes and herons were caught in the same way as crows, with the aid of pumpkins that had been hollowed out and smeared on the inside with bird-lime. Another method was to use "lime-cones", which were placed in holes in the ground. An engraving by Stradanus in Venationes *(1578) shows three men hiding behind tree-trunks, watching their cones. Their equipment is beside them; a basket of cones and a jar of lime.*

THE CRANE AND THE BITTERN

The crane was originally distributed over a wide area of Europe. During the Middle Ages, it was apparently fairly common in the British Isles, where large flocks also tried regularly to stay through the winter. It was, indeed, in England that the crane acquired its greatest reputation — as a splendid quarry for falcons and in its capacity as a highly-valued item at banquets. As a food, it was actually the subject of a thesis. (See Notes.) In 1465, 204 cranes were ordered for the famous inaugural feast in London for Archbishop Neville of York. It is doubtful, however, whether it was in fact possible to supply such a large number on one occasion.

As far as the bustard, heron, crane and bittern are concerned, it is remarkable how very much tastes seem to have changed since olden times. These birds fetched high prices in the Middle Ages and enjoyed a well-established culinary fame. Horace gives an enthusiastic description of how the crane was cut into pieces, coated with salt and pepper and fried. Gradually, however, tastes began to become more refined and interest in the large birds waned. Sven Nilsson thought it was coarse, tough and indigestible and could just about recommend crane soup as suitable for convalescents; by that time both the crane and the other large birds were no longer delicacies.

During its golden age in Britain, the crane was partly protected by royal decrees, prohibiting, for one thing, the removal of eggs or young birds from the nest. When fire-arms appeared on the scene, however, the crane was one of the worst affected birds, presumably because it was such an easy target. It is difficult to say whether it was the draining of bogs and marshes or the ravages of hunters that spelt disaster for the cranes of the British Isles. In all probability, it was a combination of both. After cranes had ceased breeding in Britain, they nevertheless continued to be fairly regular winter visitors for a time, but nowadays they are only vagrants in the British Isles.

The crane was regarded as a fine game-bird also in Germany and eastern Europe, but at the same time it was energetically kept under control on account of the damage it was believed to cause in fields during migration. In Poland, farmers built watch-huts by their fields, so as to be able to protect their crops. Elsewhere, the same hunting methods were used as those employed for the bustard — in other words, stalking-horses and long-range shot-guns. Old handbooks on hunting describe a variety of other trapping devices intended especially for cranes. One method was to dig deep, narrow trenches, fill them with the cranes' favourite food, and place snares round the edges. The idea was that

"Do you hear the cranes crying, high up in the clouds? It is a sign that the ploughing season is here," wrote Hesiod. Frederick II, the falconer-king, was well acquainted with the flying formations of cranes, which he had seen in his native southern Italy. (After a miniature in a copy of De arte venande cum avibus *from 1308.)*

Evidence that cranes occurred in Ireland during the Middle Ages is to be found in Giraldus Cambrensis' Topographica Hibernica *(1183–1186), from which this magnificent crane comes strutting forth. Manuscript in the British Museum.*

the crane, in its attempts to reach the tasty morsels at the very bottom, would thrust its head through the snare and get caught.

The *bittern* has perhaps never been included in "blue-blooded" hunting, but its importance to this occupation can be compared with that of the heron and the crane, both as game and from the gastronomic point of view. In common with the crane, it is a bird that has been badly affected by agricultural developments since the eighteenth century. Although it is distributed over a wide area of Europe, it has nevertheless greatly diminished in numbers, and has disappeared from many localities where it was fairly common in the past. This is the case in, for example, Scandinavia, Ireland, Scotland and England. It had already disappeared almost completely from Sweden by the late nineteenth century, and it is doubtful whether it could be listed at all as a regular nesting species there during the first decades of the twentieth century. In the 1920s, however, isolated bitterns began to be heard here and there. Later, in the 1940s and 1950s, surprisingly enough, bitterns staged a veritable invasion of central Sweden. In suitable places along the shores of Lake Mälaren, it was possible to hear seven or eight males booming from different points of the compass at one and the same time. This provided a vision of the Sweden of yore, when "the sonorous note of the bittern booming from the beds of reed" was a traditional item in nature-poetry.

The bittern was considered easier to digest and ranked as a greater delicacy than the heron. It was important, however, to make sure that no bones were broken before cooking, for otherwise there was a danger of the whole roast tasting of fish. The bittern was hunted mainly with bird-dogs. According to some accounts, however, falcons were also used to catch it; a fairly easy matter in the summer, when the bittern flies at regular intervals between its young in the reed-beds and its fishing grounds.

The latter are often situated some distance away from its nest. In the evenings, the bittern may occasionally rise very high in the heavens over the marsh, and this was, indeed, an opportunity for a beautiful display of the art of falconry.

According to William Turner (1544), the bittern is renowned for its sluggishness and is easily driven into nets by a well-trained stalking-horse. People also tried to catch it by setting snares, and by putting out yarn dipped in bird-lime at the "crossing-points" which the bittern was believed to use in the reeds.

As already mentioned, the bittern belonged to *"la grande cuisine"* and was seldom missing from great banquets. Old diet-lists state that its meat was wholesome. A Frenchman who had specialised in bittern-hunting warmly recommended the piece of fat to be found on the rump between the bird's thighs.

When the bittern strikes its characteristic defensive pose, with its bill pointing skywards, it is not easily spotted in the reeds. "Stellaris is that kind which Englishmen denominate buttour or bittour and the Germans call pittour or rosdom. Now it is a bird like other herons in its state of body generally, living by hunting fishes on the banks of swamps and rivers, very sluggish and most stupid, so that it can very easily be driven into nets by the use of a stalking-horse. So far as I remember, it is nearly of the colour of a pheasant, and the beak is smeared with mud; it utters brayings like those of an ass." (William Turner, 1544.)

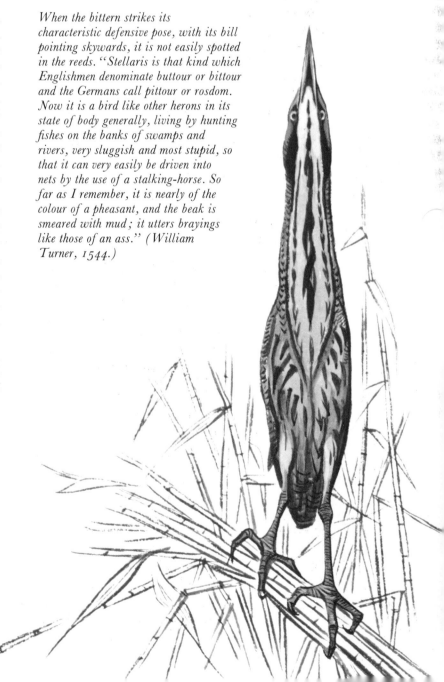

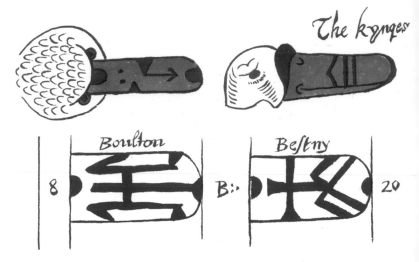

Boulton

Beſtny

(Left) Frontispiece of The Orders, Laws and Customes of Swanns, *1632. (Above) Various beak markings of the sixteenth and seventeenth centuries from* The Rolls. *With the aid of the former, "The Master and Governour of the Royall game of Swans and Signets" was able to keep a check on the swan community in England. (After Ticehurst.)*

THE MUTE SWAN AND WHOOPER SWAN

The most royal of game birds, symbol of nobility and beauty. When the zoologists of the past described it, they were transformed into poets. In spite of its having being protected as a royal bird in many areas, it has been subjected, nevertheless, to so much persecution that it has completely disappeared from certain regions but has also increased considerably in others. The distribution of the mute swan in the Old World is therefore very widespread but irregular. In Europe its existence is to a very great extent dependent on man, and in large areas of the continent it lives in a semi-tame state; this is particularly true of the state of affairs in the British Isles.

It was believed for a long time that the mute swan had been introduced into England by the Romans or by some knight returning home from the Crusades. Nowadays, however, it is regarded as an indisputable fact that the swan is really a native British bird. No one has managed to establish exactly *when* it was raised to the rank of a royal bird, but there are documents which prove that this took place already prior to 1186. This meant that the king was the owner of all the swans existing on unenclosed waters in the kingdom but he often

bestowed on his favourites the right to hunt swans in certain stretches of water or counties as a mark of favour.

There were several reasons for keeping swans: they were a respected status symbol, they were a highly appreciated present from one great man to another, they were also considered an investment and, not least, roast swan belonged to the banquet table. In order to keep track of all the swans which flourished under the protection of these different interests, a special government office was established already in the Middle Ages, with the task of keeping an eye on the royal swans and of checking those owned by the nobility and the latter's rights in this connection. The result was that the swan became the object of bureaucratic concern on a scale which, neither then nor later, was of benefit to any bird.

The Master of the King's (or Queen's) Game of Swans was the supreme authority responsible for "the swan estate". He travelled about the country, inspecting the owner's marks which every swan was required by law to have on its beak or foot. He checked and revised the herd books in which a record was kept of all swans. He settled disputes between private swan owners and the Crown,

passed judgment on breaches of the strict protective laws and, all in all, exercised considerable power. The system functioned with undiminished vigour for several centuries, but in the course of the eighteenth century, marking began to cease in several places, on account of flagging interest on the part of the landowners. As a result, the swans returned fairly rapidly to a wild state and slipped out of the clutches of the authorities.

The owning or hunting of swans also became a royal prerogative in other parts of Europe, mainly in the countries around the Baltic. The mute swan was declared the property of the Crown in some German and Baltic principalities. In Denmark and Sweden swan hunting (both mute and whooper swans) was dear to the king's heart. Particular fame is attached to a decree issued by Gustavus II Adolphus in 1621, according to which all hunting of swans was forbidden within a radius of sixty miles of Stockholm, the Swedish capital. The death sentence was imposed on offenders.

Nowadays, the mute swan is very common in southern and central Sweden, but it was not until the nineteenth century that it started to acquire its present range; previously, it occurred in large numbers only at Ekolsund Manor, thirty-six miles west of Stockholm. Swans were sometimes sent, however, from the southern Swedish province of Skåne to the royal palace of Drottningholm during the moulting season.

In the summertime, huge flocks of mute swans gathered along the coasts of the southern Baltic, where a strange method was employed to hunt them; people hunted the birds during the moulting season. This most barbaric practice took place at the end of July or beginning of August and meant that the grounded birds were chased by the hunters, in boats, who rained blows on them, seized them, or shot as many as they could manage.

This "sport" was the delight of the Danish kings

and, in Skåne, from the sixteenth century onwards, it was a privilege reserved for the governor-general and, later on, the provincial governor; as a matter of fact, it was not until the second half of the nineteenth century that this remarkable form of hunting finished for good. In the North German principalities swan hunting was regarded as an asset to the economy of the country. The down was used for powder puffs, the skin for bedroom mats or for fur coats, and the quills for pens. The meat was dried in the sun, or smoked as breast of goose and, in many places, the broad black feet, about which Shakespeare wrote in *Titus Andronicus*: "For all the water in the ocean/Can never turn a swan's black legs to white/Although she lave them hourly in the flood" . . . were used, dried, as candlesticks. In other words, it paid to shoot swans and take them to market.

No one knows whether there were more swans in the southern Baltic in the past than there are today, but, in any case, more were killed. When the Danish king hunted swans at Gedser at the end of July 1692, no fewer than 420 swans were killed at one hunt, which was such a remarkable feat, even in those days, that it was considered to be worth an offering at Kippinge Church on the following day. We learn from contemporary accounts that these royal swan hunts were arranged on a magnificent scale, with a huge gathering of boats, oarsmen and guns.

In other parts of the Baltic coast, swan hunting was practised on a more modest scale than in Denmark. In Pomerania, swan hunting covered both mute and whooper swans and took place during the migratory season. The hunters hid in reed-huts out on the low sand-banks, where the swans were in the habit of roosting after feeding at sea. They were shot either at dusk, when they flew in low over the beaches, or at night in the moonlight.

Many eye-witnesses have described swan hunting

in Skåne. The provincial governor summoned oarsmen and boats from the fishing villages along the coast, and each village was obliged to mobilise a certain number of boats and men who were placed at the governor's disposal, without any right to compensation. At midnight the large flotilla set off for the bay where the hunt was to be held. The master of the hunt had to estimate the rate of progress as accurately as possible so that the whole company arrived in position at the same time, at daybreak. Then the boats were rowed out as quickly as possible and formed a chain so as to shut off the bay with the moulting swans. Inside the bay, the hunters closed in on the terrified flocks of swans which tried to break through the chain of boats. The time had now come for a terrific battle in which guns, cudgels, oars and anything else available provided handy weapons. A fair number of swans were also caught with the aid of hoops fastened to poles.

The distribution of the whooper swan is considerably more widespread than that of the mute swan. In Europe, however, it is restricted to the extreme north-east of Finland and Norway and the interior of Swedish Lapland and of Iceland. A few pairs have also bred in the north of Scotland. In Scandinavia, its breeding areas have decreased very appreciably as a direct result of man's hunting activities. Some place-names with *emt* (a name for the whooper swan in Old Swedish) show that it bred, in historic times, as far south as the central Swedish province of Närke. In the nineteenth century it bred on several lakes in the province of Jämtland, some two hundred miles further north, but nowadays it is found only in a few scattered places in marshland in the forests of northern Lapland.

The whooper swan is one of the large birds which have suffered most. It was hunted intensively in its wintering grounds in central Europe. On its return to its northern breeding areas, it was greeted by salutes from heavy shotguns, or was caught in gins and snares which were placed by the narrow stretches of open water where the sea birds were obliged to break their journey while waiting for the ice to melt on the forest lakes. At their breeding grounds, the eggs were stolen from their nests or the still unfledged young birds were caught and kept as domesticated birds by settlers in the wilds. The English egg-collector, John Wolley, who collected eggs in Lapland in the middle of the nineteenth century, relates, in *Ootheca Wolleyana*, that the vicar of the small northern Finnish village of Utsjoki ate swan's eggs for breakfast in the spring and that the remains of whooper swans had been found at Lapp sacrificial sites.

Generally speaking, it may therefore be said that the whooper swan has been subjected to extreme pressure on the part of man. If the first modest attempts at protection (hunting was forbidden March 15 to August 1, 1808) had not been made as early as they were, it is possible that our whooper swan would have suffered the same fate as the large trumpeter swan — its homologue in North America. The latter species was almost completely wiped out by settlers and trappers during the nineteenth

Mountain lakes in Jugoslavia just north of Trieste are a traditional wintering area of the whooper swan and there hunters used a white screen mounted on runners to creep up to the shy birds.

century, but was saved, as if by a miracle, and there are now two or three thousand of these birds in existence (Voous 1962).

Naturally, it is uncertain whether the whooper swans in Lapland have become so extremely shy on account of this ruthless persecution. It is, however, difficult to explain why the behaviour of the same species is so completely different in Iceland and Scotland. In Iceland, the whooper swan behaves in approximately the same way as the mute swan of the lowland lakes. I once saw a pair of whooper swans calmly walking along with their newly-hatched young down to a volcanic lake where I was standing, fully exposed to view, by the shore. This would be inconceivable in Lapland. It is therefore not true that shyness is typical of the species as a whole. Indeed, it is as easily domesticated as the mute swan. This was often the case in Lapland with young birds, and in Russia and other places in the east of its range the whooper swan has long been a popular ornamental bird.

In Iceland, the whooper swan was formerly hunted, usually, only during the moulting season. A certain Jón Stephanson gave an account of a curious "hunting method" which according to him was an ancient tradition in north-eastern Iceland. When the swans had moulted and flew in large numbers along their age-old migration routes towards the coast, the hunters lay in ambush, armed to the teeth with rattles, dogs, drums and anything else that made a noise. When the flock of swans was exactly overhead, a frightful noise broke out and some of the young and inexperienced swans were quite simply scared out of their wits, and came tumbling down to the ground as if they had been hit by bullets! We are told that this "hunt" is repeated year after year with great success. The author of the *Manual of the Birds of Iceland*, from which this information was obtained, points out, however, somewhat impertinently, that it is strange that this most remarkable method has never been mentioned in any of the many accounts published about the home of the Icelandic sagas.

Among the more important of the numerous tricks which have been used in Scandinavia to approach the shy whooper swans were, of course, different kinds of camouflage. In the far north, white clothes were worn, as for seal hunting, and from one of the age-old wintering grounds of the whooper swans, just north of Trieste in Jugoslavia, comes the description of a white screen on runners, which the hunter carefully pushed across the ice. In France, a stalking cow was used for swan hunting, but decoys, in the form of tame swans, tethered in suitable spots, were also used. Swan decoys survived into the present century on the most famous European swan lake, Tåkern in central Sweden. As recently as 1942, I saw one of these swan decoys, made of tow yarn and cloth, in a boathouse at Hånger, on the western shore of Tåkern. A local resident told me that these decoys were "formerly" put out on the ice, by the first open patches, to entice the wild swans to descend. The meat was sold to a sausage factory in the neighbourhood.

As already mentioned, many more or less bestial methods were used to catch swans, and the account of Linnaeus's journey in Skåne includes a description of the hook and line technique employed by Baron B. W. von Lieven — according to the diary kept by Linnaeus of his journey, a man of "exceptional genius". An apple or other fruit which floats in water was fixed to a hook. A stone was attached to the line and was placed on a pole driven into the bottom of the lake. The top of the pole reached the surface of the water. When the swan swallowed the apple, it simultaneously pulled the stone down from the pole, and was drowned as a result.

Humanism long left its mark on people's views on the whooper swan. When the Finnish writer, Petrus Hahn, wrote an essay entitled De Cygno ejusqve cantatione *(Åbo, 1697), with the illustration shown here, he quoted the writers of antiquity and maintained, mistakenly, that the whooper swan's long neck, the source of sweet sounds, has twenty-eight vertebrae. (After Bernström.)*

... "When it alights on the ground to eat, the very fear of it is enough to drive the eagle and other birds of prey away from carrion. It only leaves weak and small birds in peace. It kills hares and foxes and other small animals by striking them with its wings, after which it carries them off in its claws." (Olaus Magnus, 1555.)

THE CAPERCAILZIE

"No bird, except the ostrich, grows as heavy as the cock capercailzie. Because it is so fat it sits motionless on the ground practically the whole time, and is easily caught by the hunter. It lives in the Alps and northern Europe. It loses its taste in aviaries. It kills itself in old age by holding its breath."

The author of the above was Pliny — the first person to describe the capercailzie, if we ignore a doubtful reference in Aristotle to a large bird in Scythia which hatched its two eggs in the skins of hares or foxes, and which defended itself by hitting out with its wings like an eagle!

Mediaeval scholars added to Pliny's description and even Olaus Magnus, who certainly ought to have seen capercailzies in real life, produced a grossly exaggerated description of the capercailzie. For a long time the naturalists of central Europe considered the capercailzie to be a mysterious and terrifying semi-mythical bird of an enormous size. This belief was due to the capercailzie being practically exterminated already in the Middle Ages in Germany and France, where the large forests were ruined and hunting knew no bounds.

It was, not least, on account of its rarity that the capercailzie came to be included among "blue-blooded" game, together with the swan, pheasant, bustard and — at any rate in the heyday of falconry — the heron. Gradually the capercailzie's range became restricted to the Pyrenees, Alps and mountain areas in central Germany as well as Scandinavia and eastern Europe down to Greece. On the Continent it has become, essentially, a bird of the mountains owing to the fact that it requires coniferous woods in order to thrive, and has had to retreat to hilly areas, as a result of more and more land being brought under the plough.

The capercailzie was once fairly plentiful in Britain, but was completely exterminated during the eighteenth century. It is not even mentioned in the hunting law of 1831. It is true that there is a doubtful record of an old cock capercailzie having been shot in 1815 near Fort William, but probably the last of the original stock was shot as early as 1760 or thereabouts. There were one or two unsuccessful attempts at the beginning of the nineteenth century to reintroduce the capercailzie, but in 1836 the attempt met with better luck.

It was then that some thirty capercailzies were sent over from Sweden to Lord Breadalbane's estate, Taymouth Castle, in Scotland through the good offices of the distinguished bear hunter, Llewellyn Lloyd. There they throve and multiplied so rapidly that by the 1860s there were some thousand capercailzies on the estate. Since then, these birds have spread over large areas of Scotland.

Nowadays, its principal haunts are in the northern parts of Scandinavia and Russia but, on the whole, numbers have declined considerably and vary very much locally. In recent years, this decline has been ascribed to the fact that, during the first days of their lives, capercailzie chicks are extremely sensitive to weather conditions. It is also said that the Atlantic type of climate, an increasingly noticeable factor, is responsible, more than anything else, for the decline of the capercailzies in northern Europe.

It is hardly possible for us to imagine just how plentiful the capercailzie once was in northern Europe but, with the improvement of fire-arms at the beginning of the nineteenth century, the species was ruthlessly decimated. Above all, the use of calls for shooting in August was sometimes catastrophic, since frequently the whole half-grown brood, as well as the hen capercailzie, perished.

In northern Europe the shooting of displaying capercailzie has never been considered to fall within the sphere of "blue-blooded" hunting, having instead been definitely regarded as something for the peasantry. This method has been forbidden since the beginning of the nineteenth century. On the Continent, however, shooting the capercailzie at its display grounds is considered to be a commendable occupation from every point of view, both as a first-class sport and as a method of preserving game. It is felt that when shooting displaying birds, the hunter has an opportunity of checking and thinning out the numbers of capercailzie in their territory and, above all, of weeding out the excessively old birds. The latter are the bullies of the display ground and drive the young cocks away to the detriment of breeding.

It was a popular occupation in olden times to catch woodland game-birds. In the main, traps and snares were used for the purpose. There were several versions of the deadfall type (2 and 3). The idea was to lure the capercailzie into touching a spindle, whereupon the heavy logs fell down on the bird and killed it. Snares (1) were made of annealed brass wire or twisted horsehair and placed across paths between rocks, or close to the upturned roots of fallen trees, where capercailzies are fond of having a dust-bath. Fences of twigs were often constructed along the sides of the paths in order to guide the birds to the snares. Red whortleberries were also scattered on the ground to attract the capercailzies. Both methods of catching the birds were used exclusively in the autumn, from early October onwards.

1

2a

b

3

The robin is the first bird to start singing on a spring morning, often well before daybreak. Not more than a few minutes later, the capercailzies start displaying. The peasants of old who shot these birds at their display-grounds used to call the robin "the capercailzie clock".

Nevertheless, even if this sounds sensible, the shooting of displaying birds is odious from the ethical point of view. The majority of hunters no doubt agree nowadays that game should be left in peace during the mating season.

The peasant hunters and poachers of old had many infallible signs to go by when hunting displaying birds. They never went to the display grounds before the woodcock had begun its roding and the robin had sounded its first notes, which usually occurs a good while before daybreak.

The first phase of the display took place on the roosting branch, usually one of the branches in the middle of a big pine. The display consists of three stages; first there are the clicking sounds, then a plop, and finally a hissing noise. During the latter phase, the cock, according to an ancient popular belief, neither sees nor hears anything, in his ecstasy. During the four or five seconds that the hissing lasts, the shooter has a chance of taking two or three big strides towards the display ground without the capercailzie noticing him. In that way he advances until he is within range and able to aim at the steel-blue spring night sky before lowering his gun towards the large bird absorbed in its courtship.

With or without a gun, these capercailzie mornings in the forest are full of a wonderful, ethereal, atmosphere. It is a dawn before dawn in a primaeval landscape where the light of daybreak seems to rise from the frost-covered moss on the rocks.

These shoots were most successful during the first week of courtship, in the spring before the hens had begun to gather round the cock capercailzies and warn them of the approach of the hunters.

The tremendous abundance of capercailzies in Scandinavia diminished with the improvement of

On nocturnal shoots with torches it was customary in some areas for the gun to hang a sheep-bell on his arm. The constant tinkling reassured the capercailzies. They soon got used to the tinkling sound from the advancing gun, so that it did not matter if he happened to step on a dry twig here and there.

fire-arms and, to a large extent, on account of the unrestricted shooting during the courting season in the springtime. Another cause was the availability of cheap iron shot used by the peasant hunter. People spoke sadly about the "iron age of hunting". The capercailzie became extinct in many of its traditional haunts in southern Sweden as early as the 1820s.

Hunting in the autumn with torches also occurred on a fairly large scale both in Scandinavia and in central Europe, where, however, this method was used mainly against pheasants. As a rule, when torches were used for a capercailzie shoot, the roost was located in the evening by listening to the birds making their way there. The sound of their wings then carries some two or three hundred yards. Barked sticks were used to mark the way to the roost, thereby enabling the hunter, accompanied by a torchbearer, to make his way there. The capercailzies were blinded by the light and remained perched on their roosts, so that the shooter had no difficulty in bringing them down. Unfortunately, the hens suffered most from this form of hunting since they were the easiest to detect, thanks to their light plumage.

Shooting capercailzies in treetops was — and still is in districts rich in forest birds — a very popular hunting method which, indeed, might prove disastrous if it was practised ruthlessly. It is almost only cockbirds that alight in the tops of pines in the winter to eat needles and shoots. They gather in flocks which, in years when there was an abundance of forest birds in olden times, might consist of between 150 and 200 of them.

To ensure a successful hunt the snow had to be loose, the air still and not too cold. The old treetop shooters used to wear white sheepskin furs and used muzzle-loaders and sporting guns which allowed long-range shots, since the capercailzie is a wary bird and seldom lets a skier approach closer than a hundred yards. On account of the flock of capercailzies keeping together and seldom moving any great distance, it was not so rare for a solitary gun to finish off a flock down to the last bird. When we read the amazing lists of kills from the dark days of hunting in Scandinavia — the first decades of the nineteenth century — we cannot help wondering that there are any capercailzies at all today.

The custom of hunting forest birds with *"tree-barkers"* is a very ancient one in northern Europe. It is probably one of the very oldest methods of hunting. It required a close co-operation between hunter and dog, and was of great economic importance for the inhabitants of the wilds in times when they did not have weapons suitable for wing shots. The fact that hunting with tree-barkers has declined in recent years is perhaps due to modern quick-firing fire-arms, and because the shooting of sitting birds is not considered sportsmanlike. In Finland hunting with tree-barkers continues to be extremely popular, and national championships are even arranged for this singular method.

The small reddish Finnish spitz has proved to be the most suitable tree-barker. It is a primitive species which seems to have the right characteristics of a tree-barker in its blood, in an entirely different way from other dogs.

Great indeed are the demands made on a good tree-barker. It must be quick and attentive. It must have a good nose. It must be placid by temperament and have an even and steady bark. When it flushes a capercailzie in the woods, it must follow the flying bird as far as it can and then listen carefully for the sound of the bird landing. Then, using its scent, it must make its way to the tree where the bird is. The dog must stop a short distance from the tree and stand there barking calmly, thereby indicating to the hunter that it has tracked down the quarry. On no account must it rush to the trunk and scratch it with its paws, or jump about and bark excitedly, because this would frighten the bird away. This method is used above all for hunting capercailzie and black grouse — the hazel hen has been found to be too nervous and light-winged — but even the pheasant is easily brought to bay by the Finnish spitz. This might seem to be an anachronism — the primitive dog of the wilds against the blue-blooded bird from Asia Minor.

Hunting with *pointers and setters* is regarded by many hunters as the classical form of the sport. For this, one must be able to handle both a dog and a gun well. English bird dogs are usually preferred since the white patches on their coats make them easy to spot in the open. Hunting with pointers is best done somewhat latish in the morning, after the capercailzies have left their roosting branches and are on the ground, eating berries. The old cock capercailzies, however, are considered to be very difficult to approach as they very cunningly slip away in the undergrowth and take off under cover of bushes and thickets.

Stalking is no doubt one of the hardest ways of hunting forest birds. In addition to knowing the countryside very well, the hunter must be able to move as quietly as a Red Indian and possess great knowledge of the habits of the birds. Anyone who has managed with great difficulty to creep up within range of a cock capercailzie which is calmly walking about gobbling berries among moss-covered tree-stumps and boulders in a spruce thicket must admit that stalking — here as in all other cases — not only provides excitement but also an aesthetic insight into nature which other, possibly more dramatic, methods of hunting lack.

In the autumn, the capercailzie is fond of visiting fields of stubble to eat shelled corn, preferably in fields where, for some reason, the stooks are still standing. In some areas, these capercailzies are successfully shot in the stubble with the aid of hides.

In districts where there is an abundance of forest birds drives may also take place. For this, a small area of ground is beaten, and a small number of beaters and guns take part. The capercailzies usually fly past at high speed, and may present a rather difficult target.

THE PHEASANT

Although the pheasant has been native to Europe for many hundreds of years, I still feel that no hunter or naturalist regards it as anything but a pure stranger among our fauna. Of course, it is quite at home in various latitudes and is so common over a wide area that it is familiar to the majority of people. Nevertheless, the sight of it rising from a ditch, like some superb rocket, to fly off across the fields on rigid wings, makes it very difficult — in the moment of excitement such an encounter always occasions — to accept the pheasant as an ordinary wild bird. There is always something domesticated about its appearance and behaviour.

The English writer and critic, John Ruskin, compared the cock pheasant's plumage to "a Byzantine pavement, deepening into imperial purple and azure, and lighting into lustre of innumerable eyes". This poetic description still holds good. It is an exotic bird with a fairly well documented history in Europe, although there remain many interesting question-marks.

It is not possible to say how and when the pheasant was introduced into Europe. For a long time people believed that the *Argonauts,* during their search for the Golden Fleece, took the opportunity of capturing some pheasants at the mouth of

the River Phasis (Rion) in Colchis — its scientific name, in commemoration of this as it were, is *Phasianus colchicus* — which they later released on their return home to Greece.

As a matter of fact, the first reliable date for the European pheasant is provided by the works of Aristophanes of Byzantium, where the pheasant is mentioned as a domestic bird kept by wealthy families (Aristophanes lived from 250 B.C. to 180 B.C.). Martial, Aelian and Palladius are other classical authors who drew attention to the pheasant, above all in its capacity as a much-appreciated delicacy. Palladius (fourth century A.D.), for instance, describes in detail the best way of fattening pheasants. He recommends noodles dipped in oil, cornflour and wheatmeal.

The subsequent extension of the pheasant's range in Europe was a somewhat haphazard affair, as will be seen from the map above. It is an accepted fact that this bird was taken westwards to France and Britain by the Roman legions, but it is mentioned for the first time in English documents in 1059. In Germany, the pheasant is believed to have occurred in enclosed pheasantries as early as the days of Charlemagne; it was not until much later, however, that it was found in a wild state. Wherever it was

(Above) The pheasant's invasion routes into Europe, according to various sources. The starting-point is believed to have been the country south-east of the Black Sea, whence the Argonauts, according to legend, took the pheasant with them to Greece.

(Right) Undoubtedly one of the oldest European pictures of the pheasant is a miniature in Frederick II's famous hunting book De arte venande cum avibus, *from the mid-thirteenth century.*

According to John Ruskin, the pheasant's plumage is like "a Byzantine pavement, deepening into imperial purple and azure, and lighting into lustre of innumerable eyes".

introduced, people praised it for its superb meat, even if one mediaeval doctor somewhat surprisingly described it as being hard to digest! If this was indeed true, the roast pheasant eaten by the doctor cannot have been hung long enough, as any initiated eater of pheasant will guess.

With the reader's kind permission, I shall digress a little on the pheasant as a culinary item. After all, this is justifiable since the pheasant was originally considered to be solely an article of food. Brillat-Savarin described the pheasant as "a riddle whose solution is known only to the initiated, for they alone understand how to appreciate its excellence to the fullest extent". He went into great detail as to how it should be prepared, how the ripeness of the hung pheasant for the spit can be determined only by the instinct of the connoisseur. He also disclosed what kind of fat to use, how to make a pheasant stuffing consisting of a mixture of minced woodcock and beefmarrow, and so forth. A pheasant prepared according to these directions "would be food fit for angels, if they still make journeys down to earth as in the days of Lot". Has a similar gastronomic

Interest in pheasant shooting increased remarkably about 1800, when improved fire-arms facilitated rapid wing shots. The illustration shows a fowling-piece, signed Joseph Manton, London, 1810.

epitaph ever been written about any other kind of game? (See Notes.)

In central Europe, the pheasant made its appearance later than in England — in the Rhine Valley not until the thirteenth century, and in south-eastern Germany somewhat earlier. In Denmark, the pheasant is mentioned for the first time in 1562, when an English falconer was granted permission to trap falcons there, on condition that he gave the king a brace of pheasants. The first appearance of the pheasant in Sweden was as booty during the Thirty Years' War.

As recently as the eighteenth century, the pheasant was to be found in Sweden almost solely in enclosed pheasantries, and under the supervision of pheasant-keepers employed specially for this purpose. Writers of hunting handbooks from the early eighteenth century, such as von Fleming, stated categorically that the pheasant was not to be found wild, although it sometimes escaped from captivity and returned to a wild state. He also provided instructions on how to bring the fugitives back to the fold again.

It is something of a mystery to us why it was so difficult at first to introduce the pheasant into Scandinavia, since it appears to be perfectly happy in our climate. Nevertheless, the pheasant's history in Sweden and Denmark is a series of setbacks and disappointments, before its luck suddenly turned during the second half of the nineteenth century.

In Sweden, attempts were made to rear pheasants at the royal palaces as early as the mid-eighteenth century. These endeavours were apparently unsuccessful. At the end of the eighteenth century, John Fischerström, who was interested in economics, warmly recommended the rural population of central Sweden to rear pheasants, which "enjoy an excellent reputation as poultry", but no serious attempts appear to have been made until well into the nineteenth century. (See Notes.)

When improved fire-arms began to facilitate wing shooting, an interest in the pheasant as game was kindled in different parts of Europe. In many places, particularly in England and France, pheasants were released from captivity. In Sweden — north of the province of Skåne, where pheasants had occurred earlier — it was, indeed, an Englishman by the name of Oscar Dickson who first succeeded in the feat of getting the pheasant to survive the cold, disease and homage of the guns. This event took place in or about 1880, and his success was probably due to his employing experienced pheasant-breeders from England. It was then that pheasant-farms were successfully started in several places in central and southern Sweden. However, it was not really until the 1920s that the pheasant began to appear in the countryside, to the great astonishment of the general public, who were not aware of what was going on. Nowadays, between eighty and ninety thousand pheasants are shot in Sweden every year. This is a figure that would have given the royal gamekeeper, Ström, something to think about if he were still alive.

In many areas, interest in pheasant shooting, especially with the use of beaters, has become a

On a pheasant drive every miss by a gun is revealed to his near-by companions.

Ludwig VIII's lantern for nocturnal pheasant shoots is still to be seen at Kranichstein Castle. Alongside it, detail of a picture by the court painter, Seekatz, showing Ludwig VIII on a nocturnal pheasant shoot at Kranichstein.

veritable passion. The pheasant has been regarded by many people as being the only true game-bird. Indeed, there are instances of conscientious game-keepers having wiped out all other animals which were under the slightest suspicion of being detrimental to the well-being of the beloved pheasant.

At the end of the last century, the English writer and naturalist, W. H. Hudson, deplored the fact that gamekeepers on English estates went so far in their love for the pheasant that they had the impudence to shoot nightingales, on the grounds that the latter's singing might possibly keep the pheasants awake at night! Hudson, and surely many non-hunters too, considered that the pheasant had become nothing less than the curse of the British bird world. (See Notes.)

Catching pheasants with the aid of a mirror is described in both words and pictures in The Hunting-Book of King Modus.

Old English hunting literature contains many enthusiastic accounts of pheasant shooting with spaniels or pointers. The hunt is especially exciting when spaniels are used, since one never knows when the next pheasant is going to be flushed from a thicket. The whirring sound of the pheasant taking wing is said to give especial delight to anyone fond of this kind of bird shooting. The less experienced gun may easily panic, however, and fire his shots without due reflection. Many of the earliest wing shots, armed as they were with their clumsy flint-lock muskets, nevertheless attained an astonishingly high degree of proficiency. "It is just as easy to hit a pheasant when it is flushed as it is to hit a flying haystack", as a modest English sportsman put it at the beginning of the nineteenth century. However, as mentioned above, the most important form of pheasant shooting is the large-scale drive, where shooting ability is subjected to a severe test, and where any misses on the part of a gun are mercilessly revealed to his companions.

On some estates in olden times, shooting at night by torchlight was another method used. It is a well-known fact that the pheasant is very regular in its habits, one of which is to fly to its roosting-place at a certain time every evening. A loud noise of wings and clucking sounds accompanies this event, so that the hunter can easily make out where the pheasants are perching. Ludwig VIII of Hessen-Darmstadt, in particular, was very fond of shooting pheasants on their roosts in the castle grounds, and for this purpose he had a lamp made, the light of which was reflected by a mirror. He was accompanied on the hunt by a servant, whose task it was to look after the lamp, a man to keep his gun loaded, and a dog-handler with retrievers. When the pheasants' night-quarters had been found, the lamp was lit and the birds remained sitting there, paralysed by the dazzling light.

One of the oldest methods of catching pheasants is described by the *Roi Modus* from the fourteenth century. The pheasant was apparently enticed into the cage-trap by laying a trail of husked corn up to the opening. To speed up the proceedings, however, a mirror was placed by the trigger-device on the cage door. The author of the *Roi Modus* tells us that the pheasant flies into an uncontrollable rage when he sees another cock pheasant. So when he attacks his own reflection, he walks straight into the trap.

II

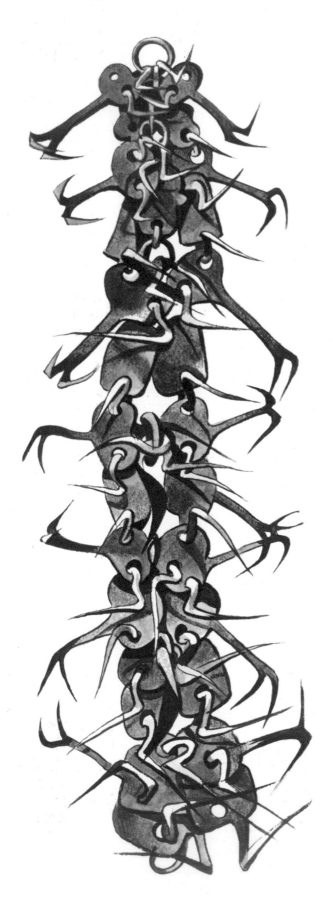

Dog-collar intended for wolf-hunting, sixteenth century. Musée de Senlis. Below: Dog-collars of a smaller Scandinavian type were also used for wolf-hunting. (Ehrenstrahl, Drottningholm Palace, 1674.)

THE WOLF

"Beware of false prophets, which come to you in sheep's clothing, but inwardly they are ravening wolves," says Jesus Christ in the Gospel according to St Matthew (7:15). This is one of the innumerable examples of the extremely deep impression which the wolf made on people in olden times as a symbol of evil, of divine punishment, as a scourge of mankind. In its personification of the devil on earth, no other animal — not even the flea or the rat — has surpassed it.

The hunting of wolves, indeed, became at an early date a matter for the community as a whole, and was soon covered by a series of laws and regulations, the aim of which was to make every able-bodied man play his part in combating these animals. Gradually, this constant watch against the wolf-plague began to resemble a general mobilisation, and in some countries the way in which the "war" was waged acquired the characteristics of a military operation.

"A wolf belongs to the man who catches it," to quote the Scandinavian mediaeval laws. Although the wolf was one of the animals that might be hunted by kings — in France, which was badly affected by the wolf, wolf-hunting came under the heading of *"La Vénerie Royale"* — it was at the same time an outlawed animal, the killing of which was considered to have divine approval at all times and under all circumstances.

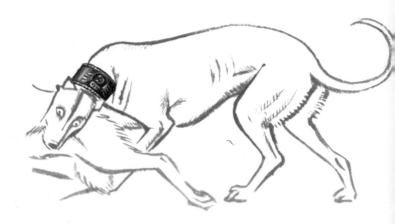

During the Middle Ages, there were laws under which some court fines were calculated in terms of fresh wolves' tongues. There was a time when the yearly tax in Wales was fixed at 300 wolves' heads. All in all, every conceivable method was employed to keep down the number of wolves. It was no less than a necessity, and a prerequisite for survival, which we today, in our praiseworthy efforts to protect the remnants of the European wolves, are often tempted to belittle.

The seriousness of the wolf-menace has varied considerably over the centuries. It often coincided in sinister fashion with alternations between periods of peace and war. In times of war, the wolves were able to feast on the dead and wounded on the battlefields. In addition, the lack of weapons for the civilian population enabled them to extend their range unimpeded.

France was one of the countries of Europe most infested with wolves, and the hunting of these animals was run on an organised basis for a very long time. As early as 1467, Louis XI created a special wolf-hunting office, whose senior member was recruited from the highest families of the land. A report on the hunting records was submitted direct to the king each year.

The power and importance of the corps of wolf-hunters may have varied somewhat over the years, but its most brilliant days occurred during the seventeenth and eighteenth centuries, when *la Grande Louveterie* became a veritable armed service, equal in status and importance to the army, from whose regiments its officers were in fact recruited. *Le Grande Louvetier* — the chief wolf-hunter, if one may call him that — was responsible for seeing that units of the corps went to the aid of those parts of the country that were seriously affected by wolves, and where the local forces were not large enough.

As a rule, the big, royal wolf-hunts took place in the autumn. They were often organised in the form of drives combined with coursing. The wolves that were not killed during the chase by the pack of

"La Grande Louveterie" was organised on a military basis and naturally the royal wolf-hunters wore special uniforms. (Musée de Vénerie, Senlis.)

hounds, or by the mounted huntsmen behind, were driven towards a partly enclosed hunting-ground, with nets and five-foot-high firing-screens, behind which hunters lay in ambush. When everything was in order, *le Grande Louvetier* gave the signal to attack, and the wolf or wolves were frightened from their daytime retreats by the tracker dog or part of the pack. The pace of the drive was gradually speeded up by releasing fresh, rested dogs on the scent. At the same time the pack was followed by the horsemen riding at full gallop. As a rule, the wolf was tired out fairly quickly during the furious chase, and the head wolf-hunter, or one of the distinguished members of the hunting party, rode up and either gave the animal the *coup de grace* with his spear or killed it with his gun. The latter weapon began to come into use on these occasions at the start of the eighteenth century. Frequently, the animals were also driven in towards the screens and nets, and were dealt with there.

Even during the first half of the nineteenth century, the wolf-plague was still a terrible reality in France, and as soon as there was a move to cut down *la Grande Louveterie* as an economy measure,

A wolf that ran riot in the French province of Gévaudan in the 1760s is one of the most famous animals in history. According to a more conservative estimate, this wolf is said to have killed more than fifty people on its own, the majority of them women and children. Louis XV sent an army totalling some 20,000 men to kill it, but in spite of more than forty huge drives it managed to escape, until it was killed in 1765 by thirty-five buckshot and one bullet. (After a contemporary print.)

*The Norrland wolf-hunters carried ski-sticks fitted
with wrought iron spearheads.
(Below) In central Europe, large hounds were used
for wolf-hunting. Seventeenth-century
German wheel lock musket. (Musée de la
Chasse, Gien.)*

after the Revolution, for instance, this immediately
led to a substantial increase in the amount of
damage done by wolves. Complaints were sent in
writing to the authorities demanding immediate
counter-measures. Statistics show that these protests were justified. At the end of the French
Revolution in 1797, general wolf-hunts were ordered
throughout France, during which 7,350 wolves were
killed. Forty people were killed or seriously injured
by wolves that year, tens of thousands of sheep,
goats and horses were torn to pieces, and in some
districts not a single watch-dog was left alive.
According to the *Moniteur universel*, no fewer than
2,416 wolves were killed or captured in eighteen
months (1816–1817). Curiously enough, only 522 of
these were female animals. (See Notes.)

Thanks to the untiring struggle against the wolf,
its depredations were gradually slowed down in
several western European countries. In England,
the last wolf is believed to have been killed in 1680,
in Scotland some ten years later, and in Ireland at
the beginning of the eighteenth century. The date
at which it was totally wiped out in Holland and
Belgium has not been established. The same thing
occurred in Germany some time in the nineteenth
century, but isolated wolves still stray across large
areas of central Europe. The truth of the matter is
that the wolf continues to be fairly widespread in
Europe, for example, in the Iberian peninsula,
Italy, the Balkans, eastern Europe and northernmost
Scandinavia. It also occurs locally and periodically
in France. In Denmark, the last wolf was shot in
1813. (See Notes.) In the mid-nineteenth century,
the extermination of wolves began in southern
Sweden and gradually continued northwards.

A contributory cause of this "victory" over the
arch-enemy was probably the change-over to new
agricultural methods, in particular the great redistribution of land-holdings. The latter meant an
increase in populated areas and cultivated land.
Without a shadow of doubt, the disappearance of
the wolf constituted a new era for the people of
Europe, an immensely significant watershed between the old and the new, if we consider, along with
the Danish writer C. F. Bricka, *"how different is the
atmosphere created by a wolf howling on a winter's night
from that produced by a locomotive's whistle piercing the
air."*

In Sweden, the wolf was hunted in a variety of
ways, depending on the terrain, the season of the
year, and the availability of helpers and so forth. In
Norrland, where it was impossible to organise
drives or enclose hunting-grounds, owing to the
shortage of people and the nature of the desolate
countryside, they had in the main to resort to *hunting*
in the original sense of the word, a war of extermination, the outcome of which depended entirely on
the physical performance, strength and endurance of
the hunters. In contrast, in the more densely
populated areas of Sweden, the wolf was decimated

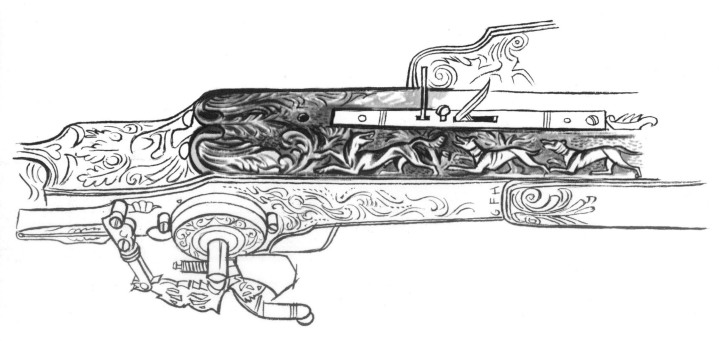

A widespread type of dead-fall for wolves (Sweden). (A) Drop-log, (B, C, D) supporting posts, (E) extra weight of logs and stones, (F) brass trigger-wire, (G) partly buried anchor-log, (H) groove in the post in which the trigger-spindle (I) is inserted, (J) rope holding up the drop-log, (K) thin twig of juniper or young spruce, (L) peg connected by a wire to the trigger-wire. How the dead-fall is triggered off: When the wire (F) is touched by the wolf, the trigger-spindle is jerked out of the groove (H), causing the peg (L) to revolve and release the catch holding the drop-log.

by more traditional methods, such as beats, sometimes with thousands of participants, or by means of ingeniously constructed trapping-grounds, which will be dealt with below. At the beginning of the eighteenth century, that enthusiastic hunter, Frederick I of Hesse, also introduced the "hunting at force" of wolves, and enclosed beats with the use of lengths of canvas or firing-screens of the Continental type, but these varieties of hunting never acquired any real importance in Sweden — they were arranged only occasionally for the august pleasure of the Court.

As regards wolf-hunting in Norrland, this usually took place when the snow was deep and loosely packed, so that a wolf was obliged to take big jumps all the time if it was to escape the hunter on skis, and as a result, tired very quickly. Hunting over crust-snow was less successful, since in the majority of cases the wolf did not sink into the snow. The feats known to have been performed by the wolf-hunters of Norrland when hunting on skis sometimes seem as fantastic as the deeds of the ancient Greek heroes, and put the Olympic Games in the shade.

Only in exceptional cases did the wolf-hunter carry fire-arms for the chase; they would have weighed him down too much. He carried a minimum of equipment — some sun-dried reindeer-

meat, coffee and bread, a knife and a lasso. He tore off his garments one after the other during the wild chase (they were picked up by his companions who brought up the rear), and towards the end he was often wearing nothing but shirt, trousers and tipped boots. If the wolf had eaten well and was rested, several days might pass before the hunter caught up with it, and was able to beat or stab it to death with his ski-stick, one end of which was fitted with a wrought-iron spearhead. The story goes that a lone Lapp once killed a wolf in this manner after a week-long chase.

Sometimes, however, people were more fortunate. At the end of the nineteenth century, a seventeen-year-old Lapp boy managed to kill four wolves in one day. As proof that this primitive and extremely exhausting method of hunting was indeed worth while, it may be mentioned that in one Lapp parish alone — Gällivare — seventy wolves were killed in this way late one winter in the 1830s.

Nowadays, the few remaining wolves in Sweden are protected by law, but it is still possible to meet middle-aged Lapps who hunted wolves in the old manner in their youth.

Trapping techniques in Norrland consisted mainly of the use of jaw-traps, which were placed at crossing-points, since the wolf's habit of keeping to the same tracks was well known. Use was made also, however, of wolf-pits, in which a dog was tethered to a pole in the middle to attract the wolves. According to Ekman, the gravity-snare, which was much used for trapping wolves on the

Shooting wolves from a sledge on a winter road (note the pig on the sledge), and plain wolf-sword for winter travellers. (The Nordic Museum, Stockholm.)

Greiff's wolf-pen was built with walls of high poles. The covered pitfall was situated in one corner. The idea was to lure the wolves to the pitfall while they were looking for a way out through the fence. (Inset) Cross-section of the pitfall. The hole was concealed by fir branches, placed crosswise, elastic enough to snap back into position after a wolf had fallen through, and look like a level floor to a succession of wolves.

Continent, has been observed in Sweden only in the Torne Lapp district in the north.

In former times, people travelled mostly in the winter, when ice formed bridges across moorland bogs, rivers and lakes, thereby facilitating travel by sledge through areas where roads were otherwise few and far between. It was then that the wolves were at their boldest and hungriest. One of the everyday problems of the Scandinavian traveller was to protect himself against the wolf-packs, which were particularly fond of following the loaded sledges, holding out as they did the promise of both horse-meat and human flesh. There is a story from Russia of how all the members of a wedding procession were killed by wolves on their way home from church.

As a matter of fact, a very popular form of hunting was based on the interest that wolves showed in sledges.

In addition to the driver and the hunter, the sledge carried another person too, and also a pig. The third person's task was to use various means to induce the pig to scream and make a lot of noise, thereby enticing the pursuing wolves within range.

In Sweden, the war against wolves was put on an organised basis in the laws of King Christopher, as early as 1442, when it was made compulsory for everyone to take part in wolf-drives. Later, conscription came to be maintained under more or less military conditions until far into the nineteenth century. The only members of a parish who were entirely exempt from joining the wolf-drives were the vicar, the parish clerk and almswomen. Gamekeepers and royal foresters had to produce a prescribed number of skins from predatory animals before they received their pay. The constantly recurring drives were a troublesome burden to the villagers, who often had to abandon urgent work in

the fields in order to take part in hunts, which might last for several days. In addition, it was a big drain on parish funds to maintain or make the high, large-mesh nets required by law. In the eighteenth century, however, the authorities agreed to the replacement of these nets by the less expensive hunting-cloths.

The law of 1808 relating to the hunting and trapping of wild animals stipulated that every province was under the obligation to maintain *three complete sets of hunting-cloths for drives,* and that each county had to construct and maintain a *hunting-ground* of the authorised type. According to the regulations, a set of hunting-cloths consisted of sixty-four bundles of painted canvas, each bundle having a length of forty fathoms (a fathom being equal to six feet), and twelve wolf-nets, each twenty fathoms long and five fathoms high.

People were summoned to a beat from the pulpit or by beacon. The arms to be carried were a hunting-spear, axe or cudgel. The master of the hunt decided who were to carry guns.

At the end of the utilitarian-minded eighteenth century, there was also an increasing tendency to streamline wolf-hunting considerably, in order to make it more effectual and less expensive for the local authorities. (See Notes.) In particular, experi-

ments were carried out with so-called hunting- or carrion-grounds, partially enclosed pens to which the wolves were attracted by depositing within them the carcasses of all cattle in the area that had died from natural causes. Under the hunting regulations of 1808, no carrion was allowed to be placed nearer than eighteen miles from the common hunting-ground, with the result that the hungry wolves made their way to the appropriate place. The wolves were generally coaxed into the hunting-ground as early as October, but they were left in peace, so as to get used to the place and eventually perhaps stay there the whole time. Lanes were cleared in the woods round the hunting-ground, so that when there was fresh snow it was easy to see whether any wolves had made their way to the carrion. The first drive usually took place in fresh snow just before Christmas.

The best planned types of hunting-ground could be "emptied" by a mere dozen men. This was an enormous improvement, compared with the number of working hours lost through the drives of former times. The drive was organised as follows: the open "ends" of the hunting-ground were quickly shut off with canvas, and sometimes nets too, after which the beaters advanced through the enclosed woodlands, to the accompaniment of a

(Above) Hunting-cloths from the 1830s in the Nordic Museum, Stockholm. (Left) Hunting-ground of a type frequently used in the first half of the nineteenth century. When the enclosure was to be cleared of wolves, the bottom end was shut off with nets and cloths. (Right) Diagram of von Greiff's hunting-ground. Nets were erected at the top end (A), while screens were placed at (B), behind which the guns stood. (C) and (D) were markers to keep the chain of beaters in line.

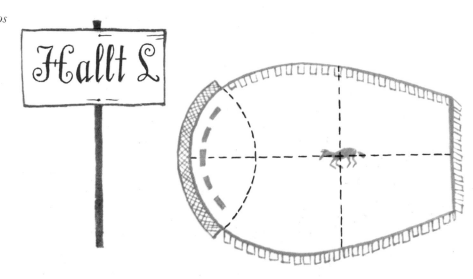

tumultuous noise of drums, shooting, hare-rattles and shouting. The wolves were usually frightened into running straight down the whole length of the hunting-ground and then rushing up a slightly inclined ramp, which led to a small, square enclosure surrounded by a high fence, where they were then easily captured. Great care was always taken never to kill the wolves in the hunting-ground, since if the animals were killed there, all future trapping in the area was believed to be out of the question.

At an earlier date, instead of the trapping-pen, firing-screens were often erected, from behind which the wolves were shot with ease as they were driven past.

An example of the further evolution of the hunting-ground is the wholly enclosed "wolf-pen" constructed by the famous royal gamekeeper, von Greiff. It worked on more or less the same principle as the hunting-ground described above. It was completely enclosed, however, by a log palisade. The logs were so placed that they sloped sharply inwards towards the pen. By putting out carrion at some distance from the wolf-pen and gradually moving it nearer and nearer, until it was finally placed inside the enclosure (naturally taking care the whole time not to disturb the animals), it was possible to lull their suspicions, so that in the last act they jumped over the sloping fence of their own free will, and were caught. Since the fence inclined sharply inwards, the wolves were unable to jump back again to freedom.

Old documents reveal that widely differing views might sometimes be held among wolf-hunting

experts as to which methods were the most profitable. A hunter such as von Greiff, who held progressive views for his day, made bitter remarks about the ignorant people, in his opinion, who at two sessions of parliament proposed that winter hunting at the carrion-sites should be replaced by old-fashioned summer hunts. The huge drives which the legendary Anders Schönberg arranged for Frederick I had, of course, produced enormous kills, but they cost a lot of money to run successfully. At the last of these summer drives, which the then ailing gamekeeper arranged for the King in the province of Värmland on September 1, 1737, five bears, three wolves, three lynxes, one fox and twelve elks were counted beside the royal screen after a day's shooting. *"We have today held a shoot and we shall never see its like again,"* the King declared with a sigh, when he afterwards thanked his devoted gamekeeper.

According to Greiff, hunts of this kind were out of date. He also considered that the summer drives were an extremely risky business, and often disastrous to growing crops through which the drive might have to pass.

Linnaeus's disciple, the zoologist and clergyman Samuel Ödmann (1750–1829), also had decided views on wolf-hunting. He maintained that neither the drives nor the wolf-pens nor the pitfalls were of any consequence in the extermination of wolves, in comparison with poisoned carrion, and in particular, "Baron Lieven's carrion sausages". B. W. von Lieven, hailed by Linnaeus as a man of great genius during the latter's journey in Skåne, carried out successful experiments with poison, which was put inside sausage-casings and then inserted at different places in the carcasses, which were placed out in the open. The Baron believed that this method had enabled him to wipe out all the wolves in Småland at the beginning of the eighteenth century, and in return for a small payment, he undertook to rid the whole country of wolves within a year in the same way! (See Notes.)

"To exterminate them (the wolves) is an aim beyond the realm of possibility, since our forests form a continuous belt of boundless woods and mountainous regions, from which these vermin descend yearly to settle down and breed," declared von Greiff in his notes in 1828. Little did he dream that less than 140 years later the wolf in Sweden was to be so rare that the authorities would have to protect it as a natural relic!

THE ROE DEER

In olden times, the roe deer was sparsely distributed in Europe in comparison with the position today. Relatively little space was devoted to it in early hunting literature and it occurs extremely seldom in the ornamentation of weapons or hunting accessories. Not even during the Stone Age does the roe deer appear to have succeeded to any real extent in inspiring artists.

It also seems to have been rare in ancient Greece and Rome, and the early naturalists dwell mainly on its culinary attractions.

The Arabian writer, Avicenna, points out enthusiastically that the meat of the roe deer is the most wholesome of all game.

A long search is necessary to find the roe deer in the art of the sixteenth and seventeenth centuries, and when it occurs with dead game in still-life pictures it is usually relegated to the company of hares, herons, ducks or small birds — an indication of the "social status" assigned to it. In many places the roe deer held an inferior position in the ranks of game, and those that managed to escape the attention of wolves and foxes were, indeed, often caught in the traps and snares of the common people.

In *The Hunting-Book of King Modus* a pivot-snare for roe deer is described as being suitable for use by "the poor man", when he wanted to catch a roe deer that had been causing damage. The *King Modus* also recommends roe-deer hunting for people who own neither a lot of land nor many hounds; the roe deer does not run as far as the red deer and does not require nearly as many hounds. In other words, an excellent quarry for the common man. All this went a long way towards keeping the roe-deer population at a low level, and any king who wanted venison for the table used to keep roe deer in a hunting-reserve, which was fenced in to protect the animals from beasts of prey and poachers.

Even early zoologists drew attention to the contradictory nature of the roe deer. Although gentle and graceful on the surface, it nevertheless often has an irascible temperament. The soft eyes of the roe deer may often be both hard and wild at close quarters. In *Der vollkommene Teutsche Jäger* (1749) Fleming, writing about the roe deer, says that it has "the characteristics of the goat but is violent by nature".

Similarly, people were surprised at this likable animal's terrible cry of alarm; it is a cry that truly makes the blood of experienced woodland wanderers run cold in their veins. The question of when the roe deer's rutting season took place was the subject of lively discussion far into the mid-nineteenth century, when scientists managed to prove that it occurred as early as the late summer.

It is natural that this paradoxical and mysterious animal came to play a considerable role in folk-medicine, and that most parts of its body were also believed to possess magical properties — not least of an erotic nature.

Since olden times, the roe deer has in fact occupied a curious and intermediate position in

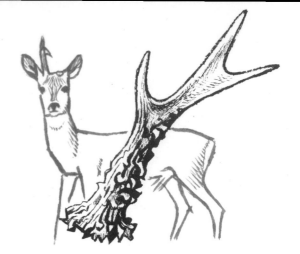

The roe deer and the red deer were game reserved for the king and the privileged classes in the Middle Ages. Anyone finding a discarded antler, however, was allowed to keep it; but Olaus Magnus points out that "it is nonetheless easier to find discarded antlers than to see a hind calve or the wild ass bray in the salt desert". The antler was used in folk-medicine and fetched a fairly good price.

European hunting. On the Continent it has been assigned a place at the bottom of the ladder, or possibly half-way up, while already in the oldest Scandinavian provincial statutes it was referred to as "the king's animal", and thus belonged to the group of blue-blooded game.

In all probability, the reason why the roe deer's rating varied was simply that stag-hunting played such a predominant role in the sport of the privileged classes on the Continent, while the small numbers of red deer in Scandinavia increased the roe deer's status, both at royal banquets and for hunting in northern Europe.

The Vasa kings were very keen that the decrees relating to the roe deer in the old statutes should remain in force. Gustavus Vasa, for example, personally, and in threatening terms, warned his governor at Stegeborg to eat beef instead of venison, if he wished to remain in the King's favour.

According to the provincial statutes of Västmanna, the hunter escaped reprimand, however, if a roe deer was caught by mistake in a wolf-net during a drive — but otherwise the right to hunt with nets was exclusively a royal prerogative in Sweden.

Olaus Magnus (1555) points out that the hunting of roe deer (and red deer) was permissible for the privileged classes alone, but that anyone happening to find a discarded antler was allowed to keep it.

It was with the rapid decline of predatory animals and the end of feudal hunting-privileges during the first half of the nineteenth century that the hunting of roe deer came into its own. The roe deer is "the blue-blooded game of democracy", as a writer on hunting once put it.

As far as Sweden is concerned, the roe deer's position in the early nineteenth century was most serious. The abundance of wolves, as well as unrestricted hunting, had practically exterminated the roe deer in most of Sweden. If the latter so much as showed itself, it was immediately subjected to furious persecution by anyone who could fire a gun.

By about 1830, the Swedish roe-deer population had dwindled to a small number of animals on two or three of the large estates in Skåne. It is no exaggeration to say that it was Count Corfitz Beck-Friis of Börringe who saved the Swedish roe deer from complete extermination.

He appealed to his hunting neighbours to limit their roe-deer hunting for a few years. As a result, the species increased and began to spread northwards, re-establishing itself in its former range! In the course of the last few decades, the roe deer has extended its range further north, so that it is occasionally met far up in Norrland, where it seldom survives the snowiest winters, however, without the assistance of human beings.

For many centuries, the most widespread method of hunting roe deer was to chase them into nets. Medium-sized greyhounds, also used for fox-

Stalking roe deer was not one of the most reputable forms of hunting in the Middle Ages, when the roe deer did not usually rank very high as game. In addition, it was a fairly uncommon species and played an unusually modest role in the history of hunting. These three crossbowmen stalking a roe deer are a detail from an illustration in The Hunting-Book of King Modus.

hunting, were employed for this purpose. Stalking and the use of calls to lure the roe deer within range have also been popular methods, and were recommended already in the mediaeval handbooks.

During the rut, the roebuck is completely dominated by its violent passions and is easily decoyed within range, whether the gun prefers to whistle softly and seductively like a goat — probably the commonest method — or whether he amuses himself by challenging the buck with hoarse and angry howls of defiance. In the latter case, it is not unusual for the infuriated buck to charge through the undergrowth straight at the suspected rival, with the intention of running its antlers through his body!

In former times, when roe deer were lured within gunshot, there was a large selection of calls available for the sportsman. The most convincing effect, however, was obtained by the gun using a leaf held in his hands — as a matter of fact, in Germany this form of hunting, "*blatten*", got its name from the leaf. The method survives in Germany and Denmark, where bucks are still hunted in the summer.

In Switzerland, roe deer were hunted so much that already in the early nineteenth century, as in Scandinavia, they were in danger of disappearing completely. Rordorf, who gives us a very detailed description of hunting conditions in Switzerland in the late eighteenth and early nineteenth centuries, maintained that the roe deer had been driven away by hunters with harriers. He describes in grim detail how powerful dogs were used for roe-deer coursing on crust-snow — the most efficient and most usual form of hunting this game in Switzerland. Rordorf does not hesitate to mention that he himself managed to shoot five roe deer in an hour on one occasion.

"A profitable but deplorable shoot," Rordorf sums up.

In view of such a state of affairs, it was really not so strange that the roe deer became increasingly rare in the Swiss Alpine valleys.

The unstable political climate in central Europe during the first half of the nineteenth century also

had a considerable effect on hunting and game. The forests that had once been the property of the electoral princes were now state-owned, and from a forester's point of view, were in an extremely bad condition. An immense effort was put in hand to make them economically profitable. Large areas of the ancient "Hercynian forest", mentioned already by the writers of antiquity, were transformed into an extremely valuable source of timber. Country that was formerly covered with beech and other deciduous trees underwent a change and rapidly became darker in colour, thanks to quick-growing pine and spruce plantations.

Forestry became an important science, and as a result of these efforts inspired by economic considerations, game began to feel the squeeze — above all, of course, deer, which were thought to damage the valuable plantations.

As far as Germany is concerned, the 1848 Revolution is regarded as a black year in the history of hunting in that country. Private hunting privileges were abolished and common hunting rights became more or less unlimited. Destructive and indiscriminate shooting of anything that stirred in the countryside was the result, both in Germany and in other countries where, in the fair name of democracy, game ceased to be protected by law.

In view of this, it was most regrettable that the roe deer should have been given the honorary epithet of "the blue-blooded game of democracy".

Unrestricted shooting and the quick-firing fowling piece caused a substantial decline in the size of black-grouse displays, already in the early nineteenth century.

THE BLACK GROUSE

It is often difficult to obtain an idea of the abundance of game in the past merely on the basis of records of shoots or of more general estimates. This is particularly true of woodland birds which in the good old days occurred in numbers that we find difficult to believe as the state of affairs today is so radically different. These birds were especially numerous in northern regions of Europe where still at the end of the last century flocks of up to two hundred cock capercailzies might be seen alighting in the snow-covered pines in forest bogs in the winter or where flocks of black grouse might be flushed on the moors "so that there was a sound as of thunder in the air", according to contemporary witnesses.

In the Scandinavian countries the black grouse was in fact the most important game bird from an economic point of view and according to John Fischerström, a leading economist of the Age of Enlightenment, about 80,000 black grouse were sold in Stockholm in 1760 and an estimated 200,000 were sent to other parts of Sweden. In good black grouse country — for example, in the

province of Västergötland and south-west Småland — two or three hunters with pointers had no real difficulty in shooting a hundred black grouse a day in the early nineteenth century.

The term "black grouse year" is used of years when woodland game birds were particularly plentiful — and when, of course, prices for the game sank to a disastrously low level. The beginning of a disturbing decline in the black grouse population in some parts of Sweden in the early nineteenth century was unfortunately, however, not a temporary decrease but the consequence of unrestricted and ruthless hunting. This resulted above all in a drop in the numbers of birds at the display grounds where indeed the greatest amount of damage was done, thanks to a time-honoured method of hunting.

While a capercailzie shoot at the display grounds was a typical example of stalking, shooting black grouse during the birds' courtship was, on the other hand, very much a matter of lying in ambush, normally in a hide constructed in advance close to the display grounds. Even in the excitement of its courtship, the black grouse remains on the alert and always makes sure that there is an escape route

Catching black grouse with the use of a pole-net and lantern dates back to the Middle Ages in Scandinavia. The "snowed-in" black grouse were not so difficult to find, if one looked for the slight depressions in the snow caused by the body-heat of the black grouse.

open — according to an old German proverb, it has "an eye in every feather".

In the winter, black grouse congregate in flocks and perch in birch trees to eat the leaf buds. The sight of a flock of these heavy and beautifully shaped birds grouped like large fruit in a birch white with hoar frost is one of the most magnificent spectacles offered by Scandinavian birdlife. It was indeed in the winter that a very important type of black grouse shooting took place when the birds were decoyed with the aid of painted wooden dummies, some more convincing than others, which were fixed to poles in a suitable birch within easy range. It was essential to turn the dummy's head *into* the wind. Experience had shown that the best time for this sport was in the late autumn in central and southern districts of Scandinavia and when in the early nineteenth century everyone began to get hold of good fowling pieces, shooting with the aid of decoys caused sheer havoc in many areas of the country. A solitary gun was often able to account for a score of black grouse in the course of a morning. In the neighbourhood of some Swedish provincial towns it became nothing but a popular craze to put dummy grouse in the trees and, of course, the black grouse population quickly began to decline in an alarming manner.

Further north, people went in for trapping more than shooting and it is surely not too rash to assume that the majority of the black grouse mentioned in the official figures quoted at the beginning of this chapter were indeed caught in traps. In the autumn, entire broods of black grouse could be caught in a very simple and efficient manner by means of erecting a series of simple

Some dummies were very lifelike — they were placed in birches for winter shooting. At the display-grounds it was often sufficient to use a ball of moss and a pine-twig as a head. (Above) Blackcock snaring device based on W. von Wright's instructions.

stick nets and then decoying the young birds by imitating the mother bird's call. Naturally, the best way was to start by catching the hen bird, the greyhen, and let her personally decoy her young to destruction. If a trapper unexpectedly happened to be interested in game preservation, he might release the greyhen and two or three of the chicks so as to ensure the continuation of the species.

Of course, people in Scandinavia experimented with several methods of catching black grouse in self-operative traps, two of the more common types of which are mentioned here. The "blackcock basket" was predominantly north-eastern European in its distribution, while the simple, but apparently very efficient, blackcock "bännan"* was a general Scandinavian method.

Nocturnal expeditions with a pole-net to catch black grouse were purely mediaeval in origin. This method was based on the black grouse's habit of burying itself in the snow and spending the night in a drift. Formerly, the black grouse was believed to allow falling snow to cover it but now we know that the bird plunges into a drift from its perch in a tree and then burrows further down into the snow. The hunter, after first finding out in good time where the black grouse were usually to be found, set out with the large pole-net and an assistant carrying a lantern. The experienced hunter immediately spotted the grouse's roost, thanks to small depressions having been formed in the snow as a result of a *drop* in the level of the snow above the warm-blooded birds. The pole-net was swiftly pressed down hard over the sleeping grouse and it was important not to let them flap about in the net and wake up the rest of the flock that might possibly be asleep in the vicinity.

This is a very ancient method of catching black grouse and is already mentioned by Olaus Magnus (1555).

* Translator's note: Cf. English "bane" — "ruin", "destruction".

The "blackcock basket" is of east European origin. It was made of long poles with a bunch of spruce-twigs in the middle. A loose wooden perch was balanced across the basket. The idea was to decoy the black grouse on to the perch, which then tipped up, precipitating the bird into the basket. The spruce-branches prevented the blackcock from escaping from the basket. (After Wright.)

THE HAZEL HEN

In northern Europe the hazel hen is so inseparably associated with its environment that one may talk about a hazel hen wood. An experienced wanderer in the woods can tell at a glance whether there are any hazel hens in a particular wood, but it is more difficult to define what is characteristic of the habitat. Preferably there should be damp woodland marshes nearby, a mixture of birches, alders and dense spruces, and preferably also an abundance of moss on the ground and of lichens on the trees; in other words, rough wooded country. When one has become familiar with the habits of these small chicken-like birds, one also recognises their behaviour, and it is possible to tell, at a distance, whether it was a hazel hen that flew out of the spruce thicket. The noisy take-off, and the brief flight, reveal the identity of the bird. The hazel hen is the most reluctant flier of the woodland members of the grouse family. It is fond of settling close to the trunk of some spruce very near the spot where it was flushed. But at the same time it is very wary, and often goes on flitting from branch to branch behind the tree-trunk, so that it remains hidden the whole time, until the danger has passed.

It is described as the most widespread of the woodland grouses in Eurasia, and it is represented by different races over the whole of Europe, with the exception of Denmark, the British Isles and the southern Balkans. It is essentially a bird of the north-east in its distribution. On the Continent, its plumage is predominantly nut-brown in colour, but in northern Europe it has the greyish hues of reindeer lichen, and is mainly found in northern parts of this region, with its southern limits more or less along the river Dal in central Sweden. There are, however, many areas containing hazel hens south of this line. The hazel hens I am most familiar with are in the east of the province of Uppland

The hazel hen gives dogs a very wide berth, so one cannot use barking dogs or gun-dogs for a hazel-hen shoot, as is the practice when shooting other woodland game-birds. Below: The colour of the hazel hen varies from one part of its range to the other. (Left to right) Siberian, Scandinavian, West-European. The fowling-piece is of French manufacture, 1730s. A flint-lock and two revolving barrels. (Musée de Saint-Etienne.)

where Linnaeus himself noted that there was a "small district" with these birds.

The hazel hen's relative lack of shyness has been its undoing. It is fairly easy to decoy with the aid of a hazel hen call, and this is indeed the method of hunting which has been the most popular all over Europe. When it hears the hazel hen call, the cock gets very excited and amorous. The Austrian hazel hen expert, Frans Valentinitsch, mentions, in his book, cases of these birds alighting on the muzzle of the hunter's gun while he was using the decoy call. The peasant hunters of Norrland normally made their hazel hen call from the wing-bone of a black grouse, but there are also excellent factory-made instruments in existence. Formerly, experienced hunters used one call for the hen birds and another for the cocks, maintaining that a very different technique was used in each case. The cock usually flies eagerly towards the calling hunter while the hen, according to the Finnish hunter and artist, Wilhelm von Wright, "is more reserved and needs coaxing before she answers, and practically never approaches the bird calling to her, but waits for him".

In contrast with other wood grouse, the hazel hen cannot be hunted with tree-barkers, for it detests dogs. Besides, dogs are absolutely superfluous since the hazel hen readily trees at the sight of the hunter. Well-trained dogs quickly get to know the hazel

In contrast to the other woodland game-birds, the hazel hen is monogamous and no display occurs. It is easily decoyed with a call.

hen's habits, however, and quietly indicate to their master where they have found the bird! It was a well-known fact that one could take one's time and shoot all the hazel hens in a tree, as long as one remembered to start with the bird perched on the lowest branches!

Albertus Magnus (1193–1280) — one of the first Swedish writers on hunting — provided the inspiration for the second half of the hazel hen's present Latin name *bonasia* by christening it *bonasa* (bona asa = good roast); but already in classical times authorities such as Horace and Martial praised the hazel hen as a wonderful delicacy.

Export figures also show very clearly that the hazel hen was in great demand for the table. In Russia alone, six million hazel hens were sent to market each year just before the First World War. It is on record that, at the end of the eighteenth century, 60,000 hazel hens were sent to Stockholm alone, while 40,000 were distributed to the rest of the kingdom. Sometimes as many as 300 hazel hens were shot, during a normal season, on a Norrland woodland estate with enthusiastic hunters.

The general popularity of the hazel hen was perhaps, one reason why the value of game birds in Norrland was calculated according to the so-called "hazel hen system", under which the bird became a kind of standard currency. For instance, two capercailzies were the equivalent of six hazel hens, two black grouse corresponded to four hazel hens; while willow grouse and ptarmigans were considered to be equal in value to the hazel hen.

In exceptionally good bird years, however, prices were disastrously low; there was quite simply a slump, and the hunter of forest birds had to be pleased if a dried fig was considered equal to the value of a hazel hen. We are told that during the great years for forest birds in the mid-eighteenth century, people were sick to death of eating wildfowl, and whole cartloads of hazel hens and black grouse remained unsold in the markets.

To give an idea of the enormous quantities of game which were sent south from Norrland, that area so abundant in bird life, it may be mentioned that from Sundsvall alone — the clearing station for birds shot in central Norrland — 15,894 hazel hens, 3,053 capercailzies, 3,038 black grouse, and 548 ptarmigans were shipped to Stockholm in 1749.

The strange pairing behaviour of the hazel hen baffled hunters and naturalists for a long time. In contrast to the other members of the woodland grouse family, the hazel hen is strictly monogamous. A partner is chosen, without much ceremony in the autumn, while the mating in April takes place without any collective display. The cock uses its twittering note to call to the hen — which, as already mentioned, the hunter can easily imitate; and if it sometimes happens that a cock hazel hen actually makes an attempt at fighting a rival, it is done with the observance of the same unassuming rules as in the case of cock ptarmigans. The hazel hen runs along with its wings drooping by its side, and its tail partially spread out. That is, more or less, all that happens. (See Notes.)

195

(Above) Ptarmigan shooting began in earnest with the completion of the railways in the northern Swedish province of Norrland.

THE PTARMIGAN AND THE GROUSE

Ptarmigan shooting is a relatively young sport. It really began only when the railways opened up the previously very inaccessible ptarmigan areas in northern Scandinavia and the British Isles.

Earlier, only the most enthusiastic bird hunters — above all, Englishmen — had taken the trouble to hunt ptarmigans, and it was indeed looked on as an almost heroic sporting achievement at the beginning of the nineteenth century. Which, indeed, it was, if one considers the conditions prevailing at the time.

Nevertheless, it sometimes happened that enthusiastic Britons, perhaps spurred on by Llewellyn Lloyd's glowing description, went off to Sweden or Norway and hired horses and carriages from inns to take them into the heart of the Scandinavian mountains in order to shoot ptarmigan in the early autumn. The transport was perhaps reminiscent of mediaeval times, the food miserable, and conditions as a whole very different from those of the Bachelor's Club; but the result of the expedition made up for all the inconveniences with which the gentlemen had to contend.

Ptarmigan shooting in the mountains meant pure air, fantastic views, brilliant autumn colours and an unparalleled abundance of game birds — at least in good ptarmigan years.

Indeed, the ptarmigan, in autumn, is as colourful as the foliage. Its plumage has borrowed its colouring from the low shrubs and lichens on the ground, its wings are as white as the patches of snow on the north sides of the ravines, and the red wattle over its eye bleams like cranberries in bogs.

Different kinds of ptarmigan-snare. (Right) A "ptarmigan hedge", with a series of snares concealed in dense dwarf-birch shrubs.
(Left) The trappers of Norrland carried their ptarmigan-snares on a plain wooden hook. (The Nordic Museum, Stockholm.)

An indication of the small number of people who hunted ptarmigan, as recently as the mid-nineteenth century, is given by the fact that there was still, at that time, a lively discussion as to whether it was possible to use a partridge dog for ptarmigan shooting. There were many who believed that the bird of the wilds would not squat long enough at the approach of a dog for the hunter to have a chance of firing a shot!

With the advent of the railways, and modern fowling pieces, ptarmigan shooting rapidly became popular among amateur hunters, and in some years quite big bags were obtained. This was partly due to the ptarmigan brood's habit of flying away from a dog in small groups, and at such long intervals that the hunter had plenty of time to pick off several birds in one place.

For centuries, ptarmigan trapping has been of great economic importance for the mountain people of Scandinavia. The ptarmigan's snow-white winter plumage and habit of burying itself in the snow fascinated the old naturalists more than anything else. Olaus Magnus describes, most poetically, how the snow-white birds hide in the snow and then "fly up into the tops of the snow-covered trees, which nature seems very kindly to have put there solely for their pleasure".

As a matter of fact, ptarmigans are trapped only in the winter, and it is not unusual for one trapper to put out some five or six hundred snares. Emptying them is a full day's work.

In the periodical "ptarmigan years" catches were sometimes enormous. In 1866, no less than 30,000 ptarmigans from the three northernmost parishes of Lapland were sold at the January market in Lyngen in Norway. This figure refers to the birds caught during the first part of the winter. Without doubt, at least as many must have been eaten or salted down at home or exported to other places!

The commonest, and most efficient, way of catching ptarmigan was by the use of snares, whole series of which were sometimes put out. Openings were made in the low undergrowth, by the snares. Trapping began when the snow had reached a depth of three feet or so, and the snares were attached to a stick which was driven into the snow — these sticks were not planted in the ground, as that made it easy for the ptarmigan to tear off the snare and escape.

In the spring, when the cock ptarmigans started their courtship displays, they were often caught by the use of snares and calls — it is unfortunate, for the ptarmigan, that it is bold and inquisitive by nature, and happily rushes right up to the trapper, who is completely exposed to view. The latter can calmly see to his catch, while new and angry cocks appear continuously, to be enticed into the traps.

The red grouse is found in Britain and Ireland. It is distinguished from the Arctic species by its predominantly dark rufous-brown plumage. This member of the grouse family, too, became popular as game only with the advent of the railways and improved fowling pieces. Then, however, great was the interest aroused.

Landowners in Ireland and in the Scottish highlands suddenly discovered, to their astonishment, that their barren moors were worth a lot of money, and wealthy hunters turned up with guns and bird dogs in superb trim. They also discovered that it was considerably more profitable to let the undulating moorlands for grouse shooting than for sheep-grazing — which, in its turn, led not only to the decline of sheep-farming, but also to a game preservation problem of a characteristic kind!

In short, matters developed, more or less, in the following way.

Since olden times the shepherds had been in the habit of burning bushes and copses in order to improve grazing facilities, but the hunters, who considered that this was harmful to the grouse, tried to prevent it, partly by renting large stretches of country, and partly by bringing about a ban on burning.

The landowners, who had realised the value of a good stock of grouse, complied with the hunters' wishes, as far as possible, and they also began to make sure that the grouse throve and increased to the best of their ability. As part of these praiseworthy efforts, food began to be put out for them in the winter, and all conceivable enemies among the animals and birds were pursued and exterminated as energetically as possible.

Naturally, the effect of all this was tremendous. On the surface, at least. The red grouse increased at a colossal rate for some years but difficulties soon cropped up. To begin with, when the moors were no longer burned, bushes began to grow again and

Grouse shooting with pointers in England, in the early nineteenth century. Pack-horses were taken along to transport the kill, which was at times enormous.

this meant less food for the grouse. They throve better in sheep pastures which were looked after according to the old methods.

In addition, as a result of various ailments and disastrous epizootic diseases, the grouse began to die off like flies. The Grouse Disease Committee was appointed in order to remedy these unexpected setbacks. After long deliberation it recommended a temporary ban on shooting, so as to enable the species to recover.

The idea in itself was a good one but the basic reasons for the decline of the grouse lay deeper than that. The increase in numbers had taken place by artificial means, and the lack of natural predators meant also that the natural balance had been seriously disturbed. Sick or inferior specimens passed on the infection, or the susceptibility to it, and this led to a gradual weakening of the species.

Modern ecology has provided us with many examples of how extremely sensitive this balancing act, between predatory animals and their prey, is to disturbances, but the Grouse Disease Committee may perhaps be forgiven for not realising this fact at the end of the nineteenth century.

Since those days a more sensible type of game preservation has resulted in really impressive numbers of grouse, and the bags with which certain experienced grouse shooters have been credited recall the two princes John George of Saxony and other mighty hunters in the seventeenth and eighteenth centuries. (See Notes.)

On the whole, the grouse may be regarded as a good illustration of how the hunter and the gamekeeper are able to influence the living conditions and prospects of a species of animal. Not least, the story of the grouse is also a useful reminder of the necessity of establishing a carefully thought-out balance between game and those who take their toll of it.

III

THE HARE

The hare was the finest species of game in the opinion of the ancient Greeks and Romans, if we are to believe an old Latin proverb. Indeed, hare hunting was a sport which was pursued with great zeal by rich and poor alike. The section on hunting in classical times includes a detailed description of the use of nets and hounds, which was certainly the most usual method of hunting hares. This method survived in fact a very long time and was practised regularly in central Europe far into the eighteenth century.

The main reason for the hare being so popular in classical times was that it was highly esteemed from the purely culinary point of view and also as an old wives' cure for illnesses. Its flesh was considered to be the most delicious of all game and in addition it was believed to possess a great number of interesting magic properties of the most varied kinds.

By eating hare regularly it was believed that one's looks could be considerably improved. To quote a court poet writing about a Roman emperor who was obviously in great need of this kind of beauty treatment:

"Happy the emperor so debonair
Who every day eats the flesh of hare."

It was also a popular pastime to hunt hares on horseback and with greyhounds. On those occasions the hunt usually ended with the dogs killing the hare before the hunter arrived. The author of an eighteenth-century German hunting book recommends hunting at force only in country with a sparse hare population, since, otherwise, the many different scents might easily disperse or irritate the dogs. At least it shows that this method of hunting hares continued for a very long time.

It is, of course, difficult to give a definite answer as to whether the apparent decrease in the size of the hare population already in the Middle Ages, at least in certain parts of Europe, was due to its popularity as game. Nevertheless, strict regulations were introduced at a very early date in order to improve the situation. For example, it was with threats of severe penalties that the emperor Ferdinand II forbade hunters to release more than two greyhounds to chase a hare. It was also forbidden to dig out a hare which in some way or other had succeeded in going underground.

Obviously, already in those days the hare was fairly uncommon on the Continent. This impression is reinforced by descriptions of royal banquets in the sixteenth century when the guests devoured all conceivable kinds of luxury food. The hare, however, was always the rarest type of game on these occasions.

During the course of a week-long drive in Italy, apart from 208 wild boars, 740 snipe and 960 duck, only five hares were bagged! These are rather telling figures!

Hare hunting did not rank very high as a status symbol. It is true that the upper strata of society hunted it, but, as a rule, it was lawful game for the common people. Above all, it was one of the animals caught in traps. As might be expected, scenes of hare hunting are among the rarest types of decoration on ancient de luxe weapons. Nevertheless,

princes showed a lively, although somewhat depraved, interest in the hare when it might prove a welcome addition to a collection of oddities! Much has been written about Siamese hare twins, horned hares and other deformed or fanciful creatures clothed in hare skin which distinguished hunters proudly added to their trophies.

The mysterious horned hares were particularly welcome hunting trophies. They were believed to exist mainly in Saxony, not surprisingly, as this was the kingdom of the hunting-mad princes John George I and II.

These horned hares were clever fakes with roe deer horns mounted on the skulls of hares. They were to be found in every self-respecting curiosity collection in Europe and were the subject of "scientific" descriptions by leading zoologists until the eighteenth century. As recently as the beginning of the nineteenth century, that excellent writer on hunting matters, von Wildungen, wrote a long report on the subject, in order to put an end to the superstition once and for all.

Of the two European species of hares, the brown hare was hunted most. In Switzerland where both kinds were originally found, the blue hare was regarded as an inferior species of game. Its market price was two-thirds less. According to Rordorf, the blue hare was only shot occasionally, for example, in conjunction with marmot hunting.

In contrast, the blue hare was greatly prized as game in the northern parts of its range in Europe — where the brown hare was introduced and spread as recently as the end of the nineteenth century. This popularity was originally due above all to the blue hare's fur, since the meat was despised as food in many places. The oldest Swedish mediaeval laws included the hare among the fur-bearing animals and in the seventeenth century a hare pelt was the equivalent of two squirrel pelts.

In both northern and southern Sweden the hare was believed to bring good luck and, consequently, there were many places where it was not killed. As a matter of fact, scarcely any other animal has played as great a role as the hare in the folk-lore and magic of olden times.

Hunting with beagles on fresh snow is an old Scandinavian method and it is still the most popular — it has been described in so many other works by hunters experienced in the use of beagles, so I shall refrain from dealing with this method here. A number of other kinds of hunting have existed and these, on the other hand, may be less familiar.

To quote one example, stalking with a muzzle-loader was a rewarding method in Norrland. It was practised above all in the autumn when the hare had already got its winter coat and there was as yet no snow on the ground.

It was also possible to take advantage of the white hare's handicap in other ways. There is, for instance, the story about the legendary bear hunter, Herman Falk, from the province of Värmland in western Sweden who used to organise big drives to hunt winter hares just before the first fall of snow. On these occasions, the chain of beaters was led by an old soldier. The latter beat a huge drum and was accompanied with great enthusiasm by hunting horns, hare rattles, gun shots and a lot of noise from the other participants. If bear hunting was a public duty for Falk, then hare hunting was perhaps the type of hunting he enjoyed most!

In the case of some hunters, hare hunting developed into a serious passion and there are actually instances of old and decrepit hunters having arranged grotesque hare hunts in the huge attics of their manor houses!

In Norrland where, by all accounts, the blue hare formerly occurred in large numbers, hunting was conducted for a long time on a fairly modest scale. This was perhaps partly due to the primitive and unsatisfactory weapons available.

Hunting with beagles was long regarded as a pastime reserved for amateur hunters, and it was

On the continent, the species hunted was the brown hare. It was not until the end of the nineteenth century that it was introduced into Scandinavia.

really only when shot guns came into more general use that the interest in hunting with beagles was aroused. For obvious reasons, however, this method was only feasible in farming country where open fields provided an overall view of the hunt and where there were plenty of opportunities for lying in wait for the quarry.

Shooting from behind window shutters was one of the strange types of hare hunting. This was above all practised in the days when the herdsman's huts were a normal feature of the forests and it was probably more a way of passing the time than a regular form of hunting.

People seized their opportunity during the light nights in the summer when the hares ran out into the pastures round the huts to feast on clover and timothy.

As far as the hare is concerned, trapping, however, played a much more important role than hunting.

On the continent, hunting and trapping were combined so that dogs were used to drive the hares into nets. Another method of beating was to move across cornfields with long ropes to which were

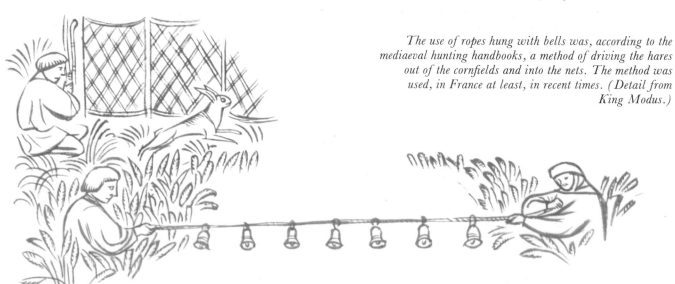

The use of ropes hung with bells was, according to the mediaeval hunting handbooks, a method of driving the hares out of the cornfields and into the nets. The method was used, in France at least, in recent times. (Detail from King Modus.)

attached a large number of small bells. This latter method was employed in ancient Greece and Rome and apparently still exists in regions of central Europe where fields are relatively small and where, besides, farmers are afraid of damaging the growing crops.

Snaring was by far the most common technique of trapping. This method appears to have been used in every period of history and in every part of the world.

In Sweden, the snares were made in a variety of ways, but as a rule they were attached to a stick which, if the worst came to the worst, the hare would drag only a short distance through undergrowth before it got stuck for good. Usually this simple arrangement was considered sufficient, but of course the trappers often experimented with various improvements. One example of the latter was "hare-scaring". This was done simply by stretching a piece of thin wire or horsehair across a frequently used hare track and only a few yards in front of the snare.

Hare-scaring was based on the well-known fact that a hare might often hesitate a few seconds and look mistrustfully at the changes occasioned by the setting of the snare. The wire was placed at this psychological distance from the trap. Experience had shown that as soon as the hare felt the wire tighten against its fur, it went wild and rushed headlong into destruction.

It is true that hares have been snared since classical times, but according to authorities such as Gjessing the *deadfall* was a considerably older item of trapping equipment in Scandinavia. Deadfalls for hares were constructed in the same way as those for woodland birds (see chapter on the capercailzie) but they were baited with slender aspen and willow

twigs which were placed on either side of the trigger wires. The deadfalls were often placed near the openings of the close picket fences of olden days.

Through the centuries, the hare's reputation as game has varied, but when, however, the hunting privileges of the nobility began to die out here and there in Europe and hunting became more democratic, interest in the hare came to be shared by all classes of society. Another reason for this was, of course, the advent of improved fire-arms which facilitated rapid and accurate shots at fleeing game. As a matter of fact, this change of attitude is not only noticeable in hare hunting; it also affected many other kinds of small animals which already in the Middle Ages were mainly classified as game suitable for the poor.

The fairly rapid rise in the status of game that fell outside both the category of royal game and the intermediate group was, however, to some extent intimately connected with the new approach to nature, whose chief prophet was Rousseau. Before his appearance on the scene, the hunt in the view of the great majority of the hunting gentry was merely a splendid spectacle or a stimulating sporting feat. Now, suddenly, there awoke an interest in nature for nature's sake.

The stealthy stalking and outwitting of an animal with the aid of knowledge and experience of its habits and biology was no longer an occupation suitable only for stalkers and peasant hunters. On the contrary, it now became a popular pastime for the aristocracy who had begun to realise the joys of simple rustic life. This fact must be borne in mind when we study the noticeable change in the attitude towards the hunting of hares and other small game.

"Hare-scaring" is an old trick used in Norrland. The idea was to frighten the hare so that it rushed blindly into the snare hung across a hare crossing point. (After Widén.)

The squirrel deadfall was placed on the south side of the tree and was baited with a piece of dried fungus, which was particularly tempting in the late winter when the squirrel's own food store was coming to an end.

THE SQUIRREL

The squirrel became a protected animal in the mediaeval laws, which shows that it was highly valued as game, primarily for its fur. It was also an amazingly popular food item all over Europe — in spite of its meat having, by all accounts, a sweet taste.

In some of the Nordic provincial laws it was a punishable offence to trap or hunt the squirrel before All Saints' Day (November 1st). As a matter of fact, the squirrel had usually got its winter coat by this date, and consequently was at its best as game. The hunting season ended automatically when the summer coat began to grow, with the approach of spring.

The demand for squirrel fur was the main reason for hunting this animal. The skins were used for a variety of purposes but were particularly popular as material for underclothes in the days when cotton-yarn was unknown. As recently as the seventeenth century, there are records of squirrel fur being supplied to the Court in Stockholm for making "Her Majesty the Queen's Nightgown".

"The further north the better the fur", ran an old proverb and it was indeed from the northernmost parts of Scandinavia and Siberia that the dearest furs came. In order to supply the needs of the courts and the privileged classes, compulsory contributions of furs were introduced in the Swedish province of Norrland. Squirrel furs were an important item in these contributions, which were counted in "timmers". A "timmer" was the equivalent of forty pelts. A large portion of the Scandinavian squirrel furs were exported to the Continent via Lübeck.

A lot of evidence suggests that the squirrel was found in considerably larger numbers in former times. Olaus Magnus, who had travelled far and wide in Scandinavia, tells us that squirrels "abound everywhere in the trees, just as densely as a shoal of fish in the sea". It should not, therefore, have been difficult for a tolerably capable man to cope with the fur contributions in those days.

The hunting and trapping methods varied considerably. What might be termed "shooting while you walk" was, and still is, one of the commonest methods in northern Europe. As recently as the 1940s I met people, living in the woodlands of central Norrland, who spent their entire time in the winter shooting squirrels. In their opinion, a dozen squirrels or so a day was a fairly normal bag in good squirrel years.

If a squirrel got stuck in a tree when it was shot, the tree was immediately chopped down. This was the normal procedure until late in the nineteenth century. A squirrel's fur was regarded as being a good deal more valuable than a pine tree! It frequently happened that a squirrel had been tracked to its nesting-hole which, despite any amount of persuasion, it refused to leave. Sometimes a shot was then fired straight through the

In Norrland, a good squirrel dog received the same rating in a person's last will and testament as a good milking cow. Already in the mediaeval provincial laws, fines were imposed for stealing or killing a squirrel. (In the background) Squirrel arrow with blunt head from Lule Lapp District. (The Nordic Museum, Stockholm.)

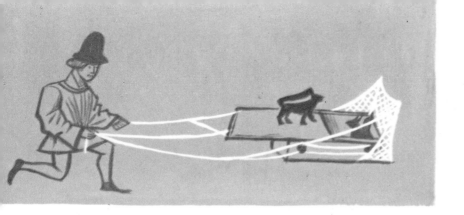

In the Middle Ages, the squirrel was not only much in demand as a fur-bearing animal; it was also a very popular dish on the dinner table. Numerous kinds of trapping methods were used. The picture above shows an ingenious trap which is recommended in The Hunting-Book of King Modus *from the fifteenth century.*

nest or the nesting-tree was felled. Experienced squirrel hunters knew, however, that the best trick was to creep, very cautiously, up to the nesting-tree, and scratch on the bark. In areas abundant in pine martens, the squirrel immediately took the noise as a sign that its arch-enemy was approaching, and left the danger area as fast as it could go.

It was very important to avoid damaging its fur when shooting a squirrel. It was preferable for the bullet to enter its head. In Norrland they clung stubbornly to the muzzle-loaders for a long time and, even towards the end of the nineteenth century, people in some areas — particularly in Finland — stuck to the crossbow, which was loaded with special squirrel bolts. These bolts had a blunt, not pointed, end. The squirrel was simply *knocked* down from the tree, and that meant a completely un-damaged fur. As far as Europe is concerned, shooting squirrels with a crossbow was the last use of this ancient weapon.

The bolts were very well made and, in order not to lose them when they missed their target, which happened very easily even in the case of a skilled shot, a trained "bolt servant" was employed. His duty was to keep an eye on the bolt and retrieve it for the hunter. An Italian, by the name of Acerbi, who made a famous journey through the Scandi-navian countries, studied squirrel shooting in detail. He was fascinated by the fact that, when the hunters took aim, they placed the butt of the cross-bow not against their cheeks, but against their midriffs — with good results.

A good dog was also required for squirrel hunts. Its task was to find the squirrels which had been knocked more or less unconscious by the blunt bolts. Good squirrel dogs were considered to be extremely valuable and there are records of wills rating a dog of this kind as high as a milking cow. Already in the mediaeval provincial laws, fairly heavy fines were imposed for stealing or killing squirrel dogs.

A strange hunting weapon was the long spiked pole which was used to seize squirrels that had been cut off in the upper branches of a solitary tree. According to an eighteenth-century account, it was used in the far north of Finland.

A slender birch rod, with a few twigs still attached, was a somewhat more humane equivalent of the spiked pole. It was possible, with the aid of this rod, to reach squirrels which had been chased up an isolated tree. All the hunter had to do was to twirl the rod about the squirrel so that the latter's long-haired tail got entangled in the twigs at the top of the rod. A quick flick of the rod then brought the animal tumbling to the ground.

There were many ways of catching squirrels.

The main method in Norrland was, perhaps, the use of squirrel deadfalls. These traps were placed on the south side of pine-trees and were baited with a kind of tree fungus, which grows on the stumps of birches, and is a favourite food of squirrels. The squirrel hunter picked the fungus in the summer and dried it for the hunting season. This kind of trapping was most profitable in the late winter, when the squirrel's larder is empty and it is obliged to look for more food.

A long slender birch rod with the top twigs still attached was one of the strangest devices for trapping squirrels. When a squirrel had been chased up a solitary tree, the trapper twirled the tip of the rod round its tail and pulled the animal down to the ground.

The map shows the distribution of the beaver in Europe today. (After Brink, 1958.)
According to popular belief, beavers bit off their castor glands and gave them to the hunter as security for their lives. If only this had really been true! (After woodcut in Aesop's fables, 1501.)

THE BEAVER

The beaver is one of the animals whose rapid decline may be regarded as a direct result of persecution by man. It is true that the beaver's environment has undergone great changes, but that hardly explains the fact that its decline in Europe began to be noticeable as early as the sixteenth century.

The reason for the beaver's popularity was, above all, its castor. It was also valued for its fur. The castor comes from two large glands, situated by the anus, which for a long time were believed to be the animal's testicles. The castor-glands were considered, according to popular medical beliefs, to possess extraordinary powers — primarily as a remedy for childbirth pains, impotence, epilepsy, stomach aches, colic, gout, toothache and so forth — and at times fetched high prices. As recently as the 1880s, over 300 crowns was paid, in Austria, for two castor-glands; this was the equivalent of a farm-hand's annual wages in Scandinavia. There is a record of one single beaver having yielded 630 crowns' worth of castor at the beginning of the nineteenth century, but prices have always varied enormously.

Apart from all this, the beaver's fur was in great demand; for a long time was more valuable than a good bearskin, so it is easy to understand why the beaver was so persecuted in every country.

In some places beaver hunting was considered to be the sport of princes, when the animal was driven from its den by hounds, and killed with tridents. Otherwise, it was uncommon for it to be hunted. In northern Scandinavia, however, beavers were shot by hunters keeping vigil on moonlit nights, or when the animals were forced to leave their dens after the ice had begun to break up in the spring.

It was, however, *trapping* that had the direst consequences for the beaver and, by taking advantage of the animal's characteristic habits, it was possible to decimate the colonies with dreadful

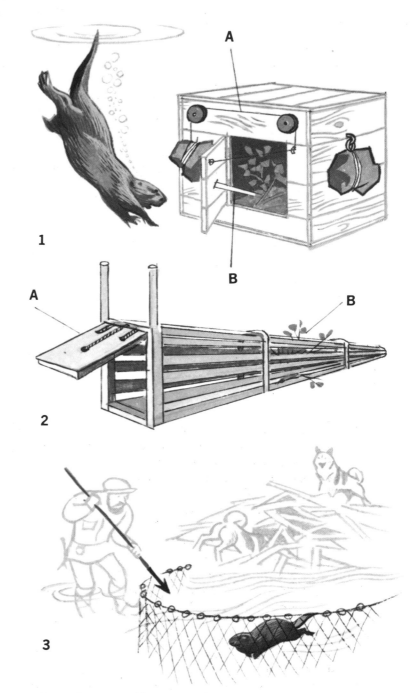

Fig. I. Beaver trap from Jämtland, according to Nordholm. (B) Trigger stick holding open the door to the trap. The trap was triggered off when the beaver took a bite at the branches placed inside and the door was pulled shut by the weight at the end of the wire (A).
Fig. II. Funnel-like beaver trap, according to Widén. The heavy trap-door (A) fell down when the beaver crawled into the trap and pulled at the aspen branches (B), thereby releasing the rope attached to the door.
Fig. III. Hunting with dogs, nets and a spear. One of the most destructive methods of hunting.

efficiency. Holes were made in the dam constructions and gins were placed there to catch the beavers when a drop in the water level forced them to repair the damage. The rivers were sealed off with nets or, alternatively, deep nets were stretched across the mouths of the dens and the beavers were forced out with the aid of dogs. On the continent, dragnets were often used. Like seines they were pulled against the current and could be tied together if a beaver got caught. Particularly in the late winter, when the beavers' food supplies were exhausted, gins baited with aspen twigs were also used with success. In one week a solitary upland farmer in Jämtland caught eighteen beavers — an illustration both of the abundance of beavers and of the efficiency of the gin. For a long time the beaver continued to exist in reasonable numbers in the northern Scandinavian forests. Already, however, at the end of the eighteenth century, there were dangerous signs of a decline in numbers as a result of the large colonies breaking up into "migrant beaver families".

The rapid decline was not noticed, however, by many people. According to an old proverb in Norrland, the hare in the forest and the beaver in the meadow belonged to the game which "never could be wiped out".

The incredible ignorance about the disastrous state of the beaver in the last half of the nineteenth century is borne out by the fact that it was not until 1864 that the beaver hunting season in Sweden was controlled. The beaver was declared a protected animal in 1873, which more or less coincided with the killing of the last specimen!

In Finland, too, the beaver was completely wiped out and, of the Scandinavian countries, it was eventually only Norway that managed to save a pitifully small remnant of the species — entirely thanks to the efforts of private persons. Norwegian beavers were introduced into Sweden in the 1920s and some from North America have been sent to Finland. In southern Germany, beavers were released in the countryside in 1967. Gradually,

perhaps, beavers will once again have an opportunity of building their dams in streams and rivers in different parts of Europe.

There are not many kinds of wild animals in Europe which have been the victims of such unforgivable mismanagement. It is interesting to see what a Swedish hunter, with a flair for economics, thought about this badly-treated animal, in an article written in 1834.

"In view of the fact that the beaver is rather rare nowadays, at least in our country, it may be concluded that it is indeed rather valuable. Soon this valuable animal will no longer be found in Scandinavia; we do not establish new beaver colonies; we destroy them.

"It is to our shame that we kill off our native animals and calmly watch other people gain control of our mercantile products." (F. v. Schéele.)

THE ARCTIC FOX

The Arctic fox was once fairly widely distributed in northernmost Scandinavia. These white foxes regularly wandered southwards, causing quite a stir among hunters. Now they are the rarest of all predators in Sweden and it is probably due to their being protected permanently (in Sweden) that they are still to be met in Lapland.

In contrast with the red fox, the Arctic fox often constructs its lairs, impressive in size, in the form of accommodation for several families. Thanks to the rich manure on top of the lair, the bright green colour of the lush grass is visible from afar. There was a time when some fifty entrances and exits were not at all uncommon. There have been instances of lairs — or "towns" as they are sometimes called — with as many as 172 openings. When the wanderer approached an Arctic fox "town" of this kind, there were sometimes large numbers of foxes lying about near the entrance holes, yapping or merely basking in the warm sunlight. Under those conditions it was not particularly difficult to shoot a few of them.

Arctic foxes were, however, mainly caught in steel traps or pivot snares of the same type as those used to trap the red fox, although smaller in size. Less care was needed when setting the trap than in

The Arctic fox is either white or bluish-grey in the winter. (Above) Steel trap for Arctic fox. The same type is used for the common red fox. The screw at (A) is turned to screw down the spring when the trap is set, but is removed once the jaws of the trap are in position.

the case of the common fox. Apparently excellent results were obtained merely by placing the steel traps close to the openings of the lair without the use of a lot of camouflage.

The Arctic fox is of little account, generally speaking, as vermin, except in isolated cases where it may do a lot of mischief. I have seen the Arctic fox in Iceland where I also saw the result of its feasting in a colony of pink-footed geese in the willow thickets close to a stream in Odada Raun. I was told, however, that as soon as the eggs were hatched, the geese moved up to the bare mountain slopes where they were better able to protect themselves.

It is to be hoped that the Arctic fox, now that it is a protected animal, will really have a proper chance of surviving in the Scandinavian mountains.

THE FOX

It is a moot point whether any other quarry has succeeded in fascinating nearly as many different categories of hunters as the fox. The retired colonel in scarlet and the shepherd in his worn-out sheepskin jacket would certainly not be lacking in a topic of conversation if they were to meet and start talking about the fox. There is something almost mysterious about the way this beautiful and intelligent creature seems to be able to excite the majority of those who are interested in hunting.

In the eyes of a Scandinavian, the fox is a highly complex and singular personality whose habits and behaviour can never be summarised in clear-cut and precise terms. On the contrary, it constantly provides the hunter with new surprises. It is a highly developed quarry — of its kind, a perfected animal, to quote the words of Brehm.

That is why fox hunting may often pose problems containing several unknown factors, and there is no key to provide the answer in advance. No two fox hunts are alike and, to judge from hunting literature, nearly all fox hunts are worth an obituary, as it were, even if only a fraction succeed in enthralling anyone other than the huntsman himself or possibly his hunting companions on the occasion. In the days when euphemisms were used to refer to the wild animals of the woods so as not to harm human beings, the fox was called "the wanderer of the woods" in several parts of Sweden.

The fox, that woodland animal par excellence, a quarry which, with almost supernatural cunning and craftiness, makes use of the thousand and one ways afforded by the woods of escaping from the hunter. Whatever may have been felt about its reputation as vermin, the fox has nevertheless always been respected as an exceptionally worthy animal to hunt.

For us Scandinavians, with our attitude towards the fox and towards animals in general, it might perhaps be difficult to understand the almost religious devotion paid by the English to fox hunting. There are actually some people who are dubious whether it should in fact come under the heading of hunting in the accepted sense of the word since, after all, the fox hunter follows the chase unarmed and it is up to the pack of hounds to do the killing at the end of the pursuit. It should perhaps instead be described as a form of riding in view of the classic books on fox hunting always having maintained that great riding skill is an absolute necessity in order to enjoy the chase. The majority of Scandinavian hunters no doubt consider the English method of fox hunting as incomprehensible as bull-baiting, cock-fighting and similar bloodthirsty

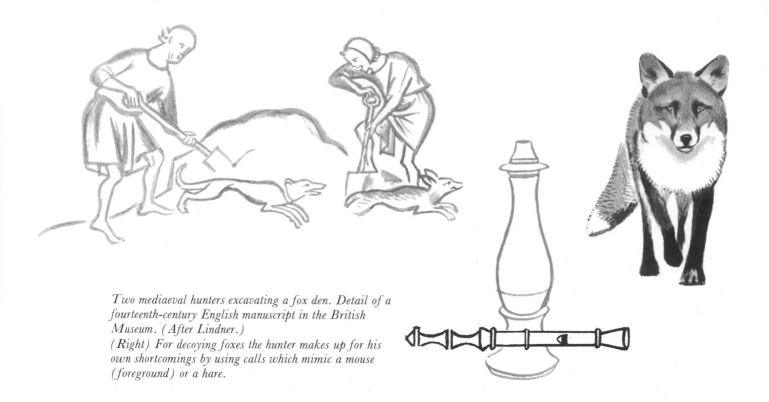

Two mediaeval hunters excavating a fox den. Detail of a fourteenth-century English manuscript in the British Museum. (After Lindner.)
(Right) For decoying foxes the hunter makes up for his own shortcomings by using calls which mimic a mouse (foreground) or a hare.

events which are incompatible with our temperament and our feelings about animals.

This matter is of course connected with a more humane form of hunting which has become noticeable, particularly in Scandinavia, during the last fifty years. As recently as at the end of the nineteenth century, a Swedish hunter was able to summarise his impressions of fox coursing (when the fox is harried to death by greyhounds in an open field) as follows: "It is most amusing to watch the fox's manœuvres when he sees that he is pursued by the greyhounds". A thoughtless remark like that would be absolutely out of the question in our times. The hunter's attitude to hunting and the quarry varies considerably, depending not only on national characteristics, religion and his general philosophy of life but also on the level of civilisation as a whole.

Part of the plan of campaign in the traditional fox hunt is for an experienced gamekeeper, with a good knowledge of the area, to go round the hunting grounds the night before and seal off all the earths and lairs there while the foxes are out on their nightly expeditions, thereby cutting off all their normal ways of retreat. The hunters and the foxhounds assemble the following morning. The num-

ber of hounds in a pack varies, but for normal hunts it is usually in the region of forty or fifty. To begin with, the hounds are released in the copse where there is good reason to believe that the fox is to be found. In the meantime, the piqueurs (the whippers-in), by riding to windward of the copse, arrive in good time to see the fox making for the open fields. It is now the task of the whippers-in to try to make the hounds keep to the scent and to prevent them from being confused by all manner of tricks employed by the fox.

Then the horsemen follow the pack's wild chase across the countryside until the hounds catch up with the exhausted fox and kill it. All the dramatic, comic or merely annoying events which since the eighteenth century have provided artists with an inexhaustible source of material for their illustrations of English fox hunting centre round the main phases of the hunt as mentioned above. No type of hunting has been more thoroughly documented. Indeed, reams of more or less poetic or "scientific" analyses have been written about every phase or subtlety of the sport; the intellectual capacity required of the huntsman has been scrutinised with irresistible solemnity; there exist detailed accounts

Lying in wait for foxes is an ancient method, with an atmosphere of its own — especially when it is done through an open shutter in a byre window on a moonlit winter's night. Old handbooks recommend the hunter to hang a brush harrow outside the window so that the ever-watchful fox will not notice the gun barrel protruding through the opening!

of not only what the ideal hunting morning should be like but also how the true hunter should most suitably take advantage of it!

It might be added that at the beginning of the twentieth century between 9,000 and 10,000 foxes were estimated to have been killed in fox hunts in England. Furthermore, foxes were also introduced from Scandinavia and elsewhere into counties with a poor supply of foxes. (See Notes.)

The sport of beagling comes into its own in places where woods alternate with open country. As far as Sweden is concerned, it is for this reason that the southern and central parts have long been beagling country while in the extensive forests of the northern province of Norrland, other hunting methods have had to be adopted. The latter include coursing on skis, shooting from behind cover in the winter but, above all, a number of trapping techniques. On the whole, coursing was done in the same way as that described in the chapters dealing with the hunting of other large predators. In other words, it was necessary to find fresh tracks in deep loosely-packed snow, after which the quarry was pursued until it was exhausted.

A very ancient form of hunting is the method employed everywhere in populated districts where the fox has become used to looking for offal and refuse on manure heaps in the winter. In many

In the past, foxes were hunted in loosely-packed snow in Norrland. The method was the same as that used for other predatory animals.

places they have for years, perhaps for generations, accustomed the foxes to looking for carrion within easy range of the byre windows. Now and then during the winter the farmer or his son can keep a look-out for foxes by an open window shutter. This is a sport which provides both excitement and a tense atmosphere. The rattling of the chains of the cows, their heavy breathing, the squeaking of mice from the byre floor, the warm steamy darkness. And outside, the winter night gleams an almost blue phosphorous colour in the moonlight.

As a matter of fact, the fox is incredibly careless if lured into an ambush with the aid of a *mouse* or *hare call*. These instruments have proved to be very efficient in the hands of an experienced hunter.

This method is used in the mornings and evenings when the fox goes hunting along the edges of fields and in woodland pastures. The squeaking of a mouse, which is easily imitated by pressing one's lips together and sucking in air between them, is surprisingly effective and, providing that the fox is

Particularly in Norrland where there were not many opportunities for hunting foxes on account of the large tracts of unbroken forest, various trapping methods were used to catch the fox. (Extreme left) Cleft log, which is described in detail in the text. As can be seen from the picture, in contrast with the impression often given in books, the cleft log was not too high to allow the fox, once it was trapped, to sit or at least half-sit in the snow below. (Above) A simple type of pivot snare which was also used for trapping Arctic foxes. (Below) Closed box trap where the lid fell down and imprisoned the fox when the trap was triggered off.

sufficiently hungry, it will come as quickly as a dog being called.

In the past, foxes were mainly caught in traps. People used fox pens, similar to those used for wolves, fox deadfalls, snares, iron collars, poisoned carrion (the seed of the poison nut tree), pitfalls, box traps but, above all, they used various types of steel traps.

In the northern parts of Scandinavia, the trapping techniques survived a longer time than in the south where the opportunities for hunting were considerably greater. This was especially true of the baited steel traps that were laid on fox tracks — in view of the fact that the fox often followed the same tracks more than once — and which were very widespread and much used. Trapping was done in the winter. When the trapper had found a suitable fox track, he carefully dug up one or two sets of footprints with a spade, placed the thoroughly cleaned and "scented" steel trap — it was smeared with goose fat and junipers — in the hole, put back the snow with the footprints as a lid over the metal and, as far as possible, removed all signs of his having been there. Steel traps used for this type of trapping were not baited.

A primitive trapping method, presumably very ancient, was the cleft log. It was fairly widely used in northern Scandinavia and was in use until the Second World War. It is perhaps still in use in a few places (see picture on page 211).

According to a 1938 survey on the use of the cleft log trap to catch foxes, this method was clearly rather profitable. A trapper might have up to thirty or forty baited traps of this kind and catch some thirty foxes each winter. The best time to employ this trapping technique was in the late winter when the snow lay tightly-packed and the fox was hungry and bold.

The "wanderer of the woods" is an animal that has always managed to fascinate man. This, if nothing else, is obvious from the immense amount of literature on the subject, ever since the Bible urged the people of Israel "to catch the small foxes, the ravagers of the vineyards" and Aesop in his fables wrote about its cunning and wiliness. In folklore and poetry the fox has played as big a role as the wolf and the bear. In the field of folk medicine practically every part of the fox is used more eagerly in the television age than ever before as a remedy for the most varied illnesses and complaints.

We should be thankful for the presence of the fox in the countryside. It is an animal that is an equally fascinating subject for study both for the hunter and the non-hunter; it is without a doubt, of its kind, a perfect animal.

There are countless examples of the legendary cunning and intelligence of the fox. It is not so unusual at a fox hunt in England for the hunted fox to climb up a suitable tree in order to confuse the hounds.

THE BADGER

Despite the badger being well known to the majority of hunters, the most extraordinary misconceptions about this animal survived a long time. According to one theory, it was related to the pig — in old pictures it is sometimes shown with a pig's snout. Indeed, in many country dialects in Scandinavia as recently as the nineteenth century the name used for the badger meant "burrowing pig". In England, boar and sow are the names sometimes given to the male and female badgers, respectively. German hunters once maintained that there were two distinct species, the "pig" badger and the "dog" badger, and that their habits were totally different. In addition, it was believed that the badger obtained nourishment during hibernation by sucking the secretion from the stink gland close to the base of its tail and thus lived on food from its own body; as a matter of fact, there was a similar theory about the bear which was believed to "suck its paws" during hibernation. According to one of the more fantastic theories, the legs on one side of the badger's body were believed to be shorter than the others so as to enable it to negotiate the deep ruts made by carts on woodland tracks!

During the Middle Ages, people were extremely keen on "burrow hunting", in other words, pur-

Detail of sixteenth-century tapestry showing different methods of catching badgers in their earths. (Left) Smoking out the badger and waiting for it with a mattock. A badger dog is lending a hand. (Centre) Excavation of earth. (Right) A self-operative net placed at one of the entrances to the earth. (Extreme right) Weighted trap placed at one of the exits of the earth.

suing the foxes, badgers, rabbits and hedgehogs that lived in burrows. At the courts of many princes there were specially trained hunt attendants whose sole occupation was this form of hunting. The most important equipment used by the "burrow hunters" was the sturdy mattock, which could also be used as a weapon, as well as funnel nets which were stretched across the entrances to the earths. The funnel net was often provided with a drawstring which drew the net together into a sack when the badger rushed into it. Normally, however, the hunter lay in wait and dealt with the badger as soon as it had got entangled in the net. Short-legged dachshunds (the name is derived from the German word *Dachs* = badger) began to be used for badger hunting already during the Middle Ages.

The most important implement of the "burrow diggers" was a sturdy mattock, which was used both as a weapon and for the excavation of the earth. Dogs bearing a resemblance to dachshunds occur already in mediaeval illustrations. (After Jacques du Fouilloux.)

(Left) Fork and tongs used for badger hunting.
(Above) Italian net for badgers and porcupines. It is
evident from descriptions of the nets used in central
Europe across the mouths of burrows that they were
considerably deeper and more reminiscent of sacks.
(After Bresciano, 1626.)

There were many different versions of the funnel net. It could be made to tip up so that the sack containing the captured badger swung up into the air like a pail on a well sweep.

Naturally, however, the troglodytic and nocturnal animal was also the object of purer forms of hunting, especially lying in ambush by the animal's earth and shooting it when it went out hunting in the evening. In addition, there was coursing with beagles or other large dogs. Several writers of eighteenth-century hunting books warmly recommended this "entertaining and exciting" method which spread from central Europe to Scandinavia where, according to Ekström, it was the commonest form of badger hunting in the early nineteenth century. Rordorf tells us that in Switzerland in the eighteenth-century badger coursing was a frequent occurrence on the steep slopes of the vineyards.

In coursing, the first thing to do was to find out whether the badger had left its earth on its nightly hunting expedition, which frequently might take it several miles over the neighbouring countryside. If the badger was in fact out, the entrances were blocked, with the exception of two or three where funnel nets were put in position. The hounds were then released and as soon as they were heard to be closing in on their quarry, usually after a fairly short time had elapsed, the hunters hurried after them after first posting guards by the funnel nets. If the badger gave the hounds the slip or at once took

to its heels, it always made straight for its earth and could be caught in the nets.

The sending of hounds into the badger's earth was formerly considered to be the simplest and surest way of hunting badgers, although, with bad luck, it might mean a lot of toil and sweat if a hound happened to get stuck or hurt underground. Like all members of the weasel family, the badger has an extremely sharp bite and an eager and inexperienced young hound can easily get hurt. (See Notes.)

As already mentioned, C. U. Ekström, a rural dean, mentioned the use of beagles as the commonest form of badger hunting in southern and central districts of Sweden. Ekström's description of the badger and badger hunting (1833) is one of the most detailed articles we possess on the subject. In contrast with the majority of his closest colleagues, he relied mainly on his own personal knowledge, acquired over years of field studies of badgers. He was generous enough to allow these animals to run wild in the deanery kitchen garden and oat fields. Ekström also mentions several methods used to trap badgers, including, above all, of course, the still frequently employed "box", which was placed by one of the exits of an earth after all the other holes had been blocked. In addition, Ekström refers to the steel traps which were placed at badger crossing points, and deadfalls similar to those employed for foxes. The latter kind was, however, only used in exceptional cases.

In the southern Swedish province of Blekinge bandogs
were used for badger hunting at night. When it is
attacked, the badger rises up on its hind legs with its back
against a tree and snaps in all directions.

THE STOAT

It is wise to take tales about the alleged abundance of certain game in olden times with a pinch of salt. The primary aim of the mediaeval writers, in particular, was not to give a factual and scientific account of nature; their enthusiastic descriptions were often written with completely different aims in mind. When Olaus Magnus produced his history of the Scandinavian peoples he tried, in a high degree, to glorify the Scandinavian countries. He wanted to make them both exotically attractive and worthy of respect. For this reason it is not so strange that the wild animals there had to be abundant enough to be reminiscent of Paradise.

It is in this light that one should read Olaus

for the squirrel; in other words, it was only legal in the winter when the fur was at its best. In some parts of Norrland far into the seventeenth century, a considerable proportion of the taxes consisted of stoat pelts, varying from one to eleven a year, all according to the size of the homestead. In many places in Finland, stoat pelts were also included in the clergy's tithes. The information that the mighty Bo Jonsson Grip once sold 275 timmers, the equivalent of 11,000 pelts, shows that the stoat really was numerous.

It was in northern Scandinavia and Russia that the fur obtained its coveted pure white colour, and there was a considerable export of stoat pelts, or ermine as the white fur is called, from northern Europe to the countries on the continent. Ermine

(Above) Stoat trap according to Olaus Magnus in The History of the Scandinavian Peoples, *1555.*

has been a royal status symbol since olden times, and in England, at least, it was monopolised by the crown because of its rarity. Sweden was in a more fortunate position, however, for there it was also an article for everyday use as, for instance, lining in clothes.

Stoats were generally caught in deadfalls of the same type as those used for pine martens. Sometimes the trap consisted of nothing more than a plank with a weight and was placed in the floor of a barn or in a shed in an outlying field frequented by stoats owing to the plentiful supply of mice.

Stoats were also caught in small steel traps which were so set that they gripped the slender body. Olaus Magnus's assertion that they were also caught in pitfalls does not, however, seem very plausible.

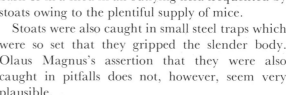

Magnus's description of the huge numbers of stoats in the Scandinavian forests. If we are to believe him, the woods literally teemed with stoats. These highly coveted fur-bearing animals thronged around the trapping equipment and snares of the Northmen to such an extent that as many as eight were caught at the same time in one and the same deadfall! The hunters also kept specially trained dogs which went out on their own to hunt stoats, which they then carried home and laid in a neat pile at their masters' feet.

The fact remains, however, that stoat trapping really was of great importance during the Middle Ages — hunting very likely occurred only on a very limited scale. According to the old provincial laws, the trapping season was approximately the same as

For reasons easily understood, the stoat has never been subjected to systematic hunting, even if it was occasionally shot in the past, like the squirrel, with blunted arrows and more latterly with firearms.

The classic weapon for otter hunting was the trident. Detail of sixteenth-century tapestry at the Victoria and Albert Museum, London.

THE OTTER

As in the case of the beaver, people found it rather difficult in olden times to define the exact position of the otter in the animal world. It was long believed to be a kind of mysterious intermediate form between a mammal and a fish — with special emphasis on the fish aspect, bearing in mind fasting regulations as far as the clergy were concerned!

For a long time, too, the doubt prevailing as to the true nature of the animal played a dominant role in otter hunting. On the whole, it was caught with the same equipment and by means of the same methods as those used for fishing. Originally, otter hunting was classed, for legal purposes, under the heading of fishing. As a result, the otter was not included in the hunting privileges of the nobility — a state of affairs which in the Middle Ages gave rise to a lively debate in which both fishermen and the gentry stood up for their rights. (See Notes.)

The otter was persecuted for several reasons; mainly on account of the damage it caused, but to a large extent also because of its valuable skin and because it was an interesting and exciting animal to hunt. (See Notes.) It was therefore enthusiastically hunted by all strata of society. In the Middle Ages, the major courts of central Europe maintained special *bevararii* whose sole duty was to be responsible for otter "water hunts". At the English Court, the person in charge of otter hunting held an important position.

The classical type of otter hunting was done with dogs which drove the animal towards the hunter, whose only weapon was a trident. This method was practised during the Middle Ages and into the present century, especially in England and Germany. The trident was preferably not more than three pounds in weight. A shaft of ash was recommended and its length was supposed to correspond approximately to the hunter's height.

In Sweden, too, the otter had had a price on its head ever since ancient times. The Västgöta provincial statutes stipulated that "the otter belongs to the person who pulls it out of the water". It was hunted on fresh snow or was dug out of its holt. If it hid in an air pocket under the ice by the water's edge, the stream was dammed so that the water rose in the hole and forced the otter out. Gins were baited with fish and in some parts of Norrland heavy log deadfalls of the same kind as those used for hares and woodland birds were constructed and placed at right angles across streams and rivers. During the mating season, otters were sometimes shot by hunters using calls.

Although perhaps somewhat outside the scope of a description of the otter as a game animal, it may be mentioned that the otter was sometimes caught alive in Sweden and trained to catch fish for the kitchen. (See Notes.)

Otters were caught in dragnets which could be closed tight by the hunter when the animal was enmeshed. (Right) Norrland type of otter deadfall laid in river. (After Ekman.)

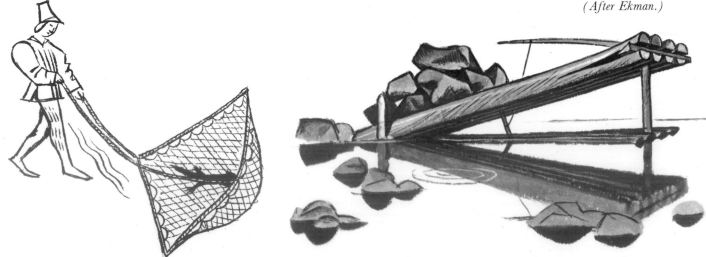

THE MARTEN

The pine marten — the noble marten as the Germans call it — is essentially a denizen of the coniferous forests. Its fur is the same deep brown as the bark of a spruce and the yellow patch on its throat is reminiscent of wolf lichen. The squirrel is its only rival in the art of scampering through a dense coniferous wood, completely unimpeded by the laws of gravity.

It hunts alone and ranges far afield. The systematic hunting of martens has always been a matter of luck, even if scores of peasant hunters have had a shot at it and have perhaps been fortunate. The great attraction was the high prices paid for the skins.

It hunts alone and ranges far afield. The systematic hunting of martens has always been a matter province of Jämtland. Twenty years later, the price appears to have dropped to three crowns in the skin markets of Norrland before rocketing up to seventy crowns some years later. Since then, the pelt has risen in value constantly while the number of martens has dropped in large areas of Sweden.

Once good weapons became available, marten hunting took place mainly on fresh snow, preferably on days without a breath of wind, when the marten's passage from tree to tree is marked by a cloud of snow falling from the branches.

When a marten is chased and finds itself in a tight corner, it often disappears into a tree and hides in a hollow or in a squirrel's nest. Sometimes its tracks reveal that it had lain down to sleep long before the hunter happened to locate it.

On such occasions, despite every means of persuasion, the marten often refused to leave its shelter. In the good old days, this problem was most ingeniously solved by means of chopping down the tree concealing the marten; in the eyes of a hunter a sturdy timber pine with the promise of a good supply of matchsticks was less valuable than a marten.

If, on the other hand, the marten lay low in some abandoned squirrel's nest, a shot was simply fired

The "mårdrivil", a barbed staff, from Norrland was an implement used to persuade unwilling pine martens to leave their dens. The barb was twisted into the animal's body. This specimen is from the province of Härjedalen. (The Nordic Museum, Stockholm.)

straight through the nest from the ground below! If the tree was decayed and hollow throughout, it was of course tempting to smoke out the uncooperative marten. This method was not encouraged because, if the worst came to the worst, the fire might scorch the valuable fur and make the whole undertaking less profitable.

Sometimes — for example, in Norrland, according to Widén's reports — funnel nets, similar to those used on the Continent for badgers, were placed in front of the holes in the trees.

Elsewhere, the marten was caught in deadfalls — somewhat sturdier than the squirrel deadfall, and provided with hollowed-out recesses on the inside of the halved logs so as not to damage the precious fur.

The beech or stone marten, found in southern Europe, is hunted in rather the same way as the pine marten although their natural environments differ considerably.

If the pine marten had treed, the tree was felled without second thoughts. It was best to have two men for this; one of them felled the tree and the other stood by, ready to shoot the moment the pine marten darted out of the hole.

THE GLUTTON (WOLVERINE)

In prehistoric times the glutton was distributed over large areas of Europe and was still to be found, in the early Middle Ages, in Poland and the Baltic countries. Today, however, it is one of the rarest mammals in the world. The total number of gluttons in Europe has been estimated at between 500 and 1,000, of which some 150 are shot each year, most of them in European Russia.

In the past, the glutton was usually hunted, in northern Europe, in the winter, when people pursued it on skis. As a physical feat this method of hunting must rank with the pursuit of wolves. Indeed, there are many who consider that it is a great deal more exhausting. The glutton is, in fact, incredibly tough and possesses great powers of endurance. If the hunt takes place high up in the mountains and the going is good, the hunter may be obliged to pursue it for several days; there are cases of its having taken ten days to overtake a glutton.

The Lapps have many names for the glutton, as indeed they have for the bear. One name is *vätke*, which is derived from a verb meaning, approximately, "to carry constantly". When the glutton dragged food home to its young in the den, it left behind easily recognisable tracks which revealed its hideout to the hunter. After hunters stopped chasing the glutton up hill and down dale, the excavation of the den became the most important method of hunting. Normally, an attempt was made to smoke out the glutton on these occasions.

One of the reasons why the glutton was so fundamentally misunderstood by the earliest zoological writers was the fact that it was so difficult to approach. Olaus Magnus, too, contributed to the general confusion with his highly imaginative description of the glutton. He borrowed delightedly, from a Lithuanian colleague, the legend about the insatiable glutton which gorges itself so full of meat that its skin tightens like a drum, whereupon it looks for two trees growing close together. It squeezes itself between them and in this way regurgitates its food so that, with fresh courage, it can return once more to the feast. While the glutton is busy with these stimulating activities, the hunter has a good opportunity of shooting it with his arrow, in the opinion of Olaus Magnus.

Even later writers like Lloyd, for instance, were convinced of the glutton's abnormal greed. He maintained that it would bite a chunk out of a piece of granite if it was chained to a stone wall. The mistaken beliefs had indeed made a deep impression. No wonder that the glutton received its unflattering name. It is sometimes called a wolverine but, as it belongs to the weasel family, this does not seem to be a very suitable name.

In the northern Swedish province of Norrland the glutton has been hated since time immemorial. It scatters herds of reindeer and breaks into the larders of the Lapps. As a result of all this, there is no other predator for which so many different kinds of traps have been devised: spring traps, several kinds of self-releasing spears and set guns, and deadfalls. A feature of glutton trapping is the fact that it is not necessary to spend so much time on cunning and craft. In fact, the glutton is a bold animal and used to breaking into larders if necessary.

The glutton deadfall was a bulky and rather clumsy arrangement but apparently efficient. It was carefully constructed of heavy logs and the method of setting the trap was not particularly involved. As will be seen from the illustration, it worked when the glutton, after running into the trap, grabbed the bait, thereby at the same time pulling away the wedge from the hanging logs. The latter then fell down and crushed the glutton.

(Above) The oldest known picture of a glutton is to be found on a small flat piece of bone that was discovered in a cave in Dordogne. (The Louvre, Paris.)
The glutton is a bold animal and the methods used to trap it need not be particularly discreet. The glutton deadfall was a fairly bulky contraption which was placed in the open without any attempt at concealment.

THE LYNX

Not so very long ago the lynx was distributed over large areas of Europe. Indeed, it was common in suitable places until the beginning of the last century. It is not an easy matter to state for certain the immediate cause of the lynx's very rapid decline in numbers and why it was gradually able to hold out only on the outer edges of Europe — in the Balkans, southern Spain, Russia and Scandinavia. The growing scarcity of unbroken tracts of desolate country rich in animal life and the intense persecution on the part of man nevertheless contributed greatly towards the lynx being forced to retreat from central Europe.

The lynx had a price on its head both because of the destruction it was believed to cause among cattle and small game and because of its fur — once upon a time rated as the dearest fur in Europe, a luxury item for royalty.

It is not so strange that lynx hunting was a great event in central Europe when the lynx began to approach extinction. The lynx was hunted there all the year round — in the summer occasionally with the use of calls, when the hunter imitated roe deer or hares. Further north, however, hunting took place mostly in the winter when the fur was at its thickest and was most valuable. The winter was also the easiest time to approach the lynx, when there was fresh snow on the ground.

In Sweden the lynx was usually hunted with dogs which the hunters followed on skis or on foot. Young lynxes, in particular, tired fairly quickly and climbed up into a tree. When the dogs arrived they stood under the tree and started to bark.

Old lynxes did not give up so soon and fought the dogs to the bitter end. There are many descriptions, both in words and pictures, of how the lynx threw itself on its back in a last attempt to defend itself against overwhelming odds. As a matter of fact,

To a greater extent, perhaps, than the other predators, the lynx has come to acquire a mysterious, almost legendary reputation. Popular belief credited the lynx with fantastic characteristics. It was maintained that amber came from the animal's urine and that when the lynx, like other members of the cat family, scratched soil over it, this was taken to indicate a grudge against mankind. Its gaze was said to be sharp enough to penetrate thick timber walls. According to one mediaeval account, its skin was so luminous that it could be used as lighting in a powder magazine.

many dogs were seriously injured during lynx hunts. Ekman tells us of one case when a solitary lynx was attacked by sixteen dogs, thirteen of which it managed to cripple in the final struggle.

Lynx coursing also took place even without the use of dogs, particularly in Finland. The hunters pursued the lynxes on skis in deep loosely-packed snow. On such occasions they had to maintain a furious pace from the very start. The actual hunt, however, was never nearly so wearying as wolf and glutton coursing.

SEAL HUNTING

When the first missionaries preached the Gospel in Greenland, the Eskimoes are said to have asked them whether there were also plenty of seals in heaven! This tells us a great deal about the dominating role which the seal and seal hunting played in the lives of the hunting peoples of the northern oceans.

Of course, in the seas round Scandinavia the seal has not acquired the same paramount importance. In many coastal areas, however, particularly by the Gulf of Bothnia, seal hunting on the spring ice has been a great event for centuries. Life on the *"fälan"*, as these hunting expeditions in the Gulf of Bothnia were called by seal hunters, offered hardship and adventure galore. The hunters usually spent three months out on the ice before the spring sun finally put an end to the long hunt.

There is surely no other type of hunting in Europe which demanded (and still demands) greater physical exertion from those involved than seal hunting on the spring ice. Nevertheless, the cold, the monotonous diet, the privations and the almost constantly wet clothes seem to be a mere drop in the ocean compared with the thrills and excitement which spur on every man taking part in these hunting expeditions. He goes off to the hunt in the same spirit as the sea dog who goes to sea, leaving the trivialities of everyday life behind him. Very often indeed it was the freedom rather than the money that tempted the coastal peasants out on to the ice.

In February, the seal hunters of the Bothnian Sea set out across the pack ice — on the "fälan". Two or three months may pass before they return home to the coast again.

"The 'fälan' is a mighty attraction", was the laconic comment of one of the last seal hunters in an interview only a few years ago. This also goes to show that this ancient form of seal hunting had become more and more a kind of off-beat sport.

As a matter of fact, there is much to suggest that matters had been like this, more or less openly, for centuries! When a provincial sheriff by the name of J. D. Cneiff wrote an article on seal hunting in the Finnish province of Österbotten in 1757, he devoted a lot of attention, in the spirit of the times, to the profits that might be made. He estimated that every person participating in a seal hunt generally made about sixty-six copper thalers, after the deduction of overhead costs. He summarised his impressions in some very critical remarks in which he showed that the three months spent on the hunting expedition "profited neither the voyager himself nor his dependants at home but were, if anything, harmful on account of his long absence from work". This statement, naturally enough, did not remain unanswered for very long by more enthusiastic friends of seal hunting.

There are detailed descriptions of seal hunts of considerably earlier date, but one of the most interesting is the one described by the Finn, Jacob Wijkar, who wrote a thesis on seal hunting in the Gulf of Bothnia in 1707. (See Notes.) In the latter work — as a matter of fact, the first dealing solely with hunting in Finland — there is a detailed account of the preparations for life on the "fälan";

The seal hunter's equipment. White sheepskin coat, "skredstang" with rests for the gun, harpoon, telescope. In the background, the "fäl" (cf. "fälan") boat and tent.

the type of boat used, the kind of food supplies taken, and so forth. On the whole, to judge from this account, no great changes have taken place in the "fälan" down to the present day.

The boat used in the eighteenth century on these expeditions looked more or less like the one in the picture opposite. It usually carried two small dinghies which were used to cross open water and channels in the ice. The hunters spent the night in the boat under a tarpaulin roof.

It was from here that they set out on their hunting trips in the icy wilderness — usually once a seal had been sighted through a telescope from the boat or from the top of some block of ice in the neighbourhood. The hunter was dressed in a sheep-skin coat or other white clothes. Extreme stealth and caution was necessary for the advance across the ice, so he used a ski some nine feet or so in length — in Swedish, *"skredstång"* — on which the long, heavy seal gun was mounted on two ordinary fork rests. The ski and the hunter were hidden by a white canvas screen which was fastened across the ski tip. The seal hunter then shuffled along with infinite care on the "skredstång" towards his quarry. In olden times when fire-arms did not have such a long range, the hunter had to get as close as possible and occasionally he tried to confuse the seal by scraping the ice with the front flipper of a seal as well as by imitating its call. (See Notes.)

An exceedingly ancient hunting method was the clubbing of seals. In remote and uninhabited areas where the seals are not afraid of man, clubbing may be catastrophic for the entire seal population. Proof exists that several of the most valuable species of seals have been brought to the verge of extinction as a result of this wholesale slaughter.

In several places off the Baltic coast of Sweden, the grey seal was killed by clubbing. This occurred,

The seal hunter shuffles forwards with the "skredstång" towards his quarry. The white canvas screen prevents detection. The three species of seal most commonly hunted in Scandinavian waters. (Top) Ringed seal. Centre: Common seal. Bottom: Grey seal. In the background, seal hooks which were placed in a ring on much-frequented seal rocks.
(Below) The clubbing of seals has sometimes proved to be disastrous for a number of species of seal.

above all, on the low-lying rocks near Harstena in the Östergötland archipelago where, far into the 1930s, grey seals sometimes appeared in flocks of tens of thousands during the mating season. Stealthily, the hunters crept up on to the islets at dawn, rushed into the crowds of seals and hit out in all directions with their heavy clubs. In order not to slip on the slimy rocks, the men wore iron spikes on their boots.

On the island of Gotland — where for centuries seal hunting had been the kind of hunting of greatest importance for the island's economy — the grey seal was hunted in a similar manner, but instead of a club, they used the *"kutapilk"*, a harpoon which is depicted in Linnaeus's *Journey to Öland and Gotland*, 1745. (See Notes.)

A variety of different kinds of trapping equipment such as vertical nets, horizontal nets, seal chests, seal hooks and so forth have all been developed on account of the seal's habit of climbing up on low rocks for a rest.

One may wonder at all the cruelty that has been shown through the ages to this animal, in its way, beautiful and gentle-eyed. Perhaps it stems from the irreconcilable hatred of fishermen for the seal because of the damage it does to their nets. Perhaps it springs from the more or less vague idea that the seal is an insensitive animal of the oceans with fish blood in its veins.

GEESE

Since the hunting of the eight species of geese regularly found in Europe — the Canada goose is not a native species — mainly occurs during the migratory season and since all the methods employed are rather alike, it seemed best to group them all together under one heading.

Wild geese were an important species of game already in prehistoric times. The superbly realistic paintings of geese in the Egyptian tombs as well as the descriptions furnished by ancient Greek and Roman authors are also proof that the interest in these heavy, meaty birds has kept alive through the centuries.

There is no doubt that in the past geese were far more abundant in the marshes and on the plains and steppes of Europe than they are today. It is not absolutely certain, however, that hunting alone is to blame for the geese practically disappearing from some of their former winter quarters or intermediate stopping places. Geese have been known to change their migratory routes and they may suddenly appear in places where they have never been observed before. That is what happened in the case of the barnacle goose, huge flocks of which used to break their journey in the past in the southernmost part of the southern Swedish province of Skåne. They all but disappeared from the latter area at the end of the nineteenth century. It is interesting to note that there is a mysterious report of white geese

with black wing tips which, according to Pliny and Olaus Magnus, migrated across the Scandinavian countries. It is tempting to interpret this to mean that the migratory routes of the Arctic snow geese once lay across Europe.

Unfortunately, a great toll was taken of the geese, both in their moulting season in the summer and down in their winter quarters in the south. Hunting moulting birds was often disastrous for the local goose population. We are reminded that it was of great economic importance in Lapland, for instance, by the fact that the Lapps refer to the moulting season as "goose week".

Specially trained dogs were used to round up the helpless birds which were then beaten to death with sticks. It was considered wasteful to use ammunition on them. As was the case with whooper swan cygnets, goslings were caught alive and reared on farms. In that way people were provided with a living larder! This is how the goose was actually domesticated in former times.

The hunting of geese in the spring also took place on a considerable scale in Norrland. It started as soon as the first flocks arrived in open water and in the marshes some time in April. Since the geese had to make use of limited space in the open stretches of water, snow-free shores and on bare patches in the fields, it paid indeed to catch them with snares, metal traps and baited hooks. Whole series of

It was above all brent geese (top) and barnacle geese which, according to a widespread belief in the Middle Ages, were born from fruit which grew on sunken pieces of timber. The "fruit" were gooseneck barnacles. The slightly curled tentacles which protrude from the shells were thought to be the down of the goslings.

snares were laid out along the shores and iron collars and jaw traps, baited with their favourite aquatic plants, were placed in shallow water.

We gather from Aeschill Nordholm's account of Jämtland hunting in the mid-eighteenth century that these various methods were nevertheless not considered very satisfactory. Nordholm complains vehemently that no one had invented a really efficient means of catching geese and whooper swans — it was mostly a matter of luck if they were shot, in view of their legendary shyness.

He declares that it is perhaps true that some people are against the birds being disturbed in the mating season. At the same time, however, he stresses that there is not the slightest reason for sparing them, since, after all, they leave the country on migration and consequently fall into the hands of foreign hunters! *"In such cases one should enrich the fatherland and not the foreigner,"* as he very patriotically sums up.

The spring and summer hunts were, however, on a smaller scale than the severe thinning out of the numbers of wild geese which took place every year down in their winter quarters or during migration.

Wherever the geese stayed, they were hunted and trapped in a great variety of ways. In the Kurische Nehrung in northern Germany, the hunters approached them with lanterns at their roosting places, once their night haunts had been discovered. They were hunted extensively on the Frisian coast, both for the sake of their meat and on account of the great damage they were believed to do to the young corn, not only because they ate it but equally much because of their droppings which were considered to be highly corrosive. In a few places people even put out scarecrows for the geese.

In eastern Europe, Puszta Hortobágy was re-garded as one of the leading areas for goose hunting. Thousands of geese, including the small attractive red-breasted goose from the coastal tundra by the Arctic Ocean winter there. In addition, moulting grey lag geese have been hunted on a considerable scale along the eastern stretches of the Danube.

The brent goose and the barnacle goose which mainly winter in the British Isles, have been hunted enthusiastically since time immemorial — not least as a welcome change in diet at times of fasting. As a matter of fact, like the otter and the beaver, they were regarded as being most closely allied to fish.

The origin of this belief was a mediaeval superstition that the brent goose and the barnacle goose were hatched from fruit that grew on flotsam and driftwood. This bird fruit was later identified as the magnificently coloured *gooseneck barnacle* which clings in its thousands to the hulls of boats, the foundations of jetties and other timber in water. Other birds, too, have been connected with this superstition — the little auk, for example, which often drifts in towards the coasts of the British Isles in the winter in the wake of westerly gales from the Atlantic — but it is the small Arctic geese which have stubbornly managed to retain their reputation of being born from sea fruit. There are cases of goose hunters in remote parts of Britain who believed in the mediaeval misconception as recently as the 1920s.

In the chapter on the use of disguises for hunting, mention is also made of the camouflage that was used particularly for stalking the extremely cautious geese, for example, the "dummy cow". Many other types of camouflage were of course employed and there was no limit to the variations on the theme; it all depended on the hunter's imagination and the opportunities offered him.

The weapons used included very heavy calibre guns, taking huge charges of shot, and guns with extremely long barrels — as much as eight or nine feet in length. They had to be transported on wheeled rests resembling gun carriages and were aptly called "barrow guns". (See Notes.)

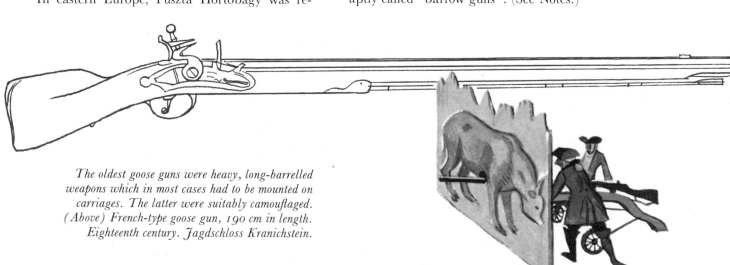

The oldest goose guns were heavy, long-barrelled weapons which in most cases had to be mounted on carriages. The latter were suitably camouflaged. (Above) French-type goose gun, 190 cm in length. Eighteenth century. Jagdschloss Kranichstein.

Two sixteenth-century hunters creeping towards ducks. The men are using heavy calibre wheel lock muskets of the South German type. The ducks (left to right): mallard, wigeon, pintail, shoveler, garganey.

DUCKS

Duck hunting did not enjoy a high reputation from the Middle Ages until the eighteenth century. It was essentially a "pastime for the lower orders" while the upper classes devoted themselves to the pursuit of nobler game.

The reasons for this state of affairs were obvious. The fire-arms of the time were clumsy to load and unsuitable for rapid wing shots. Besides, the whole business of duck shooting was lacking in the splendour and elegance which made stag hunting, for example, so popular during the centuries when pomp and circumstance were the order of the day. A squire out on his own might possibly shoot birds to improve his marksmanship, but it was a pastime without any real status value, from the mediaeval point of view.

Hungers Prevention or the whole Arte of Fowling, was the telling title of a book on bird shooting which was published in 1621. This sport was very much a matter for the poor man.

If a fowling expedition was to be a success, the hunter had to get as close as possible to his quarry and had to use the longest and heaviest gun available. If the target was a tightly-packed, motionless flock of ducks, the shooter stood a fair chance of killing one of the birds with his shot, providing that he did not use too small a charge.

Various types of camouflage were used in order to get close to the wary ducks. The hunters hid in holes dug in a sandy beach or in the ground near the places frequented by the ducks; they used reeds to camouflage large rafts which glided with the current within easy gunshot of the ducks; they shot the ducks when the latter flew between their roosting quarters and their feeding grounds in the mornings and evenings.

As in the case of geese and other shy birds, the hunter had to use a good deal of imagination in the choice of camouflage. If we are to believe the mediaeval hunting handbooks, it does not matter *what* one wears; the main thing is to look as little like a human being as possible! Naturally, a lot of tricks are used to lure the ducks within range — decoys when shooting sea birds, for example, and "hunting with a red dog". This method was recommended by many duck hunters in olden times and demanded a thorough knowledge of the habits of these birds. It was based on the principle that

The fowling pieces were useless for long-range shots at sea birds. It was necessary to use stealth in order to get within range. The hunters along the lagoons outside Venice hid in holes in the sand. (Right) Camouflaged raft drifting with the current towards the reeds concealing the ducks. After von Hohberg, 1682.

The inquisitive ducks were enticed within range by means of letting a dog, preferably a red one, run down to the shore. With the advent of improved fire-arms, bird shooting was quickly transformed from a poor man's occupation to a sport for the gentry. Costumes from 1804.

ducks are inquisitive by nature and are readily lured within range by a dog or fox acting in a mystifying manner. They swim as close as they can to the mysterious animal and are easily shot by the hunter hiding nearby. (See Notes.)

Various methods of trapping played, however, a more important role than shooting. Trapping was done above all at the winter quarters of the ducks along the German, English and Dutch coasts, where they formerly occurred in enormous numbers.

It is often easy to be misled by the enthusiastic accounts, passed down by our forefathers, in which we are told how abundant birds were in the good old days, but as far as ducks are concerned, there is a certain amount of evidence which perhaps lends some substance to their claims. The most efficient type of trap was the "duck tunnel". It resembled a huge, large-meshed hoop net of the type used for pike and was placed at the end of a short artificial canal. This method acquired a solid reputation over the years — it was in fact the most lucrative occupation for the penniless owner of a strip of coastal land.

As a rule, small lagoons were dug behind the shore and the duck tunnel was placed at one end of them. On either side of a lagoon there was a close fence leading up to the mouth of this huge net. The fences were erected when the net was to be used. Tame ducks were employed as decoys and placed at the entrance to the canal trap.

Ducks which alighted by the tame birds, either because they were inquisitive or because they wanted company, were lured without difficulty into the canal, where they were driven into the net by water dogs. These enormous duck tunnels were often left in position for long periods at a time but they were mainly used in the late autumn or winter.

Some records of catches made in these duck tunnels have come down to us and they illustrate the abundance of ducks in former times as compared with the state of affairs today. In a single tunnel net in northern Germany in 1784 no fewer than 67,000 ducks were trapped while in the 1880s eleven nets were required for a catch of 56,000 ducks!

Duck nets of this type were to be found everywhere along the North Sea and Baltic coasts from the Middle Ages onwards. The birds were decoyed by tame ducks and were then carefully driven into the net by water dogs. 67,000 ducks were caught in a single net of this kind in 1784. Freely reproduced from a seventeenth-century Dutch engraving.

SEA BIRDS

The term "sea bird" is ued here of the diving ducks which migrate in large numbers along the coasts of the Scandinavian peninsula, mainly in the spring and autumn, on their way to and from their summer quarters. Quite a few of these species of birds stay and breed on the coast but the long-tailed duck — perhaps the species of most importance for hunting — spends the summer in the northern-most parts of Europe. Not so long ago, sea birds were one of the corner-stones of the coast-dweller's economy and there is much to suggest that the excessive toll taken of these birds was a prime cause of their rapid decline in the early nineteenth century.

In some parts of the Baltic, the downward trend became noticeable already in the late nineteenth century — for instance, the large trapping nets were no longer considered worth while at that time. As recently as the mid-nineteenth century, however, sea birds on passage occurred in numbers which we today find difficult to believe. Even cautious observers (C. U. Ekström, for example) described the flocks of long-tailed duck as "the flying armies of the Baltic Sea" and the famous Scottish indus-trialist, Alexander Keiller, resident in Gothenburg (Göteborg), did not hesitate to declare that the masses of sea birds in the Great Belt during the severe winter of 1853 numbered "billions"! There is a story of a fisherman by the Bothnian Sea who, at about the same period, killed so many long-tailed duck in a single patch of open water in one winter that the down alone weighed over sixty-five pounds. It was not unusual for him to get between twenty and thirty long-tailed duck with a single charge.

"The flying armies" were, of course, considered to be inexterminable and people did not believe that there was any reason for limiting the numbers killed. If anything, quite the reverse. As recently as 1854, a writer by the name of F. Heins made an outspoken appeal for stepping up the trapping of sea birds in nets:

"Millions of wild duck are born and die, few of which benefit mankind. This cannot be the will of Providence, but is solely our own fault!"

There is no doubt that it was primarily man who was responsible for the great drop in numbers which took place afterwards, not merely as a result of constant shooting, but also thanks to large-scale egg collecting and trapping with nets.

Apart from everything else, greatly improved fire-arms, technically speaking, made their appearance at the beginning of the last century. This develop-ment led to an increase in both springtime shooting in the skerries and in the disastrous shooting of moulting birds. The result was that already by the

Bird nets were mainly used for long-tailed duck. The illustration shows a Finnish type of net which was used right up to the twentieth century. (After Dahlström.)

end of the century, sea birds were considered by old men in the islands to be only a tenth as abundant "as in the old days".

The island parson, hunter and naturalist, C. U. Ekström, maintained in an excellent survey of sea bird shooting that it "should" be the most profitable type of shooting, as well as the most pleasant, in Scandinavia. That was in 1832. Many years were to pass, however, before it was finally promoted to the rank of sport. (See Notes.)

In Ekström's day, sea birds were shot in the autumn and spring in the traditional manner; that is to say, from *emplacements* which looked like stone parapets and were erected out in the archipelago. *Decoys* — artificial birds made of wood — anchored with sinkers on the sea bed were placed in the water in front of the emplacements. The gun took up his position at dawn so as to be on the spot when the hosts of birds came in from the sea, where they had spent the night. (See Notes.)

Shooting caused havoc in the spring, too, in the first open patches of water where large numbers of the first migrating birds crowded together. In some places, people lay in ambush by these "pools" and, rushing forward, used sticks to knock down the densely-packed birds.

In Norrland, decoys were seldom used — although they were sometimes to be seen in the far north of the country. Instead, the local inhabitants were very fond of hunting moulting birds and for this they used dogs and fishing-spears. On a good day, a hunter and his dog were apparently able to kill between seventy and eighty birds in this way in the space of five or six hours.

In olden times, when fire-arms were not very reliable for shooting birds and ammunition was much too dear for the poor inhabitants of the islands, sea birds were caught in the Baltic mainly with the aid of high nets of a very characteristic type. Since this method of trapping was of great importance, both for the islanders' larders and for the relative

decline of the long-tailed duck, a detailed description is perhaps called for.

The use of nets was based on the well-known fact that every morning and evening the long-tailed duck fly at a fairly low level across the skerries to and from their night quarters out at sea.

Since they are very definitely birds of the water, they are consequently very careful to avoid flying over dry land and choose instead the straits between the islands. It was in these narrow and frequently used sounds that the trappers erected their bird nets. High poles were raised on either side of the strait and between them was stretched a line along which the net ran like a curtain on rings.

The net was more than nine feet high and up to seventy yards long. The methods of hanging up the net varied between the Finnish and Swedish archipelagos, but the principle remained the same. In position, the net was meant to hang tautly between the poles, a foot or so above the surface of the water. The line on which the net was hung was worked by the trapper — and it was on him that the outcome of the proceedings depended.

When the flocks of long-tailed duck came in low over the water, the trapper had to be ready to let out the line a fraction of a second before the birds collided with the net. The latter then dropped into the water, entangling the ducks in its meshes. If, however, the trapper failed to release the net, a subdued noise was heard as the birds flew happily through the meshes, and the net quivered slightly.

According to the ornithologist and island parson, Samuel Ödmann — he, too, went in for trapping

When sea birds alighted in dense flocks in the first patches of open water in the spring, they were slaughtered on a huge scale.

with nets during his years on the island of Värmdö — a net cost a maximum of ten thalers, which sum was the approximate equivalent of a hundred pairs of long-tailed duck. In olden times, there was no difficulty in catching that number in one morning. Already during Ödmann's sojourn in the archipelago in the late eighteenth century, the decline in the numbers of sea birds had become noticeable and by the 1830s only the net poles remained as memorials to a vanished golden age. It was no longer considered to be worth the effort to catch birds with nets.

In the Finnish archipelago, the use of nets for trapping birds lasted considerably longer and was to be found as recently as about 1900 in the parish of Hitis. (See Notes.)

The principal species of sea birds shot along the coasts of Scandinavia are — apart from long-tailed duck — eider, scaup, velvet scoter, goldeneye, goosander and merganser. Decoys are placed close to the shore in more or less the same way for all the above-mentioned species. They are all gregarious birds which unsuspectingly seek company when they see other birds resting on the water, but the

Nesting-boxes for goldeneye were placed near water to make it easier to harvest the eggs.

hunter heightens the effect, the more decoys he puts out — this is particularly true of the long-tailed duck.

The great Welsh hunter, Llewellyn Lloyd, who lived in Sweden from the early 1820s until his death, was certainly one of the very first to go in for Scandinavian sea bird shooting purely as a pastime. In his big work, *The Game Birds and the Wild Fowl of Sweden and Norway* (1867), he recommends sea bird shooting as a particularly exciting occupation. "You never know what species of bird is going to be attracted by the decoys next time!" But he also stresses the drawbacks — the hardships and the danger of catching bad colds.

Apparently egg collecting was done on a very large scale. As recently as the 1860s, the islands were so thoroughly stripped of all kinds of eggs of an eatable size each spring that the sea birds, at any rate on the Swedish west coast, decreased in a most alarming manner. As an eye-witness summed up laconically: "The water fowl along this coast are being wiped out in order to improve the taste of pancakes."

The erecting of goldeneye nesting-boxes for egg collecting is a very ancient custom in Sweden. On eighteenth-century survey maps goldeneye nesting-boxes are sometimes used to mark boundaries — a fact which at least emphasises their position as permanent features of rural economics in olden times.

The goldeneye nesting-box was emptied several times in the spring, but never so much that not even one brood was finally hatched. According to some accounts, a hen goldeneye might lay as many as forty eggs if her nest was raided. This form of "encouragement" was done the whole time in such a sensible and careful manner that the bird was not frightened away. This was a relic of the old home and family economy when man still realised how dependent he was on the maintenance of a balance between supply and demand and how in the end he was always the worst affected by any exploitation of nature!

Hides of stone were used in various parts of the northern hemisphere for catching eagles. This method dates back a long time especially on Vaerǿy in the Lofoten Islands in Norway and is already described in works from the seventeenth century. (Left) Old white-tailed eagle.

THE EAGLE

One of the more depressing episodes in the long history of hunting is the furious persecution of birds of prey. It started already in the eighteenth century in Germany under the name of *Greifvogelvernichtungsaktion* and culminated at the end of the nineteenth century.

The scarcity of the larger birds of prey, which is now affecting the industrialised countries of Europe, is for the most part a result of the successful campaign of hate which, in the sacred name of game preservation was pursued with every available means — even the most savage and the most primitive. There is scarcely any other question on which the hunter has had to do such radical re-thinking as in the case of his attitude to birds of prey. It is not more than a hundred years since otherwise sensible hunters believed that the buzzard and the osprey were an underestimated threat to game. A similar period of time has passed since the authorities paid bounty money for mouse-hunting short-eared owls and since an understanding of the healthy balance between game and their natural enemies was entirely non-existent.

In the section on hawks and falcons, the use of eagle owls for hunting predatory birds was mentioned in some detail. Here we shall add a brief description of how eagles were hunted in northern Europe — especially when the bounty system made hunting and trapping a paying proposition.

The hunters were ruthless. Various types of steel traps were set above the newly-hatched youngsters; nesting trees were felled; the hunters fired at the nests from the ground; the adult birds were shot when they returned with food for their young.

There was absolutely no limit to the cruelty. (See Notes.)

A device called the *eagle line* was a trapping method often employed in Jämtland. A roughly twined line was stretched between two rocky pinnacles. Hanging from the line were hooks baited with meat. The eagle alights beside the bait, whereupon the line sways about so violently that the eagle in its impetuosity swallows the piece of meat and is caught on the hook. There is also a version with snares instead of hooks.

A peculiar method of trapping eagles has been practised right up to the present day on Vaerǿy in the Lofoten Islands, on the Norwegian Arctic coast. A similar method has also been employed on the Atlantic coast of North America, in Scotland and perhaps in other places, too. According to Hans Lidman, it was reported from Norway as early as the 1660s by the Italian traveller, Francesco Negri, and the method was fully developed already at that date.

It is called "going to the eagle's nest". The trapper builds a low half-buried stone hide, which hardly protrudes above the level of the surrounding ground. On one side of it he makes a narrow opening, concealed by a boulder, in front of which is placed the carcass of an animal. The latter is secured by a piece of string which leads to the trapper.

Trapping occurs mainly in the late autumn when eagles are hungry and bold and the days are short.

When the eagle settled down on the carrion and began to peck at the meat, the trapper hauled in both the bird and the carcass and quickly grabbed the eagle's legs and pulled his catch into the hide.

THE WADERS

It is a well-known fact that account books and housekeeping records become precious historical documents once they have aged a little. The famous housekeeping records kept by the la Straunge family at Hunstanton Hall, Norfolk, between 1519 and 1578 show how documents of this kind are sometimes of great value to anyone interested in the history of hunting. The la Straunge records give us a good idea of the game that appeared on the tables of the more distinguished families of England in the Middle Ages. We are also told how game was hunted and the degree of esteem in which the different species were held, and so forth.

We learn that the wader family was well represented on the bill of fare; this is perhaps not so strange when we remember that in the sixteenth century England was covered with marshland and saturated water meadows where sandpipers, redshanks and other waders were to be found in enormous quantities. Those that were supplied to Hunstanton Hall were usually caught in nets or snares, but some were also recorded as having been shot with the cross-bow.

Woodcock and snipe were most in evidence. Next came curlews, redshanks, small waders and other birds usually associated with the seashore. In some parts of central Europe, as a matter of fact, the

Ruffs were among the waders most in demand and were caught both at their display grounds and during migration.
(Top right) A common type of clapnet with artificial decoys intended primarily for lapwings, which was placed in water meadows. (After J. C. Aitinger, 1653.)

curlew was considered to be blue-blooded game and was a popular quarry which was generally shot at its haunts on passage with the aid of a stalking-horse. In Norfolk, curlews appear to have been shot particularly in the late autumn, in November and December, when they gathered in colossal flocks. It was — and still is in many places — also usual to lure them with a curlew call.

The ruff was also highly prized for the table in the days when it was still abundant in central Europe. When Thomas Pennant travelled through Lincolnshire, he was amazed at the enormous numbers of birds to be found in the marshes. The ruff was so common that a single trapper sometimes caught as many as seventy-two with nets in one morning, and it was not unusual for a fowler to catch a total of between forty and fifty dozen ruffs in the course of a season!

The ruffs were usually taken back to the farm

where they were fattened on bread and milk so that they would fetch a better price.

This system was also employed in other countries including Sweden. During his journey through Skåne, Linnæus saw flocks of tame ruffs walking about with chickens and geese outside the byres at Marsvinsholm Castle.

A wader which, perhaps more than other species of game, has been affected by civilisation is the great snipe. Already by 1860 or thereabouts, a Swedish naturalist and hunter was able to note that "scarcely any game can have decreased in number as much as the great snipe". The reasons given for this are, firstly, the ruthless shooting and trapping which occurred at the display grounds in the spring and, secondly, the increase in cultivated land which rapidly limited the supply of suitable breeding places.

A similar state of affairs existed on the continent where the decline in numbers, particularly in the western areas of central Europe, began as early as

without any appreciable decrease being noticeable the following night!

At least equally disastrous was the shooting of great snipe in the autumn when they often appeared in huge numbers in suitable places on migration. Snipe were so fat at the beginning of September that the skin on their breasts sometimes burst when they hit the ground after being shot!

According to all reports, the great snipe was considered to be easier to shoot than any other bird that was hunted with gun dogs. Even with the comparatively poor fire-arms of earlier days, huge massacres were possible in good snipe country. In 1847, for example, 500 great snipe were shot in Kungsängen meadows just outside the Swedish university town of Uppsala! It was far from uncommon for a hunter to account for sixty or seventy in one day. Shooting was facilitated by the fact that even when near-misses were whistling past all round it, the great snipe continued its usual placid and slow gait.

the first half of the nineteenth century. In France and Britain, the great snipe has not been of any real importance for sportsmen, since these countries lie outside the predominantly easterly migration routes and only solitary birds are to be seen there; hence, as a matter of fact, the older English name of solitary snipe.

In contrast with the common snipe, the great snipe is a rather sluggish and tame bird. These features have proved the latter's undoing.

In Scandinavia, the great snipe was shot or caught mainly at its display grounds. At the big courtship displays that still took place in central Sweden in the mid-nineteenth century, about sixty snipe might be caught in a single night with nets stretched in all directions across the display ground,

During the 1860s, the open season for this valuable game bird lasted the whole year in Sweden and the toll was, as one writer put it, unlimited. The great snipe is one of the most frightening examples of the possible result of thoughtless shooting. When at last it was protected by law, matters had gone too far and today it is one of the rarest and most threatened species in Sweden.

The great snipe may be an easy bird to shoot but the common snipe is the complete opposite! This is no doubt one of the reasons why the latter species is still so widely distributed and common. Only very skilled wing shots were able to bag any appreciable numbers. In addition, of course, the common snipe does not display collectively as is the case with its larger cousin.

(Left to right) Labrador retriever:
Golden plovers and curlews — in a
number of places the latter came
under the heading of blue-blooded
game. Curlew call.

THE WOODCOCK

One of the main attractions of a Scandinavian spring is the roding of the woodcock, at its height on warm, misty evenings when the trees are bursting into leaf, while thrushes and robins pour forth their song in the tree-tops. At first, the woodcock's display flight starts half-an-hour or so after sunset, but later in the spring it is less punctual. In the middle of the summer, the season's young male birds also begin their roding in the short period of darkness.

For a long time the shooting of woodcock during their courtship flight was regarded as one of the highlights of hunting in Scandinavia. This was an attitude that astonished foreign observers such as Llewellyn Lloyd, who points out in his great work on hunting in Scandinavia that this form of woodcock shooting would be regarded in England as little better than sniping! (See Notes.)

On the whole, roding occurs along the same routes year after year, even if the countryside should happen to change considerably in the meantime. All the gun has to do is to find a suitable vantage point and then wait for the woodcock. He may also use a woodcock call to trick the roding bird into

Woodcock hunting in the autumn has occurred on a large scale on the continent for many centuries. In the early days woodcock were caught in nets and snares but after the advent of improved fire-arms shooting accounted for a lot of them. In the mid-eighteenth century, Ludwig VIII of Hessen-Darmstadt organised big woodcock shoots at Kranichstein Castle. (Below) Detail of painting by Sonntag.

slowing down in flight and presenting an easier target. By throwing his hat into the air, he tricks the woodcock into alighting on the ground in the belief that the hunter's headgear is a bird of prey. (See Notes.)

Although the spring shooting of woodcock used to be considerable (it is forbidden nowadays), the toll taken was nevertheless insignificant in comparison with that which has occurred for centuries on the continent during the autumn migration. (See Notes.) If, as people maintain, this latter shooting has diminished considerably as compared with "the old days", the woodcock must indeed have been tremendously abundant in the past.

In comparison with the enthusiastic woodcock hunters on the continent, the Scandinavian "spring hunters", whatever one may feel about their activities, are nevertheless relatively innocent as far as the woodcock is concerned!

THE PARTRIDGE

The partridge is the classic game bird of the open fields. It was popular long before the start of the pheasant's triumphant progress through Europe. The partridge was so highly esteemed that there were times — in Sweden, for instance — when it was reserved for the king and his court.

Its range extends mainly across central Europe where it has been hunted and trapped in a variety of ways. In early times, trapping was, of course, the predominant method of obtaining the partridge. This involved the use of hoop nets and snares of different kinds. As recently as the mid-sixteenth century, it was apparently unusual to shoot partridges. We gather from the le Straunge housekeeping records, mentioned on an earlier page, that none of the many partridges taken to Hunstanton Hall had been shot. Evidently, they were generally caught in nets. (See Notes.)

At that time, it was also very usual to use falcons or sparrow hawks for hunting partridges. Since, however, falconry was reserved for the privileged classes alone, the use of various kinds of nets was nevertheless the main method of catching partridges for several hundreds of years. In particular, the tirasse net, mentioned on an earlier page, was very popular. Spaniels were used in combination with the tirasse net. They caused the partridges to squat so tightly that it was an easy matter for the hunter to pull the net over them.

As everyone probably knows, the partridge is a wily and amorous bird. During the mating season they put out their tongues at each other and are consumed with a desire to mate. (Olaus Magnus, 1555.)

The tirasse net and spaniel combination gradually developed into the use of gun dogs for bird shoots. The latter method, originally intended above all for partridges, reached perfection when the modern percussion locks appeared at the beginning of the nineteenth century. The dog's rapid search across the field, the confident and noiseless discovery of the covey, informing the hunter, flushing the birds at a word of command, retrieving the kill; all these things require careful training, which makes this kind of hunting an art.

In England, in particular, the partridge has been the object of intense game preservation, not least in the form of an energetic persecution of all kinds of birds of prey. (See Notes.)

Bird shooting with gun dogs has undergone an interesting change in England, where the partridge no longer squats as regularly as before at the approach of the dog and where, for this reason, drives have become increasingly common. (See Notes.)

Three breeds which are used especially as gun dogs for partridge shoots: setter, pointer, vorsteh. The red-legged partridge replaces the partridge in south-west Europe. Introduced in England.

THE QUAIL

In contrast with the partridge, the quail does not even attempt to spend the winter in northern Europe. It is the only one of the chicken-like birds that migrates. It winters in tropical Africa and, in the past, was caught in incredible quantities during the autumn migration, particularly in the Mediterranean countries. The marked decline recorded in the course of the last hundred years is believed to be a direct result of the large-scale trapping with nets which took place, especially on the northern shores of the Mediterranean but also in the Near East. (See Notes.)

In good quail years, as many as 100,000 quails

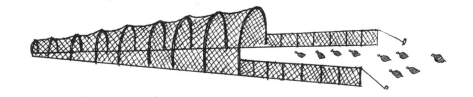

might be caught in a single day outside Naples alone, and, according to other sources, when the flocks of quails made a halt in windy weather on Mediterranean islands, the ground was literally covered with huge numbers of the birds.

Even if it is wise to deduct quite a lot from the above-mentioned figures, it is nevertheless obvious that the quail was once so numerous that the famous quail catch in the second book of Moses (16:13) does not seem at all improbable.

In the northern part of its range, the occurrence of quail has varied very much; sometimes these small birds have been fairly abundant locally. In the late nineteenth century, the numbers of quail rose sharply in the British Isles and in southern Scandinavia — possibly as the result of a series of unusually hot and dry summers — but since then they have again dropped considerably.

The classic areas for quail hunting in Europe are

the extensive grassy plains in the southern half of the Iberian Peninsula, where huge flocks of quails still make a halt on the way to their winter quarters. Andalusia, in particular, teems with quails during the migratory season and, of course, it did so to an even greater extent in the past. At the end of the nineteenth century, a shoot with five guns might account for 900 quails in one day. Abel Chapman's personal record from the same area and period was 104 quails in the course of a few hours.

It is not so surprising that the existence of this beautiful and really charming chicken-like bird has been greatly threatened in many areas as a result of the unreasonable scale on which it has been shot on passage over the centuries.

The quail's measured call, so intimately associated with twilight on a summer evening with mist over sweet-scented clover fields, is becoming increasingly rare in many of the quail's former haunts in Europe. It is only to be hoped that the decline will not continue at the same rate as hitherto.

(Right) In the past enormous numbers of quails were caught in southern Europe. In the background, eighteenth-century stick net. Germany.
(Above) Trapping with the aid of a dummy cow and a hoop net.

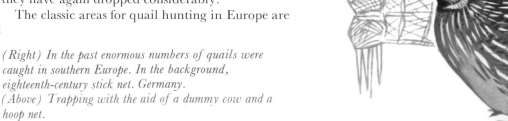

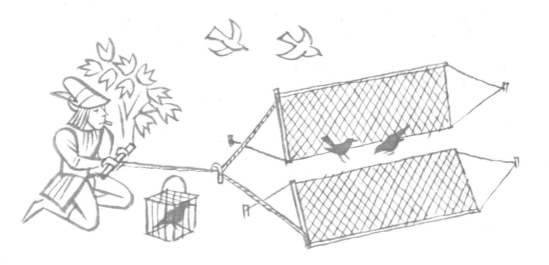

SMALL BIRDS (SONG-BIRDS)

From the days of antiquity until the late nineteenth century, small birds were caught on a tremendous scale with the aid of lime twigs. It was really only in the twentieth century that people began in earnest to describe this occupation as primitive and un-sportsmanlike. The trapping of small birds and lark shooting have, however, played such an important role in the history of hunting that they very much deserve a mention in this survey of hunting in Europe. The ingredients of the lime used for the twigs included mistletoe berries. The mistletoe, which is a parasite, is spread by thrushes — above all by the mistle thrush, *Turdus viscivorus*. (See Notes.)

It was indeed primarily thrushes, at least in central Europe, which were caught. Already in his day, Martial declared that he valued a bunch of thrushes more than one of "roses and spikenard", and everywhere in ancient gastronomic literature, authors mention time and time again the delicious small birds of various kinds.

The trapping and, to some extent, shooting of small birds were for centuries such common practice among all classes of society that there is justification in maintaining that it was almost as much part and parcel of rural housekeeping as fruit picking and jam making.

On the continent, the use of lime seems to have been the predominant method of trapping — there are frequent references to it in literature, in the works of Shakespeare, for example: "Birds never lim'd, no secret bushes fear" — while in Scandinavia different types of snares were used.

The huge flocks of waxwings and pine grosbeaks which moved southwestwards every autumn from northernmost Scandinavia and Finland were greeted in Finland and southern Sweden by merciless persecution. There existed an infinite variety of trapping methods, including different types of ring, stirrup, hanging and running snares

There are descriptions of clapnets for catching small birds dating back as far as the Early Middle Ages. When the hunter pulled the rope, the net closed over the birds that had been decoyed with grain and birds in cages.

(Below) Huge quantities of thrushes and starlings were caught in the vineyards. Often with the aid of simple snares which were hung in trees and baited with berries and grapes.

which could be hung from the branches of trees or placed on the ground, according to the needs of the occasion.

Every autumn in southern Europe there is a mass slaughter in which millions of song-birds are trapped in clapnets, *passator*, *brescianellor* and all kinds of ingenious trapping devices. Anyone who has lived in the Mediterranean knows about the murderous hail of lead which greets swallows and other migrants on their way to southern climes in September and October.

To us today this seems to be a question of wanton destruction rather than sport. A Scandinavian, at least, never ceases to marvel at the mysterious motives which cause adult people to fire a shower of lead at swallows and willow warblers.

235

Two lark mirrors from the late nineteenth century. (Left) Revolving mirror which was set in motion by the hunter or his assistant with the aid of a long piece of string. (Centre) Mechanical lark mirror which was wound up with a key. Musée de la Chasse, Gien.

THE LARK

Without a doubt, one of nature's mysteries is how the skies above our fields and meadows can still ring with the song of larks in the spring. All the more so when it is recalled how the lark has been subjected to a violent persecution, especially in the Leipzig area, for centuries the centre of the lark trade. The figures available are incredible. Leipzig larks were famed far and wide for their good taste and plumpness. The tax alone paid on the birds sent to market amounted to 6,000 thalers. The larks were trapped above all in snares and clapnets. Already at an early stage in the history of fire-arms, however, they were killed with powder and shot. When the lark in full song rises straight up into the heavens, it presents a small but nevertheless fairly steady target to an unscrupulous gun who has no qualms about shooting at the harbinger of spring. (See Notes.) Falcons were still used in the seventeenth century to catch larks for the table; according to the le Straunge housekeeping records from Hunstanton Hall, the hobby was used solely for this purpose.

A curious trapping device of very ancient origin was the *lark mirror* — a flat piece of wood on which were glued bits of glass of different colours. The "mirror" was then fixed to a short stick and placed in some suitable field for the purpose of attracting the inquisitive lark to it when it glittered in the sunlight. "Daring", a word found in seventeenth-century English literature, was the term applied to this method which was very common in England. (See Notes.) Later, the mirror was mainly used for lark shooting during the autumn migration.

Every autumn, bundles of freshly shot larks are to be seen on the counters or in the windows of butcher's shops on the continent — macabre reminders that winter is on the way and that migratory birds are moving southwards towards warmer latitudes. For centuries they have been caught or shot in incredible quantities in every country in Europe and yet every year, remarkably enough, the lark chorus is as numerous as ever and the spring sky is full of them.

Had every animal possessed the same miraculous ability to survive the ruthless toll taken by human beings, our fauna would be very different today.

Page 16

According to Obermaier's chronological table of the different archaeological periods during the Stone Age, the *Mousterian* occurred about 150,000 years before the Christian era. It was followed by the *Aurignacian* in about 100,000 B C and by the *Solutrean* in about 50,000 B C. Next came the Magdalenian in about 30,000 B C.

Page 79

It took a little while for the matchlock to attain any real importance for hunting: to begin with, it was primarily a weapon for the wealthy. The Emperor Maximilian, who in so many other respects established a reputation as an unprejudiced and progressive hunter, was one of the first to try out the new weapon. According to one story, he almost went down with his boat while shooting seabirds in Holland at the end of the fifteenth century when, in a moment of carelessness, he set light to a powder keg with his smouldering slow match.

This anecdote will serve to indicate some of the disadvantages of matchlocks. They were in fact legion. The smouldering, smoky slow match readily revealed the presence of the hunter to his quarry. Besides, the weapon was heavy and clumsy. A long time was to pass before firearms managed to oust naked steel, which entirely dominated the sport of hunting. It was for this reason that firearms first gained importance as weapons for the humble duty of providing food for the kitchen; an occupation which, characteristically enough, for example in the Danish hunting laws, never counted as proper hunting, being quite simply referred to there as a way of "striking and destroying animals". The new weapon was, in fact, fairly efficient for that purpose.

Page 80

Already in 1518 the Austrian Estates wrote to the Emperor Maximilian, requesting him to prohibit the manufacture of guns "which fired of their own accord". Bearing in mind the remarkable features of the weapon, it is small wonder that the regulations laid down by the Emperor had no effect.

Page 93

There was a remedy for this, too. A book on black magic published in 1841 helps a person in trouble:

"If anyone has cast a spell on your gun, you can load your bewitched gun with powder and spit three times, and a bullet and spit thrice. Then take your gun and go to a tree stump and fire the shot so that the bullet remains in the stump. Next take a suitable piece of wood and put it in the hole whereupon the person who has cast the spell on your gun will be tongue-tied until you remove the piece of wood from the hole."

Page 105

The dachshund, on the other hand, is never mentioned in the hunting literature of classical times and a lot has been written about its possible origin. Kurt Lindner believes that he has found the oldest illustration of a dachshund-like breed of dog in a twelfth-century manuscript of the Physiologus or "Bestiary", where a hunter is out hunting with a short-legged dog which, with a modicum of goodwill, may be said to resemble a dachshund.

Page 106

[1] According to the mediaeval *Lex Baiuwariorum* it cost six *schillings* to steal or kill a lead dog or a tracker dog. A greyhound for hare hunting was worth less and in this case the stipulated fine was three *schillings*. A rather drastic and ignominious punishment for dog thieves is to be found in the Burgundian laws. "Anyone who steals a greyhound, bird dog or harrier will have to kiss the said dog's hind quarters in front of the assembled populace and in addition pay the owner a fine of five *schillings* as a peace offering."

Bibliography: Marx-Kruse and von Sampe: Chronik der deutschen Jagd, Munich, 1937.

[2] For my account of the breeds of hunting dogs in England in the sixteenth century, the works which I consulted included John Bernström's excellent summary of "De canibus Britanicis" in the *Historical Encyclopaedia of Scandinavian Civilisation in the Middle Ages*, volume VII, Malmö, 1962.

Page 114

The following is a short extract from the book and illustrates its somewhat didactic tone:

"If you want to hunt the stag and slay it in the chase, two things are necessary: firstly, you must be able to recognise a good hunting dog by the shape of its head and, secondly, you must never be in doubt about which way to take but ride close behind the hounds wherever they may run. I shall explain to you why both these things are of help to the hunt. When the hounds stop the pursuit and start wandering about, searching, you will know where they lost track of the quarry if you have followed close behind on horseback. It often happens, as a matter of fact, that a stag turns right round and runs back the way it has come, with the result that the hounds, which are hunting it, spurred on by their eagerness, run too far; in a case like that the huntsman, who is following the chase, should not continue any further but instead turn the hounds round and return to the spot where they went wrong, at the same time shouting: 'Back! Back!'"

Page 115

Erasmus of Rotterdam expressed his views on this subject in his work *In Praise of Lunacy*, where he writes:

"Fools are also they who do not find any pleasure in anything other than hunting and who boast about the pleasure they experience when they hear the abominable noise of the hunting horn and the howling and whining of the dogs. I am fully convinced that the stink of the droppings of their hounds is just as agreeable to their sense of smell as the fragrance of cinnamon! How they enjoy cutting up the kill! Anyone can cut up sheep and oxen but only a nobleman is allowed to cut up game. Kneeling, with his head bared and holding in his hand a special hunting knife, solely intended for this purpose — no other kind may be used — he cuts up the slain animal, all the time following a particular pattern of procedure."

Page 118

This magnificent stag was captured in 1763 at Battenberg and was taken to Kranichstein where the complete series of antlers from 1763 until 1767 was preserved. It was in 1765 that this stag produced antlers with thirty-two branches. The court painter, George Adam Eger, portrayed the Battenberg stag the same year and the painting later inspired a famous engraving by the then fashionable artist, John Elias Ridinger, who specialised in hunting scenes.

In those days the trophies were always mounted on carved wooden stag heads.

Page 121

A contemporary diarist — C. F. von Schorokofsky — gave a good description of this six-in-hand. The first pair were led by the reins by a groom riding a small roan while the coachman, Fuchs, held the reins of the other stags in the team. The team could be driven at walking pace only and for not more than an hour at a time, but not before every dog in the neighbourhood was behind lock and key.

Page 122

As a matter of fact, in his diary Linnæus also expresses his anger at the depredations of the wild boars but this, too, did not appear in print. The reason for this caution is obvious. It was not very long since the wild boars had been introduced by King Frederick I, who, frequently and with great delight, devoted himself to hunting in the preserve in Öland. Consequently, critical remarks about the royal boars would not have been very much appreciated. It may be mentioned that the king's death in 1751 was greeted with joy by the sorely-tried inhabitants of Öland who, as early as the following year, were delivered from the hated beasts, thanks to a resolution by the Estates of the Realm.

On November 21, 1789, the ancient hunting privileges of the nobility were abolished in Sweden. It was then that Gustavus III signed the famous decree according to which every commoner who owned taxed land obtained the right to hunt on his own property.

Page 123

According to Anton Weck's *Beschreibung der Residens und Hauptvestung Dresden* (Nürnberg, 1680), the apothecary at the electoral court of Saxony, John Wechinger, used, in addition to other preparations, the following items in his "deer apothecary": extract of hartshorn, ashes of burnt hartshorn, the fat from a deer's eyes, a ring of deer hooves to be worn against cramp, bezoar stones from deer,

Oleum Cornu Cervi, Liquor Cornu Cervi, gelatine from boiled hartshorn, deer's heartwater (?), dried and pulverised venison, pulverised stag's testicles, a stag's penis, deer's blood, ground hartshorn, hair, hide etc., etc. A total of forty-one carefully defined preparations.

Several other pious saints have had the red deer as a symbol: Ida of Herzfeld (died *c.* 820), Catherine of Vadstena (1331–1381), Prokopius (died 1053), John of Matha (1160–1213), Meinulphus (died 850) and Felix of Valois (1127–1212). According to legend, they all met a stag with a crucifix between its antlers and to commemorate the event each of them founded a monastery on the spot where the animal was encountered.

Page 138

The evil nature of the wild boar is stressed, very graphically, in the moralising comments of queen Ratio in *Roi Modus*. In an allegorical interpretation of the roles of the red deer and wild boar, she makes the red deer — the red game — symbolise the pious, while the wild boar — the black game — symbolises an antichrist. The wild boar is black and shaggy, as indeed are the souls of the goddess. When the wild boar offers resistance, it is a sign of the same arrogance which characterises an evil person. In common with the latter, the wild boar, too, is a violent fighter whose sharp bites correspond to the knives which drunken people are in the habit of waving about on the way home from a hostelry. Wild boar love wallowing in mud and filth. When they have finished guzzling, rooting and wallowing about in the mud, they are tired and want to rest. They do this in a hole which they dig for themselves in the ground. That is what happens to the wicked who, after wallowing in sin, end up in the grave and eternal damnation.

Page 141

These "hunts" were often combined with pageants and processions, such as the generals of antiquity loved to arrange on their homecoming from a victorious war. It was, indeed, classical antiquity which set its seal on these hunting spectacles, overflowing with mythological figures among exotic animals and savages. The unfamiliar animals helped to bring variety to the lists of animals shot, and it is far from surprising to find lions, tigers and Indian mice (!) among the more commonplace game mentioned in the hunting diaries of a minor central European prince's court. In 1662, the son of John George II of Saxony, referred to above, organised a hunt of this kind which people talked about for a long time afterwards. Among the satyrs, nymphs, lion tamers, Lapps, savages playing the bagpipes, men leading bears, and other attractions, came His Royal Electoral Highness himself, dressed up as Diana, riding a snow-white stag.

Bibliography: Wildungen, L.C.E.H.F. *Weidmanns Feierabende*, Marburg, 1817.

Page 158

[1] All in all, hunting hibernating bears required an unusual measure of sang froid at the crucial moment. Misjudging matters by a millimetre or a second might spell disaster.

If all the precautions taken misfired and the hunter lost his weapon or was attacked by the infuriated bear, he hurled himself to the ground — providing he was experienced — and pretended to be dead. The bear was extremely suspicious, however, and did everything possible to find out whether the hunter was bluffing — according to one account, the bear turned the man over on to his back and deposited its droppings on the hunter's face in order to put the man's lifelessness to the test!

[2] Herman Falk was probably the last hunter in Sweden who managed to shoot three bears, three wolves and two lynxes in the course of a single hunt. These figures, however, were nowhere near Frederick I's record bag in the province of Västmanland, west of Stockholm, on September 1, 1737 when — according to the master of the hunt, Anders Schönberg — "our Most Gracious Sovereign with His Own Gracious Hand killed" five large bears, twelve large elks, three wolves and three lynxes.

Page 159

The best account is provided by some of the hunters who took part. It was not until some years later that they sent their report on the historic drive to the periodical published by the Association of Swedish Sportsmen (1875). The beaters, both men and women, were dressed in their Sunday best and it must have been a splendid sight to see the chains of beaters moving across the marshes or the forest clearings on the hillsides. When they made their second halt for the night, it was possible, from the spur of some hill, to obtain a fine view of the entire chain of beaters, thanks to all the fires which formed an arc, many miles long, from the north-west down towards the south-east. In the distance, in the pale mist of the midsummer night could be seen the glowing remains of the fires at the previous stopping places.

On the afternoon of the third day, when the beaters approached the area where the animals had taken refuge, unbelievable scenes occurred when the encircled bears scuttled among the bushes together with large numbers of hares, foxes, lynxes and the odd wolf or two. Entire herds of elks rushed past, panic-stricken by the noise around them. Strange things happened, too. At one stage, people saw what they took to be a white elk in some undergrowth, but when the animal came out into the open, it turned out to be one of the most enormous bears that any of the hunters had ever seen. It was almost greyish white "from age". The animal was believed to measure three and a half feet across its head!

In spite of the giant being shot at several times "with a burst of fire that called to mind an assault on an enemy position", it nevertheless succeeded in breaking through the chain of beaters and disappearing into thin air. This episode undoubtedly added substance to the belief in "magic bears" which were considered to be impossible to kill with an ordinary bullet.

When the hunt reached the shore of the lake, an indescribable noise arose. From all sides shots were fired into the hordes of game — particular mention is made of some moulting cranes that came under fire when they ran in sheer desperation straight out into the lake! A number of pessimists had loaded their guns with veritable cannon charges in order to protect themselves against expected attacks by bears and it was not until the hunt was over that they dared to waste shots on some hare which, as often as not, continued its headlong flight while the hunter, on the other hand, fell backwards from the violent recoil.

Page 160

It would be too much of a digression to describe here in detail all the local variants of trapping equipment which occurred in different parts of Scandinavia but it may be of interest to conclude by mentioning one of the most curious — trapping animals with the aid of mirrors and schnapps!

The use of mirrors and similar objects for the purpose of decoying animals is of ancient date and was frequently practised by the hunters of antiquity. Zoologists of former times with a humanist bent often took the opportunity of moralising upon the "vanity" of animals when they discussed the latter's interest in mirrors, but anyone who has watched a puppy growling at its own reflection in a mirror will realise that this is a case of exaggerating the intelligence of animals. However strange it may seem, a bear was nonetheless caught by means of a mirror — in the Finnish province of Tavastland — as recently as the mid-eighteenth century, according to a report by Christopher Herkapeus in an academic thesis in 1756.

The catch was made in an oatfield, where bears are fond of repairing in the late summer to gorge themselves on the sweet and juicy grain. Shiny copper cauldrons filled with a fifty-fifty mixture of water and schnapps were placed in holes dug in the ground. When the bear had eaten its fill and made its way back to the woods "his eyes alight on this well in which he sees his reflection, whereupon he begins to mumble, and intending to get hold of his image, drinks the contents of the cauldron which make him intoxicated so that he falls over and lies on his back, roaring hideously and waving his paws in the air until his killer comes"

Page 162

The courtship display of the male birds is extremely strange and takes place in the following manner: the big birds spread out their wing and tail feathers while at the same time inflating the air sack in their throats like a balloon so that they look like shapeless balls of white and rust-brown feathers and down. The function of the throat-sack was a matter of doubt for a long time and quite a few zoologists far into the nineteenth century were fully convinced that it served as a very useful water container for this bird of the steppes. The fact that some male birds seemed to lack the water sack added, of course, to the uncertainty of the scientists, but the reason is now known to be that it is easily visible only during the breeding season.

Page 164

The belief that the heron's smell attracts fish is so widespread that it actually led a modern English ornithologist, Frank A. Lowe, to investigate the matter by means of laboratory experiments. He soaked a piece of plaster in the extract of a heron's foot and another in the extract of a chicken's foot and put them together in a tank containing ordinary freshwater fish. Strangely enough, the latter immediately showed a marked interest in the heron extract but already after a few seconds they had satisfied their curiosity and then ignored completely any possible trace of heron smell. There was nothing of practical value in this black magic trick, although the fish's first reaction was undeniably somewhat bewildering.

239

Page 165

[1] As a rule, fish breeders are responsible for the worst massacres, but there are other people, too, who, for various reasons, feel that they are "bothered" by the herons. An English landowner once declared that his reason for getting rid of the herons was that "their noise was disturbing for hunting". Herons seem to have been persecuted most in Germany where in some cases decreases of between 60 and 70 per cent annually, caused by the human factor, have been recorded.

In Holland the decrease in the heron population during the 1940–55 period was put at 44 per cent as a result of land drainage, severe winters and, in some degree, systematic persecution in several areas. In 1925, the huge colony at Gooilust in northern Holland — for a long time the largest in our part of the world — consisted of no less than 1,035 nests, but now it has diminished considerably. Otherwise, in the countries of western Europe, the average number of nests in the colonies varies between fifteen and thirty, and nowadays we have nothing to equal the huge colonies in Asia where as many as sixty nests have been counted in a single tree. According to Pennant, there was, however, at the end of the eighteenth century, an oak in Lincolnshire which contained no fewer than eighty heron nests. We can understand Gilbert White when he declares in a letter to Pennant that he would willingly ride half that number of miles to see that fantastic heron tree with his own eyes.

[2] There are many contradictory accounts about this sumptuous banquet but, according to J. H. Gurney in *Early Annals of Ornithology* (1921), the game birds ordered included the following: 400 swans, 2,000 geese, 1,000 chickens, 400 golden plover, 1,200 quail, 4,000 duck of various kinds, 204 cranes, 204 bitterns, 400 herons, 200 pheasants, 500 partridges, 400 woodcock, 100 curlews, 1,000 egrets (?), 2,400 ruffs as well as an unstated number of redshanks, small waders, larks and "martynettes". According to one interpretation, the last-mentioned type of bird was the swallow. As Gurney points out, the archbishop's figures should not be taken too literally but rather as an approximate estimate of the amount required for this memorable and tremendous banquet.

Page 166

One of the earliest essays in *Archaeologia*, entitled "A Dissertation on the Crane as a Dish" (1773).

Page 179

[1] A French bishop is said to have declared in a sermon that the pheasant, partridge and ortolan bunting should be reserved exclusively for the clergy since, if that were so, these blessed delicacies, "in physical union with the pious gourmets, would be guaranteed a place in heaven".

Bibliography: Scott, W. H.: British Field Sports, London, 1818.

[2] Oscar I started a pheasantry outside Stockholm in 1846 but the breeder, the royal gamekeeper, J. B. Ström, suffered a series of setbacks. When they were hatched, the chicks caught mysterious diseases and many were suffocated by the hen turkeys that were used to sit on the eggs. Year after year, however, Ström stubbornly tried to get to grips with the problems and new eggs, as well as fully-grown birds, were ordered each year from the more fortunate establishments in Denmark. In 1850, matters at last looked promising for Mr Ström. More than 700 eggs had been collected for placing under hen turkeys, which seemed to respond well, but only two days before the eggs were due to be hatched an unexpected catastrophe took place. A division of gun-sloops had anchored in Brunnsviken, not far from the pheasantry, and when their cannon fired a salute, for some reason or other, many of the eggs were trampled to pieces by the frightened turkeys while the remainder were spoilt, allegedly by the violent shaking of the nests.

Two years later, the project was abandoned and the disappointed royal gamekeeper declared that it was impossible, in his opinion, for the pheasant to establish itself in a wild state in Sweden. It was not only unusually sensitive but also far too stupid to survive against its enemies.

Page 180

Thanks to the painstaking protection of game, numbers rose to unbelievable levels and it was said of the French king, Charles X, that he shot about 8,000 pheasants a year — at a cost of twenty-five francs each! This figure does not seem quite so remarkable, however, when it is learned that an English squire on his estate was able to shoot some 4,000 pheasants annually without any permanent ill effects to the pheasant population.

Page 184

[1] It has often been observed that there is a considerable predominance of males in wolf invasions. When large numbers of wolves invaded North Karelia from the Soviet Union in 1960–61, of the fifty-four wolves killed, thirty-eight turned out to be males and sixteen females. (Bertil Haglund, 1965.)

[2] It was particularly during the war-torn seventeenth century that the wolf plague increased considerably in Denmark and the peasants complained bitterly about this fact to the authorities. In the winter of 1674, when large numbers of cattle died on account of the unusually severe cold, the wolves broke into the byres and ran riot among the surviving animals. The situation was catastrophic for the impoverished peasants. The number of wolves increased uninterruptedly and the task of remedying this sad state of affairs was given to a German expert on wolf hunting, John Täntzer. He supplied his own hunting cloths but had full access to hunt attendants and beaters. He travelled all over the country and delivered the villages from wolves. He was responsible to the gamekeeper-in-chief, had a rent-free dwelling at Skanderborg and was paid for his services.

He published his experiences later in a work entitled *Der dianen hohe und niedere Jagdgeheimmüsz* (Copenhagen, 1682–1689). It is believed to be the first book on hunting published in Denmark. Täntzer normally caught the wolves in large enclosed wolf pens — always in the winter since he himself was entitled to the skins — and in these pens he dug wolf pits. The wolf pit was, in Täntzer's opinion, an invention for which he should have been ennobled and should have received the same revenues as from a shire.

Unfortunately, the authorities did not appreciate his qualities as a killer of wolves, if we can believe his own bitter comments. He ended up as a humble bird-catcher at the court at Frederiksborg Castle with an annual salary of 150 thalers.

Page 187

It was not only the depredations of the wolves among cattle that cost huge sums of money each year but also all the time and trouble involved in the compulsory drives for which whole parishes were sometimes called out. One example of this was the large-scale wolf drive that was held in two parishes in central Sweden in 1779. In addition to the hunt servants and officials, about 3,000 men were summoned for a three-day stretch of duty which, expressed in terms of money, meant a cost of 27,000 copper thalers, apart from the thousands of trees that had to be cut down in order to clear lanes through the woods. The result of all these arrangements was a total kill of three foxes and a wholly unsuspecting elk.

Page 188

Great care had to be taken when putting out poisoned carrion if the desired results were to be obtained. Ödmann tells us that a neighbour of his once put out the carcass of a calf which had been prepared with arsenic and the dead animal was eaten mainly by crows and magpies, large numbers of which were killed at once by the poison. Worse was to follow, however. The ground itself was polluted with arsenic and when cattle ate the grass there the next spring, some seventeen cows and three horses died immediately. So things did not go quite according to plan.

As a matter of fact, since olden times the poison most frequently used against beasts of prey had been *poison nuts*. Von Lieven also used them. They are the seed of the poison nut tree *(Strychnos nux vomica)*, native to southeast Asia, and contain *strychnine* and *brucine*. Experts considered arsenic to be unsuitable for wolves since the latter is able to vomit very easily and in that way cleanse its stomach of this nauseating poison.

Page 195

This lack of visible passion on the part of the hazel hen formerly gave rise to absolutely ridiculous notions as to how their mating occurred. According to an often quoted mediaeval scholar — Thomas of Cantimpré — the cock bird ran about in the mating season with his beak wide open until foam appeared in his mouth, whereupon the hen bird ran up to him and drank the foam so that she became pregnant. According to other writers of the same period, toads then sat on the hazel hen's eggs and hatched basilisks and similar frightful creatures after the old familiar pattern. Nonetheless, this shows that the hazel hen has long had the reputation of being a strange and mysterious bird.

Page 198

One of the most fantastic grouse shoots is generally considered to be the one that took place in August 1915 in Lancashire when 5,971 grouse were bagged by eight guns in three days!

During the same season a total of 17,078 grouse were shot in an area of 17,000 acres. This figure certainly suggests a population density of uncommon proportions.

Page 211

Even this form of hunting which, more than any other kind, is governed by etiquette has had its individualists who stubbornly went their own way. The most famous of them was the legendary John Peel of Cumberland. People said that "he appeared to have been brought into the world for the sole purpose of driving foxes out of it".

Fox hunting was a veritable passion with him. He sold some of his land to get money for the hunt, neglected his farm and had no compunction in rushing off to hunt a reported fox on the same day that his son died.

He had no time for the normal flamboyant accessories of fox hunting. His coat was grey, his manner was humble and the only item of the showy hunting equipment of fox hunters that he did not despise was the curved hunting horn. During his fifty-five years of fox hunting he always kept a pack of two dozen hounds and two horses which made up in speed what they usually lacked in beauty.

In his old age he was granted an honorary pension as a fox hunter, but he kept up his beloved sport until his death. In his home town of Cockermouth he is still looked upon today as a hero and an often-heard folk-song keeps his memory alive:

D'ye ken John Peel with his coat so grey?
D'ye ken John Peel at the break of day?
D'ye ken John Peel when he's far, far away —
With his hounds and his horn in the morning?

Page 212

In old pictures of the cleft log trap — in the works of Lloyd, Hahr and others — the log or plank of wood is so high that the fox must jump if it is to get caught in the notches on either side of the bait. The most recent investigation into the matter showed that this was wrong. Out of a large number of cleft log traps, the average one was not too high for the fox to reach the bait fairly easily while standing on the ground; on the lowest one measured, the distance from the ground to the bottom of the notch was not more than 110 cm!

The cleft log trap was a fixed piece of trapping equipment which was used from year to year. Usually it was fashioned out of a tree-stump with sturdy roots. A cleft log had either one or two notches. As will be seen from the drawing, the bait was fastened to the highest point and so firmly that the fox was unable to knock it down with its paws and was obliged to try to bite it off. In doing this its paws slipped and one of them got caught in the notch. The fox then instinctively tried to withdraw its paw and this only served to press it deeper down in the notch. It never had the strength to lift its paw and remained hanging or sitting there until it died of exhaustion or froze to death after a few hours. In its attempts to free itself the fox not infrequently got trapped with one paw in each notch!

Page 214

Respect for the badger's strong jaws and sharp teeth has been expressed in curious ways in some places. In southern Sweden cases still occurred last century of peasants putting charcoal or egg shells in the legs of their boots owing to the belief that the badger would only stop biting a person's legs when it heard the tibia being crushed between its jaws!

Page 216

[1] Gradually a compromise was reached whereby the fishermen retained the right to kill otters as long as they

241

did not use fire-arms — for the otter has been regarded through the centuries as enemy number one of freshwater fishermen. This was one reason why trapping methods developed in a very special manner in the case of the otter, and bearing in mind the fierce persecution it has had to endure it is strange that it has not met the same sad fate as its comrade in misfortune, the beaver.

[2] Like the majority of other animals, the otter was also used in pharmacy. Dried pulverised otter was believed to be a remedy for fever, constipation and other aches and pains.

[3] The story about otters in Sweden being trained to fish has been discussed and generally dismissed as improbable in foreign works on hunting. It is already mentioned by Olaus Magnus in his *History of the Scandinavian Peoples* (1555), but is also corroborated at a later date. Above all by Doctor John Low in an essay in KVAH, 1751, page 139 *et seq.*, under the title "Ways of catching Otters alive and of teaching them to fish for the household".

The training method recalls somewhat the one used for retrievers and according to the author gave fairly rapid results "since it is possible in this way, without any undue effort, to make most kinds of animals, at least tractable ones, retrieve".

He also mentions the experiments made by a farmer in Österlen in southern Sweden whose otter is said to have taken home daily enough fish for the whole household.

When the news of this experiment was read aloud to the members of the Swedish Academy, one of the officials, Charles Harleman, declared that he had seen a similar "trained" otter fetching fish for its master from the water by Kungsholm bridge in Stockholm.

Page 220

Full title: *Tractatum de phocis in sinu Bothnico capi solitis.* *Bibliography:* Borgström, C. A.: Finnish hunting literature until the mid-nineteenth century (Swedish title: Finlands jaktlitteratur till mitten av 1800-talet. Helsingfors, 1964). (Includes a Swedish translation of the abovementioned dissertation in its entirety.)

Page 221

[1] The hunting of seals by means of decoying them occurs in many places along the east coast of Sweden. The hunter lies down like a seal (in a banana-like posture) on some suitable rock and howls to the best of his ability. The seal does not see well and is sometimes tricked into coming well within range.

[2] As in the case of clubbing, the seal hunter rushed at the seals on the islet and plunged his harpoon into the nearest animal. The barbed tip came off the harpoon shaft and the fifteen-foot-long rope which was wound round the hunter's wrist was pulled away by the fleeing seal. At the very moment when the hook got caught, the hunter threw himself to the ground and got a grip on a rock with his feet, at the same time letting out some of the rope so that it did not snap. If he did not have time to get a foothold on the rock, it sometimes happened that the seal pulled him out to sea. Experienced seal hunters used two harpoons, one in either hand, and in that way were able to grab two seals at a time.

Bibliography: Säve, P. A.: "Skäl-jagten på Gotland" in "Läsning för folket", Stockholm, 1867.

Page 223

Since olden times, geese spending the winter along the coasts of the British Isles have been a favourite quarry of hunters. Fire-arms used for this purpose included puntguns. The latter were long, heavy calibre guns mounted in punts which were then poled or allowed to drift downwind towards the flocks of geese. The birds came under fire while still on the water. The gun was aimed by manoeuvring the punt since the former was too heavy to be handled in the normal way.

Page 225

This strange hunting technique was taken northwards from central Europe by the Walloon blacksmiths and, according to a hunting periodical, *Tidskrift för jägere och naturforskare* (The Sportsmen's and Naturalists' Journal), was introduced in Gysinge — province of Gästrikland, Sweden — in the early nineteenth century.

Page 227

[1] It is interesting to note here how highly the goosander was esteemed in some places for three reasons: its good taste, the food value of its eggs, and on account of its usefulness as a fisherman's assistant! The goosander acted in the latter capacity in different parts of southern and central Sweden where the peasants had learnt to utilise for their own benefit the well-known "seine-fishing" practised by goosanders. When these birds congregated in large flocks in the autumn, wire cages and wooden "fish-houses" were placed in the inner reaches of the coves where the birds fished. In this way it was possible to catch the large predatory fish which followed the shoals of small fish being pursued by the goosanders.

"Goosander fishing" is described in detail by John Ihlström, a parson, in KVAH, 1749.

A similar method of fishing with goosanders still occurs on a lake in Yugoslavia.

[2] Another reason why sea bird shooting had such disastrous results was the often puzzling lack of fear of gunfire shown particularly by the long-tailed duck. In spite of a flock of long-tailed ducks having been greeted by a murderous hail of shot, the flock immediately behind alighted in the same place! There was, as a matter of fact, a Swedish proverb which ran as follows: "*The long-tailed duck alights best in gunpowder smoke.*"

Page 228

[1] The historical and geographical origins of the sea bird net have been much discussed. There is a description of the bird net (not intended for sea birds, however) as early as the tenth century from Russia and Olaus Magnus describes its use both in the White Sea as well as the Baltic and the Gulf of Bothnia. It occurs in legislation in the first hunting statutes in 1647. The suggestion that the origins of this ancient method of trapping with nets might be traced back to the hunting practised by the upper classes in central Europe would seem to be somewhat far-fetched, not least in view of the fact that the method was never depicted in the mediaeval handbooks. After all, even the most primitive trapping techniques appeared in illustrations so one wonders why this most unique and remarkable method was omitted. The most likely answer

is that it reached the Swedish archipelagos from the East.

Page 232

[1] Llewellyn Lloyd's first lines in the chapter on the woodcock in *Game Birds etc.* (1867) are perhaps surprising but probably do not lack foundation:
"Fewer Woodcocks, in proportion to their numbers, are probably killed in Scandinavia than any other bird coming under the denomination of game."

[2] This was the origin of the woodcock's age-old reputation for being stupid — during the Middle Ages in England woodcock and idiot were in fact synonymous terms, a state of affairs to which Shakespeare referred several times in his plays.
"Oh this woodcock! What an ass it is!" (*The Taming of the Shrew*, Act I, Scene 2).

[3] As recently as the late nineteenth century, two hunters in Italy shot 862 woodcock in the space of twenty days. In a hunting reserve near Capua, 360 migrating woodcock were shot on a November day in 1869. In Ireland (the Mecca of woodcock shooting), 450 woodcock were shot by a party of sportsmen in the course of ten days.

In Hamburg, Germany, in the seventeenth century, the man who succeeded in shooting 100 woodcock during the autumn season was crowned "Schnepfenkönig" and in addition was excused paying taxes that year!

A list of birds of Pembrokeshire compiled by George Owen of Kemes in England came to light after the latter's death in 1613. We are told in this work that the woodcock is commoner in the autumn than all other game birds put together and that it was caught in nets stretched between trees — a method which, as a matter of fact, alongside a special type of snare, was the most usual one employed in the Middle Ages.

Page 233

[1] It was not until the beginning of the eighteenth century that the partridge really began to induce aristocratic sportsmen to go in for wing shooting in earnest.

One of the leading pioneers was Frederick William I of Hohenzollern, who shot partridge two or three times a week and gradually developed into a particularly skilful shot. With a small retinue of servants to load his guns and accompanied by falconers and gamekeepers, he sometimes returned home with fair-sized bags — 160 partridges on one occasion (in addition to nine hares, four pheasants and a barn owl!). Misses were, of course, legion and an eye-witness assures us that the royal gun often fired "600 shots and more" in the course of a day in partridge country.

[2] It may be mentioned that many partridge hunters and gamekeepers rounded up their beloved birds in the autumn so as to keep them indoors during the winter. As recently as the late nineteenth century, exactly the same methods as those recommended to mediaeval partridge hunters were used for this purpose! The distinguished hunter, Gustaf Banér, described in detail how he used to catch his partridges either with the aid of a tirasse and spaniels or a large hoop net and a cow-hide!

In Skåne, too, this method was practised very successfully, above all by Corfitz Beck-Friis of Börringe, who on one occasion caught sixty-two partridges in a hoop net in the course of one drive!

Bibliography: Banér, Gustaf: Jaktminnen, Stockholm, 1900. Lloyd, Llewellyn: *Game Birds and Wild Fowl etc.*, London, 1867.

[3] According to Arthur Berger, this deterioration is due to inherited changes in the habits of the partridge species. The partridges that squatted most tightly were shot while those with a less pronounced distinctive behaviour escaped and passed on their characteristics. Besides, when a terrestrial bird squats on the ground, it does so primarily in order to protect itself against a bird of prey, but since predatory birds have been almost exterminated in England, there is no longer any vital necessity for preserving the instinct to squat tightly.

Bibliography: Berger, Arthur: *Die Jagd all Völker im Wandel der Zeit*, Berlin, 1928.

Page 234

To judge from old records, the quail migration formerly occurred on a scale that we today find difficult to imagine. According to Smart's account of a journey through Turkey in the early nineteenth century, quails appeared in such large flocks in the autumn that they "darkened the sun". He also tells us that the sultan ordered *400 dozen* live quails from one of his governors in October 1829. They were delivered three days later. They were caught in nets that were suspended between lofty poles in the manner of the Scandinavian sea bird nets.

Page 235

Thanks to this way of spreading its own means of capture, the mistle thrush gave rise to a Latin proverb — *Malum sibi avis cacat* — which, freely translated, means: the bird paves its path to perdition with its own droppings.

Page 236

[1] A lark shoot which found its way into print took place in Leipzig, the famous lark town, in 1604. The electoral prince, John Sigismund, was travelling through the town one spring morning when he suddenly heard a lark singing above the street. The electoral prince stopped his carriage, took out his pistol and killed the bird with a well-aimed shot. The court poet, Frederick Taubmann, who was sitting beside the electoral prince in the carriage, immediately wrote a twelve-line poem where he praises his royal master's skill with the pistol.
The first lines run as follows:
Ecce suum tirile, tiritirlirli tractim
Candida per vernum cantat alauda solum
"Behold how she sings her tirile tiritirlirli . . ."
The first line is quoted by Linnæus in the introduction to his *Lapland Journey*, 1732.

[2] A quotation from Shakespeare's Henry VIII (Act III, Scene 2) shows that the lark mirror was sometimes used in combination with a piece of red cloth in order to increase its efficacy:
"Let his grace go forward,
and dare us with his cap, like larks."

Bibliography: Harting, James Edmund: *The Birds of Shakespeare*. Chicago, MCMLXV.

Index